RICHARD CROSSMAN

For my future husband, Joseph Teanby.

RICHARD CROSSMAN

A Reforming Radical of the Labour Party

Victoria Honeyman

I.B. TAURIS

LONDON · NEW YORK

Published in 2007 by I.B.Tauris & Co Ltd,
6 Salem Road, London W2 4BU
175 Fifth Avenue, New York NY 10010
www.ibtauris.com

In the United States of America and in Canada distributed by Palgrave Macmillan
a division of St. Martin's Press, 175 Fifth Avenue, New York NY 10010

ISBN 978 1 84511 553 1

A full CIP record for this book is available from the British Library

A full CIP record for this book is available from the Library of Congress
Library of Congress Catalog Card Number: available

Printed and bound in Great Britain by TJ International Ltd, Padstow, Cornwall
From camera-ready copy edited and supplied by the author

Contents

Tables

Acknowledgements

There are many people whose help and advice has been invaluable to me for the duration of my PhD on which this book is based. Firstly, I would like to thank the archivists at the Modern Records Centre at the University of Warwick, particularly Christine Woodland. Their encyclopaedic knowledge was a great help, as were their tips on where to have lunch. I thank them for their professionalism and friendly attitude, whether it was nine o'clock in the morning or seven o'clock at night.

Secondly, I would like to thank Darren Treadwell and Stephen Bird at the Labour History Archive in Manchester. Not only did they put up with relentless requests for documents, they also gave me some useful hints on related documents. Again, their professionalism and friendly attitude made my research much easier and was much appreciated.

Two people without whom my PhD and this book would never have been written are my supervisors – Kevin Theakston and David Seawright. They both share a dedication to their students and to the subject which is inspirational. They have encouraged me when it seemed that my thesis would never end, helped me continually and forced me to demand more from myself – the true job of supervisors. They have been truly superb supervisors and I owe them everything.

Additionally, I would like to thank my two PhD examiners, Professor Mark Wickham-Jones from the University of Bristol and Dr Stuart McAnulla from the University of Leeds. Their thorough questioning was very beneficial when I came to adapt my PhD into a book. Also I would like to thank my publishers I.B.Tauris, in particular Dr Lester Crook and Liz Friend-Smith for all their help and advice.

On a personal note, there are six people I need to thank. Firstly, without my parents my thesis and this book would never have been possible. My mum, Margaret Honeyman, is thanked for her constant support, sitting on my shoulder and convincing me that I was 'up to the job'. My dad, Peter Honeyman, has been arguing with me since birth about politics in preparation for my academic career. Their love and moral support has been essential to this study and much appreciated. I would also like to thank Holly Honeyman for her regenerative cuddles and constant smiles – my little angel. I also need to thank Jennifer Sands, my favourite office buddy and friend for life! Thanks for the endless support and cups of tea. You're the best. Ian Bruff also needs a special mention for coping with my moans, questions and constant e-mails. Thank you all.

Lastly, and most importantly, I thank my future husband, Joseph Teanby. His impact on my thesis and this book has been so great that he really should be credited on the cover. His love and support every single day have been essential, and without him, I would have given up long ago. He has kept me sane and working late into the night. This book, my darling, is for you.

1

Introduction

While Crossman was a senior member of the Wilson cabinet and an individual with a large personality, he has not been focused on by the academic community. Perhaps because of the impressive calibre of the Labour Party after the Second World War, other individuals have been concentrated on instead, including Harold Wilson, Anthony Crosland, Hugh Gaitskell and Roy Jenkins. These individuals occupied key positions within the party or government and it cannot be said that Crossman occupied either. However, his position within government, the Labour Party, and the media taken as a whole, coupled with his communication abilities make him a fascinating and useful individual to study. He was a compulsive communicator and teacher and this trait provided a substantial amount of evidence on his views, his influence and his particular areas of interest. Writing after his death, Wilson questioned whether Crossman had been ' a student, arguing with his successive permanent secretaries the intellectual verities of political decisions, or was he a teacher, rebuking civil servants and his ministerial colleagues?' Wilson went on to conclude that Crossman was, in fact, both a student and a teacher but rarely a serious politician.[1]

While Crossman's own writing is very useful, it does not provide a clear picture of his ideological views as a whole, instead focusing on singular issues and the detail of his life. The existing literature on Crossman is fairly limited in comparison to that which exists on some other key politicians of the same period. The literature only offers the reader a limited and fragmentary view of his life and career, allowing large areas of particularly important activity and policy making to be overlooked. It is particularly surprising that, despite its important role in Crossman's career, foreign policy issues are repeatedly overlooked. There is a large gap in the literature which requires filling in order for a more complete account of Crossman's career to be established, as well as to better inform the wider discussion on the internal debates within the Labour Party and the role of the Bevanite grouping within this. Without a fuller picture of Crossman, the accounts which we currently have on these wider issues are incomplete and the role which he played is overlooked or lost. This biography will fill the gap in the literature by providing a thematic study on the key issues which dominated Crossman's life and political career.

There are two full-length biographical accounts of Crossman, both written by individuals who knew him fairly well. While both the Tam Dalyell and Anthony Howard biographies are useful and provide details of Crossman's life, they deal primarily with the practicalities. Of the longer essays, David Marquand concentrated on Crossman's views on the development of socialism and social democracy, while Kevin Theakston's essay focused on his views on constitutional reform and his most notorious publication – his diaries. The handful of shorter essays tend to be either purely biographical, focusing on the key events of Crossman's life or career, or single-issue essays, limiting their scope and usefulness. These essays do not consider more than one aspect of his career or provide more than a brief overview of key events. There is no comprehensive, thematic biography of Crossman's life and thinking and while the two biographies and various essays, when taken together, do provide some useful information, much is lacking.

Methodology

Biographical studies tend to divide the academic community. Many accept the traditional view that biographies tend to be a 'gossip-sodden, unreliable form of history'.[2] This means that biography often lacks the respectability which other studies enjoy, based generally on a few flawed, historic examples. However, this viewpoint has being challenged and is gradually being replaced by a more positive attitude towards this methodology. This section will consider what a biography needs to achieve, the different types of biography and what life-and-times studies tell us about an individual and the circumstances in which they lived.

Biography has a few high-profile defenders, often biographers justifying their chosen methods, but not limited to this group. Nigel Hamilton, biographer of John F Kennedy and Bill Clinton among others, described the reaction of certain members of the academic community to biographies as being partially motivated by 'snobbery and envy'. Biographies tend to be more commercially successful than other forms of academic literature, and he suggested that this popularity had contributed to its diminished status.[3] John Derry argued that biographical studies are particularly important as 'history involves the lives of countless individuals … where the materials exist to reconstruct the life of an individual with sufficient detail and with the possibility of sustained analysis, this task should be undertaken…'[4]

In addition to considering the unique benefits of biographical studies, the various types of biographies which can be produced and their relative value, due to the nature of this biography, another important element which will also be considered - the role of diaries. Unpublished and published diaries are often used in biographical studies as they offer an insight into the life and motivations of an individual which cannot be found in other forms of evidence. The way in which diaries are written and edited is particularly important as this affects their accuracy and usefulness. Additionally, the character of the diarist is vital to consider as it obviously impacts on the content and style of the diary. It is particularly useful that for some of the period that Crossman was a member of the cabinet, we have three diary accounts of events, those of Barbara Castle and Tony Benn in addition to his own. This section will offer an example of one cabinet meeting covered by all three diarists to demonstrate the diversity of their accounts, though it is important to stress that diversity does not necessarily mean that one account is 'true' while another is 'false'. This section will consider the level of detail in the accounts as well as how much other secondary information is included. This will allow us to conclude which of the diaries is more useful in this context, though this does not mean the other diaries are without merit. Harold Wilson argued that while diaries are particularly useful, they often reflect rather more about the author than first glance might suggest. As an example of this, he noted that 'Dick [Crossman] was an avid recorder of gossip; he is a great attributer of phrases never used.'[5] While diaries are very insightful, their uniqueness must be balanced with the obvious bias which they exhibit. This section will consider the value of diaries generally and how useful Crossman's diaries are specifically.

Definition of Biography

It is important, before considering the merits of this methodology, to establish what the exact definition of a biography is. The variety of definitions which are used may be contributing to the debate over the benefits of biographical studies, as it is difficult to evaluate any methodology effectively when confusion exists over exactly what it is. Biographies can become a catalogue of events within an individual's career and life, but these tend to ignore one of the fundamental requirements of biographical studies – the creation of a life and times study. Robert Shepherd, biographer of Ian Macleod and Enoch Powell, defined the task of a biographer as considering '...what their subjects did, what happened to them and to try to understand them.'[6] Nigel Hamilton defined biography as 'the way we look at real lives'.[7] Shepherd and Hamilton, both writers of biographical studies, noted that biographies need to look deeper than the superficial events in someone's life and try to understand them within a wider context.

Ben Pimlott, biographer of Harold Wilson and Hugh Dalton, indicated that biographies need to be more inclusive and demanding than the production of a list of events. 'The aim is, or should be, to understand an individual life, the forces that shape it and the motives that drive it, in the context in which it is placed.'[8] This form of biography, which includes many excellent examples, provides the academic community with a particularly focused and nuanced account of events, allowing greater understanding of the individual, their personal views and the forces and pressures upon them. The study of an individual's life, while often interesting, is lacking in substance or worth if it is not combined with discussion of the circumstances in which the individual lived – a life and times study. It is essential that biographies avoid becoming irrelevant by focusing solely on the life of the individual.

Leon Edel, biographer of Henry James and literary writer, argued that 'all biography is, in effect, a re-projection into words of material re-assembled through the mind of the historian or the biographer.'[9] Edel seems to be critical of any historian who 'reprojects' information into a biographical study, while failing to criticise those who 'reproject' this same information into more traditional studies. It is the duty of all academics and scholars to apply accepted academic standards and to attempt to remain as impartial as possible. It seems likely that biography is being singled out for criticism unfairly, based on the often well meaning but mis-guided biographies produced predominantly during the nineteenth century. Pauline Croft, respected historian and author of a biography on King James of England and Scotland, argued that often, at the heart of the criticism, using historian Patrick O'Brien's criticisms of biography as her example, 'is a distaste for any form of history that might seem popular or accessible.'[10] It is important that the popularity of biography as a methodology does not lead academics to conclude that it is a less rigorous form of study or that it is simply a popular medium for the masses. Nor is it acceptable for academics and scholars to denigrate biographical works based on preconceived assumptions and prejudices. As with all methodologies when properly researched and written comprehensively with adherence to accepted academic guidelines, these studies can be both effective and particularly insightful. 'Without it, our understanding of past politics would be gravely constricted and woefully inadequate.'[11]

Theakston's Categories of Biographical Studies

In order to provide a brief outline of the various types of biographies which exist, the criteria set out by Kevin Theakston, respected writer on the British civil service, will be used.[12] Theakston recognised four specific motives for writing biographies and outlined how varying motives can impact on the biography which is produced and its reliability. The four categories which he identified aim to better categorise all biography and identify the strengths and weaknesses of each sub-category. This will allow us to conclude that certain categories of biographical writing and research are more useful and more scholarly than other specific sub-categories, though even the most flawed example can provide useful information.

The first category which Theakston identified was biography which was written to inspire its audience. These biographies, many of which were produced during the nineteenth century, traditionally extolled moral values and indicated a higher purpose within an individual's life. They were often written to inspire an audience with exaggerated tales of morality and excellence, hoping to set an example to the nation, to drive up both personal and public standards, although this was not true of all Victorian biographies. Theakston additionally noted that more modern studies of women in senior administration posts 'tend to have the same flavour, it could be argued, with the theme of the subjects providing role models or exemplars for women in public service…'[13] Unfortunately, the deficiencies of these biographies, written almost as a form of moral propaganda, has allowed some within the academic community to dismiss all biographies.

In more modern times, an inverse of this commemorative tradition has been produced – biographies which are written to shock and provide salacious details for the reader. Some intend simply to provide a more rounded picture of an individual than was previously available, generally producing a superficial picture which is lacking in serious academic worth. Other biographies go further, adding shocking detail, presumably to gain notoriety and more publicity than might otherwise be forthcoming. Instead of extolling morality, these seek to increase their saleability by providing personal, and generally irrelevant, details of the subject's private life.

Academics, rather unfairly, tend to focus on this type of biography, overlooking its benefits and uses. Instead, its shortcomings are utilised to criticise all types of biography. While academically deficient due to the absence of any material deemed unsuitable or unflattering and the specific slant which the author mistakenly places all details within, these types of inspirational biography do have some useful features. While this type of writing is perhaps the most flawed of all biographies with many deficiencies and problems, it is not without worth and biography as a methodology should not be dismissed without individual study and consideration.

As the content of many of these types of biographies is adversely affected by the motives of the author, the most important service which these studies provide is to retain evidence. Many documents, particularly poems, letters or other personal written material, are quoted at length in these biographies. Many have not survived in their original form and it is only their inclusion within these studies which alerts academics to their existence. Nicholson, not a great supporter of biographical studies, admitted that 'many historians would recognise that biography has its uses: for example, in turning up sources (especially diaries and correspondence) as a contingent part of a project.'[14] The preservation of such evidence is particularly useful and allows more academic studies to be undertaken using the evidence which has been preserved.

Theakston identified the second category of biographies as those connecting the study of ideas and the development of public policy. These very often involve the study of the life and career of an individual who is linked to a particular public policy initiative. These individuals tend to have played a central role either in the establishment of or development of an area of public policy, some of whom have provided valuable evidence for academics, such as personal papers or diaries. A good example of this type of biography would be Jose Harris' study of William Beveridge, in relation to his work on public health and the development of the welfare state.[15] Without this kind of study it would be impossible for a full understanding of the motivations which drove these policies or the issues which moulded them to be developed in many areas. These individuals are often considered to be extraordinary or inspirationally unique figures, 'concerned with men of quite extraordinary, individual characteristics.'[16] More accurately, these kinds of studies consider individuals who have been intrinsically involved in the development of key public policies. The initial idea or decision need not have been their own, but they were in a position to communicate the idea to others, either as a leader, a minister or an influential figure and to help facilitate action.[17] This led them to be closely linked with the policy or theory and often personally committed to it.

The third type of biography which Theakston detailed are biographies which are an essential part of a comprehensive historical understanding of government. This category shares certain characteristics with the previous style of biography considering individuals who are intrinsically linked to the wider understanding of government. This category is defined as 'a useful framework, or at least a point of entry, for the exploration of the impact of ideas on the development of government thinking and public policy.'[18] Alan Beattie indicated that the structure of the British political system, where individuals hold great personal influence and power, means that the use of a biographical approach is a useful lens through which to conduct research. 'Moreover, in the British case, the concentration of political power in the parliamentary arena (and in ministers particularly) gives an obvious importance to the actions of a small group of leaders.'[19] This form of biography allows an academic to highlight wider social or political influences which an individual was involved in. This essentially means that by studying, for example Clement Attlee, much can be concluded about the Labour government from 1945 to 1951, the motives behind certain decisions and measures and the overall state and mind-set of the cabinet specifically. This type of biography is extremely useful, as it allows a much more complete and comprehensive account of political events to be established. Due to the involvement of MPs in a multitude of different issues, it is essential to consider the specific policies which they were involved in. Other types of studies, for a variety of reasons, may well have overlooked the various links between certain issues which a biography can explore more fully and focus on the role of the individual.

The final category which Theakston identified were biographies that provide case studies which can then be scrutinised by academics and scholars to discover if an individual acted as part of his social class, position, family or as a unique individual with an individual set of beliefs and values. These case studies provide evidence which scholars can use to test hypotheses and theories. Biographies of this kind are useful as overviews which, in an age of increased specialism, enable readers to cross boundaries of period and discipline, focusing on specific traits or experiences rather than one specific time period, and make connections that would otherwise escape them using a variety of case studies. This type of biography is very useful for academics as it allows case studies which might otherwise be lost or overlooked to be used to support or refute hypotheses and theories.

The Subject of Biography

Patrick O'Brien argued that biographers either 'present their subjects as extraordinary and omnipotent, or alternatively as predictable individuals whose characteristics and actions form the basis for generalisations about the government of the day.'[20] He suggested that the very nature of biography singles out the unique or extraordinary individuals while ignoring the less unique or powerful, unless it can be assumed that these 'ordinary' individuals represent a wider trend within society. There may be a limited amount of truth in this, as biographies do have a tendency to focus on famous or powerful individuals.

The definition of a truly exceptional individual is a qualitative judgement. The title of 'hero' or 'genius' can be removed as quickly as it can be bestowed. It can also be difficult to identify just one 'genius' among a larger group. While those considered particularly successful do tend to be focused on, it is equally important, perhaps more important, to focus on those who were not quite so successful, who may not have lived up to their own potential. It is important to understand why someone was considered a failure and how their ideas, work and career compared with more successful individuals. A useful example of this would be a brief comparison of Crossman and Harold Wilson. Both were well educated and academically successful, teaching at the colleges of Oxford. Putting aside their rather different personal lives, the real divergence between the two seems to have occurred during the Second World War, when Wilson became a civil servant in Whitehall while Crossman became a propaganda expert in the War Office. From this point on, Wilson was always several steps ahead of Crossman. While luck may have been a factor, there seems to be several more tangible reasons why Wilson and others, including Gaitskell, Jay and Crosland, would be considered more successful in their careers than Crossman.

Firstly, and rather inevitably, Crossman's own personality appears to have counted against him, failing to impress many within the Labour Party's hierarchy, including luminaries such as Attlee and Bevin. His bullying manner, political naivety and inability to keep his own counsel all seem to have gone against him in various ways. Others, such as Wilson, were able to play a far more tactical political game than Crossman, but this was not the only reason for his slow rise in politics. Other outspoken and naïve politicians, while perhaps not being particularly successful in the larger arena of politics, did have specific issues on which they excelled, often holding high office. Aneurin Bevan, while not perhaps fulfilling his own potential, was able to be a successful cabinet and departmental minister, an inspirational leader of the left, and credited with the mammoth monument of creating the NHS. While Crossman had some successes as a minister, none of his major policy initiatives came to fruition. Though the external circumstances which the government faced affected Crossman's departmental work, the accomplishments of others appear much greater in the same period. However, by considering the deficiencies of his proposed legislation and how external forces prevented his plans from being instituted, we can learn much, not only about Crossman, but also about his legislation and the circumstances he operated in.

Secondly, and perhaps more importantly, are Crossman's political views. His positioning, early on in his parliamentary career, within the Keep Left group and the Bevanite group seems to have hindered his career prospects. This, combined with his views on Israel, which annoyed key members of the Attlee government, made him seem quite a dangerous man to give a position of influence or power to. Other members of the Bevanite group were able to overcome concerns about their political position, either by being so influential as to demand position, as with Bevan, or by distancing themselves when necessary from the group, like Wilson. Crossman did not fall into either of these categories. When Gaitskell became leader of the party in 1955, though Crossman was becoming more distant from the group, his Bevanite credentials coupled with his personality still limited his career prospects. It was not until Wilson became leader in 1963 that his career began to substantially improve, but even then, he did not fulfil his early potential. It is also important to note that the positions which he held in government were not those which are considered particularly key, such as Foreign Secretary or Chancellor of the Exchequer, though he was Leader of the House of Commons which was a senior and important position. This was probably due to Crossman's outspoken manner, ability to make huge gaffes, and Wilson's need to accommodate other senior members in his cabinet, such as Brown and Callaghan.

As can be seen, it is vitally important to consider why a specific individual failed to live up to their potential, as it highlights so many other important issues. In many cases, as with Crossman, it is not solely due to personal reasons or relationships, reflecting more about attitudes within the political party or group than first appears. Often, the biographies of these ministers can be particularly revealing, allow a more complete picture of the wider political arena to be created. Crossman did not occupy one of the top three ministerial positions, nor was he ever Prime Minister or Party Leader, but this means that he was often involved in discussions and conflicts which Wilson, Callaghan or Brown were not involved with, or did not think were worthy of note in their later publications.

The Wilson government contained many extremely competent ministers, many of them university educated and politically astute. Many have been focused on to a much greater extent than Crossman, but individuals such as Crosland, Benn or Callaghan are not more worthy of the title 'genius'. The experiences of a middle-ranking minister can be just as illuminating as the experiences of a leader, and often cover different ground. Patrick O'Brien wrote a rather critical article on biography indicated that only the unique and extremely powerful are worthy of study, such as Prime Ministers or Kings. [21] Pauline Croft, responding to this, concluded that using '…O'Brien's criteria only the truly exceptional require any form of biography.' Historians should confine themselves to the 'lasting achievements of significant individuals … [but] the second-rate, however defined, can often be as illuminating as the genius.' [22] The career of the 'second-rate' minister can be particularly illuminating, though it seems harsh to refer to any senior cabinet minister as being 'second-rate' in comparison to his colleagues.

The Individual as Representative of a Group

Having indicated that Crossman's left wing reputation may have been a hindrance to his career, it is important to understand how much any one person can be viewed as a representative of a specific group. While he was, for much of his parliamentary career, located on the centre-left of the party, close to Wilson, his combative attitude, previous allegiances and unofficial leadership of the Keep Left group in the late 1940s, left their mark. He was often perceived as a member of the left, grouped together with his old Bevanite friends, Michael Foot, Barbara Castle and Ian Mikardo. This perception is inaccurate and incomplete, so it becomes essential to consider the individual in order to create a more complete and subtle picture of the left wing of the party, moving away from generalisations to a more nuanced view of those individuals who made up much of this group.

To make specific assertions concerning a group, institution or a period of political history based on the biography of an individual is only acceptable if the biography is well researched and adheres to accepted scholarly requirements. It is, however, unrealistic to assume that every individual was a leader or a key participant in a wider group and can therefore testify for the whole organisation. Pauline Croft stated that 'by definition, no single individual can ever be fully representative and, again, no historian would object to the requirement of thorough contextualisation.' Here Croft urged caution 'against the fashionable habit of uncritically accepting the idiosyncratic and wildly eccentric as somehow part of the mainstream.'[23] The key point is that an academic has to be very careful about the assertions that are made based on the biography of an individual. Jose Harris perfectly highlighted the value of this type of biography stating that an individual biography is an 'inadequate medium from which to generate general theories of administrative change, but…may provide a miniature crucible in which such theories can be tested and tempered.'[24] It would be unrealistic to believe that a biography of, for example, Harold Wilson could provide a comprehensive study of Labour leaders throughout history. However, a study of the life of an individual can provide evidence and detail on specific incidents which took place within a group and how its members reacted to that. This is a fairly basic point, but it is very important as its surrender can lead to flawed biographical studies which can bring broader criticisms upon the wider methodology.

While certain views and opinions were widely held within the Labour left at this time, such as their support for the retention of Clause IV in 1959, it is important to note the specific differences of opinion. Crossman should be considered, certainly from about 1955 onwards, as occupying more centre-left ground, with his opinions therefore having less in common with other members of the left wing, such as Mikardo or Foot. Without individual study, any grouping within a party can be considered superficially, but it will lack any sort of detailed or nuanced approach.

Biographies allow the distinct opinions of individuals to be explored, allowing the academic community to reconsider whether their accepted views are correct, or if they lack discussion of the subtle differences between individuals.

The Role of Diaries

While diaries are a form of evidence as opposed to a methodology, they are often linked to biographical study, as both provide an insight into the personality and private motivations of an individual which it is difficult to gain from other methodologies or sources. Diaries, like biographies, are often considered flawed, being one-sided in their reporting, which they obviously are due to their very nature. However, due to their uniqueness and insightful observations, they are extremely useful. Peter Catterall argued that 'personal sources, such as autobiographies, diaries and letters are of greater importance for earlier periods because the quality of other sources is less.'[25] This must also be true for periods of political history where official records are either not available or are edited for publication, such as in the case of cabinet minutes. Writing in 1964, Crossman noted that certain important discussions were not noted in the cabinet minutes, making them an incomplete record of events. 'All that is recorded in cabinet minutes is what actually is decided in cabinet.'[26] In his evidence to the Fulton Committee he went further, arguing that 'the minutes of cabinet committee meetings recorded not what had been said but what ought to have been said, based on minister's briefs; that was necessary because what ministers said in the absence of their official advisers would often sound like ill-informed rubbish.'[27] Crossman used this secrecy to justify the early publication of his diaries, noting that he was in illustrious company in breaking the 50- or 30-year rule. 'From Churchill downwards, there are endless precedents for disregarding the thirty-year rule which is such a burden to professional English historians.'[28]

Information and evidence can be disclosed in diaries which under normal circumstances would not be available for at least thirty years due to the Official Secrets Act, as happened with the diaries of Richard Crossman.[29] In this case, the contents were considered so sensitive that the government attempted to stop its publication.[30] Information and detail which diaries contain may never be disclosed by any other source due to its personal nature or its mundane quality. Often the basic details of an event can be overlooked in official publications, yet this detail can be interesting and illuminating. Diaries, such as those written by Crossman, Castle and Benn can provide political scientists and historians with information which can have a profound effect on how a historical period, organisation or government is viewed. However, the personality, priorities and interests of the diarist impact on the content, leading diaries of the same period to be very different, often concentrating on divergent issues. Diaries, like all evidence, are imperfect and as such require critical evaluation. 'The actor himself is normally far from rational about his own role and motivation: confused, self-deceived and rationalising as he seeks to bring order to his jumbled thoughts and experiences even in his intimate diaries…'[31] While diaries do tend to rationalise events and thoughts, they also provide a window into the psyche of the author, which is invaluable.

Political diaries provide considerable understanding and information on a particular organisation, individual or theme, but these cannot be considered in a sterile environment with no consideration of the pressures of the external situation and the position of the author. Biographies and diaries can provide greater understanding if used together. Diaries cannot provide a full account of events and issues, with the author or publisher able to erase or pass over any unfavourable or unflattering details or issues creating a one-sided account. Biographies can be insightful and accurate without the use of diaries, but when such full, detailed and entertaining diaries exist such as those produced by Crossman, it would be unscholarly not to utilise them after rigorous evaluation.

In addition to the content being affected by the personality of the diarist, it is also affected by the methods used to record it, the style in which it is edited and, finally, how it is used. Barbara Castle made extensive notes, writing her diary entries virtually every night to keep events fresh in her mind. 'From that time onwards [January 1965], I kept a regular record of what happened in cabinet and in the Labour movement generally, typing it on my little portable late at night or at weekends when my cabinet boxes had been cleared and my husband had gone to bed.'[32] Tony Benn employed a fairly similar technique in the production of his diaries, dictating daily accounts, except for a fifteen-month period in 1966/7 when he stopped keeping a diary due to the pressures of his work at the Ministry of Technology.[33] Crossman's preferred style was to wait until the weekend and then, with the use of his own notes, cabinet minutes and departmental documents, record his entries onto an audiotape which was later transcribed by his secretary.[34] While having some obvious advantages, such as a weekly overview of events as well as providing an account of passing interests and fleeting conversations, this method does have some disadvantages. Firstly, the taping of the diaries seems to have encouraged Crossman to talk at great length, while writing might have led to a more concise account. Secondly, as the diaries were not recorded every night they do lack some immediacy in their reporting, encouraging Crossman to provide an overview of certain issues rather than an accurate and detailed blow-by-blow account. These overviews then had to be separated out into daily entries in the editing process, and some passages had to be rearranged in order to make sense of events. Additionally, there are several fairly large gaps in his early diaries when, due to illness or general boredom with politics, he stopped keeping a weekly record. Also, a chunk of entries were lost when he accidentally recorded over earlier entries on his tape recorder.

The editing of Crossman's diaries was done in two different ways. Crossman undertook the majority of the editing of the first volume himself, as well as writing the introduction to volume one of his *Cabinet Diaries*. He hired Janet Morgan, a young academic from Nuffield College, Oxford, to ensure that the edited diaries did not stray too far from the unpublished version. Her initial role was limited to that of 'checker' and she additionally wrote the bridging paragraphs which contained an explanation of events.[35] However, with Crossman's ill-health and death in 1974, Morgan became, as he had anticipated, sole-editor, completing volumes two and three and his backbench diaries in the style which he had established. The published diaries, while considerably shorter then the unedited version, are still extremely long, dwarfing many other political diaries, including those by Dalton, Gaitskell and Castle. The sheer level of detail in Crossman's diaries is somewhat overwhelming to the reader, but to have omitted more would have led the diaries to lose their intrinsic value. Studying the unpublished diaries, it is clear that Morgan was forced to omit some issues and policies completely due to Crossman's lack of sustained interest in them, such as his views on the actions of China in the post-war period, and how it would react to changing developments in the Cold War. Also removed were details and gossip relating to other politicians, such as the actions of Tom Driberg, which were omitted for obvious reasons.

Following the intense media scrutiny and the court case over the publication of the diaries, they were initially utilised by the press and members of the Conservative Party looking for embarrassing or salacious details on the prominent members of the Labour Party. Additionally, the diaries seem to have been very popular amongst the public, selling very well. However, they have been widely utilised by the academic community gathering information on the period they cover. With the publication of the Castle diaries in 1980 and 1984 and the first volume of the Benn diaries in 1989, a comparison can establish how one event was recorded differently by these three politicians.[36] A useful example can be done using a cabinet meeting, such as the one which took place on 28th July 1966. As a new member of cabinet, Benn's account might be expected to be the longest and most complete. In actual fact, his account was limited to three sentences. 'The cabinet lasted from 9.45 to 1.15 today, discussing the wages and prices standstill. I had a nice little note from Jim Callaghan saying "You have joined at the worst time I ever remember. It can be more enjoyable than this."'[37] This account is too brief and provides only minimal detail about the meeting which took place.

The Castle diaries go into considerably more detail about the cabinet meeting. Firstly, Castle outlined that the dispute was over the insertion of new powers into Part IV of the Prices and Incomes Bill, and how these were far beyond what had initially been proposed. She continued by outlining the views of other members of the cabinet, including Crossman. 'Dick was the first to exclaim that these powers went far beyond what might have been expected from the "strengthening" of the Bill agreed in the previous cabinet discussion.'[38] She then further outlined the concerns of Crossman and George Brown, before describing how Wilson ended the meeting. 'At this point, Harold had one of his bright tactical ideas. Wasn't the answer to make the orders bringing these powers into operation subject to an affirmative resolution?' It is only in the last line that Castle commented on the suggested plans, noting that 'personally, I thought we were merely postponing trouble.'[39] The account seems to adequately outline the concerns which many had to the proposed legislation, though her opinion is not extensively discussed and the entry focuses on the actions of others. This could have been due to her lack of participation in the debate.

Crossman's account of this cabinet meeting is considerably longer than that of Castle. Initially, like Castle, he outlined the issues which Part IV of the Prices and Incomes Bill had raised in cabinet, but this is done in slightly more detail than in the Castle account. He outlined the reply which Brown gave to several questions on this policy and how Wilson sent for Hansard to find out what had been said in Parliament in regard to this policy.[40] He continued by outlining who voted for Tony Crosland's proposal that the measures outlined should only apply to prices and not incomes, a vote which is not mentioned in either of the other accounts. Finally, he noted his own action:

> I said this [the implementation of the order over the parliamentary recess] was intolerable; and moved an amendment instructing George [Brown] to write into the Bill an express commitment that Part IV could only be introduced by Affirmative Revolution, requiring the assent of Parliament to a 28-day order which would lapse after that period unless renewed.

Crossman concluded his notes on the cabinet meeting by considering the secondary issues of cabinet. He noted that Wilson, when the cabinet vote was tied over the date of wage claims, asked '"what shall I do, it's a tie?" I said *sotto voce*, "Be a Prime Minister" and Richard Marsh giggled.'[41] His account finishes with some discussion of the relative strength of Brown, Wilson and Callaghan.

The three accounts vary enormously, with differing levels of detail and usefulness. Benn's account tells us nothing of the cabinet discussion other than roughly what the debate was about. Castle's description offers the reader more information, outlining what the debate centred around and the position of certain individuals, such as Brown and Crossman. However, when this account is compared with Crossman's account, it seems lacking in specific detail. While his account may have been particularly complete due to his activity within the discussion, many cabinet meetings are discussed at great length within his diaries. He detailed what he remembered individuals saying within cabinet, what votes were taken, the result of those votes and who voted in favour and against, as well as the secondary issues which were also considered. The general details of the Castle and Crossman diaries seem to be consistent, and the details which Castle outlined are also noted in Crossman's diaries, though there is a greater level of detail in his account. The Crossman diary entry seems to be the most complete of the three diaries, but this kind of comparison allows a more complete picture of events to be established, and it also allows the diaries to be checked against each other for accuracy.

Conclusion

Biographies are researched and produced for a variety of reasons and while some are unsuccessful in their aims, many are very successful, well researched academic works. Nicholson argued that 'biography was invented to satisfy the commemorative instinct: the family wished to commemorate the dead and we have elegies, laments and runic inscriptions.'[42] While selected biographies may reflect this, it is inaccurate to describe the majority of them in this way. To discredit a whole methodology based on a selective number of ineffective or misleading biographies is unacceptable. High academic standards that are expected from other methodologies are equally applicable to biographical studies. 'Bad' biography is no better, or worse, than 'bad' political history. It is unacceptable in all methodologies for the study to be superficial, uncritical or unprofessional in its use of sources, research or writing. Biography has often been criticised and derided in the past due to inadequate research methods and unscholarly practices in a limited number of examples.

While biographical study has been widely criticised, the academic community seems to be realising the benefits of this methodology. John Tosh noted that

> it is sometimes forgotten by the detractors of biography that the critical use of primary sources requires symptomatic biographical research. What the authors of these sources wrote can be fairly interpreted only if their background and day-to-day circumstances are grasped; for this if for no other reason historians need to have a good biography.[43]

Other academic subjects do not deride their most popular fields of writing and research due to the inadequacies of a few examples, while failing to recognise its benefits.

The study of political history can be undertaken using several different methodologies. To conclude that one method or approach is more suitable for a specific research project or study is justifiable but these important decisions should not be based on a selective number of examples from a given genre. Biographies can be insightful and particularly useful to the academic community. By studying the life of an individual, a more detailed and accurate account of events and issues can be established, which is the aim of all academics. It should not be assumed that one approach would be suitable for all areas of research or writing. Diversity, if the proper academic standards are maintained, can only be good for the academic study of political history.

The Methodology of this Biography

A thematic biography of Crossman has been produced as this allows us to consider his views in far greater detail than has previously been allowed and analyse how he interacted with and responded to the views of other members of the party and external events. As thematic biographies allow a greater understanding of events and policies than 'life-and-times' or narrative biographies, this methodology has been adopted here. It focuses on the issues which were important not only to Crossman, but to the wider party, taking Crossman seriously as a thinker on several different issues for the first time. Three policy areas have been focused on– socialism and social democracy, foreign policy and constitutional reform.

These issues have been chosen for two reasons. Firstly, the Labour Party between 1939 and 1974 was forced to focus on these issues due to Britain's changing circumstances. The rethinking of the aims of the party and of how socialism should be developed in the future was precipitated by the success of the Attlee government, leading to a fragmentation in the party. No study of the Labour Party in this period would be complete without consideration of this issue. Foreign policy was also an issue which created conflict within the party. The Attlee government was forced to deal with the situation in post-war Europe and its response and its foreign policy aims led to fractions within the party, with left wing groups demanding a more 'socialist' approach be adopted. Foreign policy disputes continued after the party lost power, with military commitments, the future of Germany, the Cold War and nuclear weapons all being areas of conflict. Constitutional reform was another issue which the party had considered almost since its inception. Many within the wider party asked if the existing constitutional arrangements would allow a socialist government to institute reform. Secondly, as well as these issues being important and controversial within the Labour Party, they were also important personally to Crossman. Throughout his political career and in his writing, he focused predominantly on these three issues. Any influence which he exerted was chiefly in these areas, and for these reasons, this biography focuses on these key policy areas.

This biography places Crossman in the wider context of the Labour Party and provides a detailed account of his opinions and preferred policies, as well as how these developed over the course of his career. While the left wing of the party is often considered to have been a single entity, by focusing on Crossman it is possible to see the variations within the left and the external influences which encouraged him to gradually become a centre-left figure. This approach allows discrepancies to be uncovered and explanations forwarded to account for these, exploring the detail of party policy and Crossman's views on them. This critical thematic biography focuses not on Crossman as a man, but as a party member and serious thinker on political policy. It argues that he cannot simply be labelled as a 'gadfly' or a fickle politician, as he was interested in a limited number of policies for much of his career. This book fills a gap in by the existing literature, exploring key themes in the history of the Labour Party by focusing on the views of Crossman and considering how these fitted into the wider context, providing a more nuanced and detailed account of the party and its policies. Rather than studying the leadership, as is so often done, this biography has considered the views of a middle-ranking minister and backbencher to add more detail to the existing historical account.

In writing this biography, a wide-range of material has been used, both material which is specific to Crossman and wider material on the Labour Party. This includes Crossman's diaries (both published and unpublished), his articles, books, pamphlets, material in the Crossman papers, the Labour Party archives, government documents at the National Archive and publications of the Labour Party. While many of these documents are particularly detailed and insightful when used collectively, they have tended previously to be viewed in isolation. Previous studies of Crossman have failed to use the Crossman papers in conjunction with these other sources, partially because of their detailed and personal nature and partly due to the limits imposed on their usage by their repository. This has led to some studies relying almost exclusively on the Crossman papers while others have not utilised them at all. This book has drawn upon a wide variety of sources to gain a deeper understanding of the issues considered here. While he is often considered fickle and unprincipled, this biography has concluded that many of his opinions were more deep-rooted, thought-through and sustained than previously believed, highlighting the continuity in Crossman's thinking. Additionally, it has provided a wider account of the party's views in specific policy areas, many of which are marginalised, such as the party's views on Israel

2

Biography

The Early Years

Richard Howard Stafford Crossman was born on 15th December 1907. His father, Charles Stafford Crossman, was a barrister, claiming to be from old Winchester stock through the Danvers family line.[1] Richard was enrolled from 1920 to 1926 at Winchester public school, a citadel of education frequented by the sons of the upper classes, an experience which had an immense impact on him. He was, as with all new recruits to the school, used as a 'fag', being in the service of one of the older boys who would instruct him to perform menial tasks on their behalf. This school tradition was intended to enforce discipline on new pupils, though Anthony Howard argued that it was Crossman's good fortune to have the more easy-going Anthony 'Puffin' Asquith, son of the former Prime Minister as his first fag-master.[2] While at Winchester he met a small, weakly boy, slightly older than himself, of whom he expressed a very low opinion. That boy was Hugh Gaitskell and Crossman left a lasting first impression, one which he and Gaitskell attempted, rather unsuccessfully, to overcome for much of their careers. Writing in his diaries in 1957, Crossman noted that 'if you were at school with somebody who seemed innocuous and insignificant throughout your school life and who since then has been an ascending backroom boy, it is difficult to believe in his greatness.'[3] It was in 1924 while at Winchester that he first exhibited his leaning towards the Labour Party in a mock election. Though he was defeated, Howard argued that Crossman went down 'with all guns blazing'.[4] Through his parents he had already met Attlee who played tennis with his family, and this friendship continued for much of their lives with Attlee making a point of attending Crossman's mother's funeral in 1960.[5] Attlee was already becoming a very influential member of the Labour Party, and he based his opinions of Crossman on the obnoxious teenager whom he met during those tennis matches and his political career suffered for his attitude at this time. Crossman believed that 'the Attlee's never forgave me for causing my parents so much pain, and I am afraid that I reciprocated their disapproval.'[6]

Crossman was academically gifted and extremely confident, bordering on arrogance, a trait which was exhibited predominantly towards his parents. His parents were, in many respects, Victorian and religious and while he enjoyed good relations with them as a child, the relationship began to deteriorate as he got older. He recounted tales of setting intellectual traps for his mother while sat at the dinner table during his school holidays which he believed she fell into due to her less educated mind. He reserved the blame for his father who, he believed, sat idly by at the dinner table, watching his wife's embarrassment, while remaining silent. Writing in 1962, after both his parents had died, he commented that his father 'could not forgive me for cruelly and deliberately taking advantage of my mother's lack of education. I could not forgive him for suffering in retracted silence, instead of coming to her assistance, when his own values and principles were under attack.'[7] Crossman's relationship with his father did not improve, and they remained divided on many issues. He wrote an article for the *Sunday Telegraph* in 1962 entitled "My Father" where he discussed their difficult and cold relationship, describing himself and his father as 'incompatible; it was the best, not the worst in each of us which the other found unbearable.'[8]

New College, Oxford

It was expected that when Crossman left Winchester, he would fulfil his academic potential by going to Oxford. He attended New College from 1926 to 1929, as his father had before him, and he again showed himself to be a gifted but rather difficult student. At Winchester, he had often been the second placed student in the academic rankings, with Richard Wilberforce generally achieving first place and scooping all of the end of year prizes, much to Crossman's consternation. At New College, the situation was replicated, but Crossman decided to develop his social skills, which had been under-developed at Winchester. Howard indicated that this decision was 'borne out by the typically thorough exercise in personality development that Dick immediately embarked upon the moment he arrived in Oxford.' In addition, he appears to have abandoned his Wykhamist friends while at New College, except for Douglas Jay, whom he remained close to while at university.[9]

While at New College, Crossman did not join the University Labour Club and did not take part in the Oxford Union or any political activities, despite his claim to have been forced 'to decide which side you were on" by the 1926 General Strike.[10] Instead, he associated with a more artistic group of friends, including W.H. Auden, writing poetry and participating in the production of plays. Homosexuality was prevalent within this group and Howard argued that it was probably while at New College that Crossman had his first homosexual experience.[11] It appears that Auden and Crossman even competed, for a time, for the affections of a rugby player from Christchurch called Gabriel Carritt. Unfortunately for both, the rugby player only had eyes for Elizabeth Harmen and both Auden and Crossman appear to have been frustrated, though Crossman was also rather interested in Carritt's mother.[12] His more liberal attitude to sexuality, which would surely have horrified his parents, was coupled with his atheist views, which did not fit in with his parent's Christian beliefs. Despite his religious education at home and his confirmation at a young age, he abandoned his religious beliefs, probably at Winchester or at New College, though there is no evidence to indicate exactly when this happened, and he never regained them. He was developing a streak of irreverence, pushing against accepted views to create conflict, particularly with his parents, as he was not particularly rebellious at school or at university. Crossman himself referred to it as his 'bump of irreverence', a trait which he was extremely proud of. In 1962 he wrote that his career 'has enlarged the priceless bump of irreverence I inherited from my mother...'[13]

Germany

Just before sitting his final exams at New College in 1929, where he gained a first in Greats, Crossman was recruited by the college as a Don, a position that would define him for the rest of his life. However, it was thought advisable by the College for this new and very young academic to travel a little in order to gain some experience of life before entering academia, a year of his life which Crossman believed transformed him. With generous funding from his parents and a little money from the College, he spent several months in Germany studying philosophy before travelling to Italy and Greece, later describing it as 'the most formative year of my life'.[14] He returned to Germany and then back to England to take up his college post. He travelled home, not only having seen the difficult and unpredictable political situation in Germany, causing him to take the threat it posed very seriously, but also returning with a girlfriend, Erika Gluck. Erika, who was older than Crossman, was the daughter of a German doctor, had been married twice before and had a young daughter, Angelica. While Crossman was pleased with his choice, Erika's matrimonial past and increasingly frequent drug taking (she appears to have been addicted to morphine) left his parents rather concerned and they asked her to leave their home, a decision Crossman believed made a mockery of their Christian beliefs and demonstrated a lack of charity.[15] Despite, or perhaps because of his parents' disapproval, he married Erika in July 1932. She left him for another man only a few months after their wedding, either another Don or a ski-ing instructor, though details are limited. Six months later, Crossman started travelling to Germany, initially trying to persuade Erika to return and then in order to finalise their divorce. While this was a difficult situation, it did allow him a bird's eye view of the Nazi Party's activities in the mid-1930s.[16] Due to his knowledge of German affairs and his academic calibre, the BBC asked him in April 1934 to write a radio broadcast on the political situation in Germany. This was gradually extended and he spoke on various aspects of the German political situation, making a name for himself outside of Oxford.

Zita Baker and Crossman's Political Beginnings

If the scandal caused by Erika's departure was not enough to raise a few eyebrows at New College, Crossman caused even more outrage by beginning a romance with Zita Baker, the wife of another academic at the college and a very keen Labour

Party supporter in 1934. Zita suggested Crossman as a possible parliamentary candidate for Oxford in January 1935 without his knowledge, making him a member of the party for the first time in his absence.[17] While he did not become the parliamentary candidate for Oxford, (Patrick Gordon-Walker became the Labour candidate), his political interest was sparked and he was keen to become a City Councillor in Oxford as a first step towards becoming an MP, being elected to the local council as councillor for Headington in November 1935. In his spare time he taught for the WEA (Workers' Educational Association), lecturing predominantly on the political situation in Germany. This appears to have been motivated by his desire to teach, but there is little evidence to confirm this. Initially at least, Zita was the covert and discreet driving force in his political career. In 1937, he was selected as the Labour parliamentary candidate for West Birmingham, Sir Austen Chamberlain's former seat, though he was not elected.

Crossman eventually left New College in 1937 but he recorded two different reasons for his departure. The first account, which was contained in a letter to Zita, indicated that, following the leaking of their affair, he had requested, and initially had been granted, a non-teaching lectureship, but had then decided to resign.[18] Writing in 1954 in the New Statesman, he told a different story, stating that H.A.L. Fisher had sent for him and told him that he would recommend his fellowship be renewed for another seven years. However, he argued that a career in politics might be a wise move, 'I stayed in Oxford too long and I went into politics at the top. That was the cause of my failure. Go in now while you are young.'[19] In the midst of this turmoil, Crossman published Plato Today, a book which was extremely popular and well received.[20] This, coupled with his BBC broadcasts, helped establish him as a public figure, though his banishment from New College could not have been particularly well received.[21] Zita filed for divorce from her husband, John Baker and she and Crossman married in December 1937, Crossman becoming stepfather to Gilbert and Venice.

With this more settled domestic situation, Crossman's political aspirations began to be realised. In January 1938, he was officially adopted as the parliamentary Labour candidate for Coventry (later being adopted in Coventry East, the safest of the Coventry seats when the constituency was separated) and he then waited for the next general election while establishing his journalistic career. He began writing for the *New Statesman and Nation* in 1935, becoming assistant editor in 1938, before breaking for the duration of the war, and beginning again in 1945. This was financially rewarding as well as allowing him to maintain his writing after his academic career had ended. Gradually, however, he concluded that his developing political career needed to be supplemented by continued journalistic endeavour. In February 1974, he described himself as 'an observer as well as a doer, a political scientist as well as a journalist MP.'[22] This definition seems to have been one which Crossman approved of. As part of his new role, he published How Britain is Governed in 1939, considering how Government and Parliament worked.[23]

Psychological Warrior and Crossman's Entry into the House of Commons
With the outbreak of World War Two in 1939, Crossman did not join up as many
of his contemporaries did. Instead he was appointed to the Ministry of Information
but was soon moved to the War Office which Hugh Dalton headed from 1940.
The military intelligence divisions of the War Office used both 'overt' (white) and
'deceptive' (black) propaganda, with the primary aim of encouraging a large section
of the German public to rise up against the Nazi regime. This propaganda often
took the form of leaflets and radio broadcasts. With his fluent German and his
experience of broadcasting, Crossman often took part in the radio broadcasts,
which was generally categorised as white propaganda, although inevitably he was
also involved in black propaganda. Writing on psychological warfare in 1949, he
described himself as 'a propagandist for five long years, first as director of political
warfare against the enemy in the Political Intelligence Department of the Foreign
Office, and then as a member of the joint Anglo-American Psychological Warfare
Section of General Eisenhower's staff.'[24] This job kept him away from the front
line but heavily involved in the war effort, bringing him into contact with several
high profile and influential individuals such as Harold Macmillan.[25]

With the end of the Second World War, Crossman was able to return to his
position at the *New Statesman* and was elected Labour MP for Coventry East in July
1945, an MP in the first majority Labour government with his parents' friend,
Clement Attlee, as Prime Minister. He was part of a large group of new, young
Labour MPs, who would shape the future of the Labour Party for the next thirty
years, including fellow Oxbridge graduates Harold Wilson, Denis Healey, Evan
Durbin and Hugh Gaitskell. Crossman initially followed his own political instincts
but, influenced by the very left wing nature of his constituency, over the next two
years he began gravitating to the left of the party.[26] Despite being a capable and
able backbencher, his early relations with Attlee had virtually ruined his changes of
entering the cabinet or gaining a junior position, though Crossman thought
otherwise.[27] While several of his contemporaries were promoted, including Wilson
and Gaitskell, he remained on the backbenches, dividing his time between his role
as an MP and his journalistic career. He argued that he needed another career focus
as 'life on the back benches was not a job.'[28] Writing after Crossman's death,
Wilson stated that 'whatever he was, he was never a serious politician; he was,
rather, a serious student and indeed a serious teacher of politics.'[29] Crossman's
journalistic aspirations were supplemented by his appointment in 1946 to the staff
of the *Sunday Pictorial*, a mass circulation newspaper. He often wrote on one issue
each week, writing a more simplistic, accessible article for the *Sunday Pictorial* and a
more nuanced article for the *New Statesman*.

Palestine and Zionism

Crossman spent much of his early parliamentary career speaking almost exclusively
on foreign affairs, predominantly the situation in Germany and Western Europe
following the end of the Second World War. Recording a discussion with Lord

Beaverbrook in 1953, he recorded how horrified Beaverbrook was when he admitted he only spoke in Parliament on foreign affairs and defence. 'It's no good specializing,' Beaverbrook told him.[30] However, his interest lay predominantly in the future of Europe, not wider foreign affairs, and he had not paid any attention to the increasingly volatile situation in the Middle East. Following the end of the Second World War, millions of European Jews were displaced and many were extremely reluctant or unable to return to their homes. Fearing for their safety, many hoped for a new start in a new location. The Zionist movement, which was particularly strong in the USA, was keen to establish a Jewish state in the country of Palestine, viewed by many within the movement as the traditional home of Judaism. This would provide a home for those displaced by war as well as creating a homeland for the Jewish faith. Obviously, the predominantly Muslim inhabitants of Palestine and the wider Middle East were vehemently opposed to this.

The British Government, as the UN-sanctioned protectorate force in Palestine, found itself in a very difficult position. While Britain wanted to support its traditional allies in the Middle East by protecting Palestine in its current state, the American government was keen to create a Jewish state, avoiding any political backlash which the rich and influential domestic Zionist movement might implement if their plans were resisted and avoiding any mass immigration into the US. This complicated the close working relationship which Britain and America were attempting to forge in order to ease Britain's foreign policy burdens and fight the ever-constant threat of communism, meaning that a resolution was urgently needed. Bevin's Parliamentary Private Secretary (PPS), Hector McNeil, approached Crossman in 1945 and invited him to join the joint Anglo-American Commission which Bevin was setting up in conjunction with the American administration in an attempt to find a solution for the difficulties in the Middle East. The reason for this, Crossman concluded, was 'I was not committed by any public statement about Palestine or Zionism: I would therefore approach the problem with an open mind.'[31] Bevin was hoping that a solution would be found which would satisfy both the British and American governments, and that for the duration of the commission the issue would be less divisive, allowing important foreign policy decisions to be made in the intervening period. The initial issue which the commission needed to consider was whether 100,000 entry visas should be issued to the displaced Jews in Europe. The secondary issue was the long-term future of Palestine and the demands of the Zionist movement in the US to study 'not only Palestine but the position of the Jewish victims of Nazi persecution.'[32] While Crossman was not initially particularly keen, with some persuasion from his wife, he joined the Commission, a decision which would have a life-changing effect. As he recounted, 'I told him [Hector McNeil] that I know nothing about Palestine and was quite unsuitable for the job. Hector was as friendly and as shrewd as he always is. He assured me that I had not been selected for any knowledge I possessed.'[33] Neither Bevan nor Attlee saw Crossman before he joined the Commission. He concluded that 'since he [Bevin] had pressed for an Anglo-American Committee, and must know the strength of American support for Zionism, he must be ready to accept the consequences of a report which rejected the present line of British policy in favour of one more helpful to the Jews.'[34] This assumption was not correct and perhaps highlights Crossman's political naivety.

The Commission toured across Europe, visiting Britain, and America finally concluding their investigations in the Middle East, gathering opinion on the situation from all interested groups. On the British leg of their tour, the commission met with Bevin to discuss the role of the commission. At this dinner, Crossman stated that Bevin told the commission that he would institute any proposals made in a unanimous report, something which Bevin and the Foreign Office later denied.[35] Following the conclusion of investigations, the group set about compiling their report, and it became clear that there was a difference of opinion which would not be easily resolved, between those supporting the short-term solution of immigration and those supporting the longer-term aim of partition. The majority of the commission argued that 100,000 entry visas should be immediately issued to European Jews for entry into Palestine, and eventually the pressing issue of the visas was unanimously agreed upon. The idea behind this seems to have been that large-scale immigration into Palestine would ease the immediate problems which Europe faced due to its displaced population. Crossman did not believe this was a sensible option as he concluded this would inevitably lead to segregation and conflict in the region. Instead he argued that Palestine should be partitioned into two separate countries, one remaining Islamic and one becoming Jewish. This small Jewish nation would then require protection of its borders, initially from a multi-national force due to its position in the largely Islamic Middle Eastern region, a region which was particularly unhappy about the enforced changes which were being implemented by external forces. Crossman's view was not prevalent, and in order to generate the unanimous report he thought Bevin had asked for, he supported the general consensus. He commented that he could not endanger 'the unanimity on the short-term recommendations by clinging to partition.'[36]

The report was published in the summer of 1946 and satisfied no one. The British government were very concerned about the contents of the report, believing that it was, at best, a starting point for discussion and, at worst, a betrayal of the British Government's precarious and delicate position within the Middle East by failing to make disarmament of rebel groups a condition.[37] The Middle Eastern countries concluded that such large-scale immigration would be disastrous to Palestine and the first step towards a Jewish state and refused to accept the report's conclusions. The American government and the Zionist movement did not believe the report went far enough as it did not explicitly recommend the creation of a Jewish state. This meant that all groups remained locked in dispute with no resolution in sight. The American administration, without consulting the British government, immediately announced that they would help to institute the report with the intention of establishing a Jewish state. Crossman noted Mr

Truman's 'lamentable statement', pointing out that the President had 'picked upon the single recommendation relating to the 100,000 immigrants for enthusiastic approval.'[38] The British government, who had held off making a public response to the report in order to confer with the Americans, felt the report could not be instituted by them, as it would irrevocably damage their relations with their allies in the Middle East. Crossman felt that Bevin had betrayed his promise to implement the report, while Bevin felt aggrieved that a Labour MP would agree to a report which put the British government in such a difficult position. Crossman believed that 'the government would seek, for obvious reasons, to avoid an open disavowal of our report, and would try to adapt it to its Middle Eastern policy.'[39] A subsequent referral to the UN also failed to formulate a compromise, supporting the recommendations of the commission's report without making disarmament of terrorist groups a precondition.

With an increasingly violent situation developing in Palestine, the British decided to renounce their protector status of Palestine with effect from 1st January 1948, handing the mandate back to the UN. This meant that the British government would not be forced to implement the report's recommendations and they could not be held responsible for its effects. 'The British people felt that it had been very badly used. Ruling Palestine was an unpleasant job anyway and the British soldier was being forced to do a lot of dirty work because the Americans were inciting the Jews to violence from the sidelines.'[40] Only days after this, Israel declared its independence and was immediately recognised by America, causing indignation in the Middle East, with the leader of Transjordan attempting to rally support from other leaders to militarily claim Israel back. In 1947 Crossman published an account of his time on the commission entitled *Palestine Mission*.[41] While the region remained in turmoil, he had gained an interest in Israel which he would retain for the rest of his life and he was committed to supporting the state of Israel. In 1970, twenty three years after his time on the commission, he returned to Israel to give a series of lectures on the creation of Israel and its future and the actions of the British government, showing his continued commitment to the country. His relationship with Bevin, while never good, was irrevocably damaged and any slim chance which he had of joining the Attlee government was ruined. At the 1947 Labour Party Conference, Bevin famously referred to those who had attempted to harm his position and Britain's place in the world order with a 'stab in the back', a comment not solely aimed at Crossman but certainly delivered with him in mind.[42]

The Keep Left Group and the Bevanites

Crossman, languishing on the backbenches, focused on his journalistic career and forming allegiances with some of his colleagues. In 1947, frustrated by the perceived abandonment of socialist principles and lack of left wing action by the government, he joined forces with numerous other backbenchers to campaign for a more socialist agenda, co-authoring *Keep Left* in 1947 with Michael Foot and Ian

Mikardo.[43] While the section on domestic policy demanded a faster pace of change but supported the general aims of the government's policies, the foreign policy section was considerably more critical. It argued that the Attlee government was too close to the USA and instead should be looking towards the USSR and Europe for support and trade. Crossman began criticising the foreign policy of Ernest Bevin repeatedly, earning his left wing credentials and the wrath of Bevin and Attlee. Within Parliament, he began to associate with a small group of predominantly left wing MPs which included the influential left wing minister Aneurin Bevan. The 'Bevanites' as they were later christened included the authors of *Keep Left*. Crossman and Mikardo had also worked together to produce the sequel to this pamphlet, *Keeping Left*, which was published in 1950.[44] The Bevanite group also contained, on a more temporary basis, Harold Wilson. When Bevan resigned from the Attlee cabinet in 1951 in protest over the level of public spending being committed to the Korean War, Harold Wilson and John Freeman resigned with him. Freeman left politics and succeeded Kingsley Martin as editor of the *New Statesman* in 1955, a job which Crossman had eagerly sought. While Wilson and Crossman both became associated with the Bevanite rebels, there is evidence to suggest that they were both centre-left MPs seeking support, which they received from their left wing colleagues despite not entirely fitting in with ideology. Mikardo indicated that Wilson and Crossman were not standard Bevanites, failing to fit in with their more left wing colleagues. 'Nye became, with good cause, suspicious of both Crossman and Wilson. Crossman, in turn, developed an intellectual-superiority contempt (sic) for most of his colleagues.'[45]

The relationship between Crossman and Wilson was to eclipse the relations either of them had with Bevan. They became, at least in Crossman's opinion, friends in the difficult world of politics, perhaps because neither had many other political friends. He commented that

in the inner circle of the Bevanite group he [Wilson] and I had formed ourselves into a left-of-centre sub-group, well to the right of the devotees. As such, we had gone through some very unpleasant experiences together without our friendship being destroyed – partly because we had both learnt that, if they are to last, friendships in politics are best kept cool and detached.[46]

Crossman believed that while Bevan was a wonderful speaker and committed socialist, he could be temperamental and difficult. Writing to Bevan in 1955, he stated that 'inevitably, I regard some of your actions as wild and harmful to the cause. Inevitably, you regard my unenthusiastic comment on those actions as equivocal.'[47] Crossman gradually began, in the early 1950s, to gravitate towards Wilson while retaining his unofficial membership of the Bevanites, who continued to regularly met at his Vincent Square home. It was at about this time, in 1951, that

Crossman began to keep a diary on a regular basis, the publication of which would make him more famous and notorious than his political career could have.

After the 1951 election defeat, Crossman crossed to the opposition benches and continued his work as a constituency MP. He also began to participate in the re-writing of a classic Labour Party text. *Fabian Essays in Socialism* had been published in 1889 and had contained essays by, amongst others, the Webbs and George Bernard Shaw.[48] At a Fabian Conference held in 1949 the idea of a *New Fabian Essays* was first suggested. It was published in 1952 after the election defeat and contained essays by Roy Jenkins, Anthony Crosland and its editor, Richard Crossman, as well as an introduction by Clement Attlee. This book was as influential as the original had been, mainly due to the authors who had contributed to it and their views on the development of socialism in light of the reforms of the Attlee government.[49]

In July 1952, as the Bevanite group continued to rebel against the Labour leadership, Zita collapsed and was admitted to Westminster Hospital. Crossman was shocked to discover that the hospital staff had assumed that he would move her to a private room and had therefore admitted her to the hospital. Had this assumption not been made, she would not have been admitted and Crossman was to remember this in his later political career.[50] She fell into a coma following a brain haemorrhage and never regained consciousness. Crossman was devastated by Zita's death but he gradually recovered. Later that year he was voted onto the NEC, though he had a rather shaky start.[51] This was an important step for him as he had never been, and never would be, voted into the shadow cabinet by his party peers. Crossman argued that the NEC was opposition to 'the dictatorship of the executive or, respectively, the parliamentary committee. Opposition is the lifeblood of democracy.'[52] His appointment to the NEC, in the year that Morrison and Dalton lost their seats, gave him an alternative focus to the House of Commons and his journalism.

In 1954 Crossman married his third wife, Anne McDougall in the presence of Jennie Lee and her husband Aneurin Bevan. Wilson was absent due to a dispute which had begun between himself and Bevan earlier in the year. Bevan had resigned from the shadow cabinet after expressing vocal concern over the party's attitude towards Indo-China. As runner-up in the elections for the shadow cabinet, Wilson was asked to fill his place, a proposal which Bevan had obviously either concluded that Wilson would refuse due to their own relationship, which was cordial and friendly, avoiding a rift on the left or he had not considered it. As Crossman commented 'if he [Wilson] automatically said no to Nye's place, he would just look like Nye's poodle. If he accepted, he would look as if he were breaking up the Bevanite group.'[53] Wilson accepted the seat on the shadow cabinet, which Bevan and many other members of the left were not able to forgive or forget. Crossman was put in a difficult position over whom to support, but he decided to support Wilson, and with this break he became more of a Wilson man and less of a Bevanite. He confessed in his diaries, 'I can't help feeling that Nye's action has immensely increased Harold's status in the party and reduced his own. On the other hand, I can't help liking him enormously for it.'[54] Other Bevanites were horrified with the actions of Wilson and Crossman's defence of his friend, and this led to a certain sense of alienation, even if the Bevanite meetings still continued to be held fairly regularly at his home in Vincent Square.

Later that year Crossman had another stroke of luck in what was to be a very positive year. Anne's father owned Prescote, a 360-acre farm, and with Anne's marriage he had decided to sell it. However, these arrangements were abandoned and instead he signed the farm over to her and her new husband. Crossman became a landowner overnight, and noted excitedly in his diaries that his farm was much bigger than the farm which Bevan had recently purchased, which was a mere 50 acres.[55] Prescote provided Crossman not only with a family home, but also with an income and another alternative focus to politics, which impacted on his attitude to his career. It made him a landowner, a position which was not unheard of for Labour MPs but one which did not fit in easily with the traditional characteristics of a socialist Labour MP. Additionally it meant that he was leading a very different, more affluent life to that of his constituents. While this had probably always been true, due to Prescote's location near to Coventry, this became clearer to all those in his constituency, though it does not appear to have impacted on his popularity. He noted that 'I shall have to explain to Coventry who, when they come over, were assured that Anne and I had nothing to do with the farm. Now they will have to be told that we've become country gentry after all!'[56] In 1955, Crossman left the *New Statesman* and joined the *Daily Mirror*, when it became clear to him that he would not succeed Kingsley Martin, John Freeman becoming editor instead.

Gaitskell's Leadership

When Attlee resigned as leader of the party in 1955, he was succeeded by Hugh Gaitskell, despite competition from both Bevan and Herbert Morrison. Attlee had rapidly promoted Gaitskell in his government, with him becoming Chancellor of the Exchequer in 1950. This promotion, as well as irritating Bevan who believed he should have been Chancellor, allowed Gaitskell to become a contender at the next leadership election. Attlee had make no secret of his hatred of Morrison, leading him to remain as leader longer than he had initially intended to ensure his rival would be too old to succeed him.[57] His promotion of Gaitskell made his succession more likely than that of Bevan, and this was compounded by his youth and Bevan's erratic and spontaneous behaviour. In 1974 Crossman stated that his career had not been improved by the election of Gaitskell in 1955 and he had decided to 'find some academic post where I could write my books and resume my teaching which I enjoyed better than anything else.'[58] This seems unlikely, and within four years circumstances had changed in his favour. Crossman and Gaitskell's relationship had changed over the course of their ten years in Parliament, though they were not close. Gaitskell appeared willing to build bridges and Crossman was encouraged in early 1956 to become an unofficial spokesman on pensions as well as being appointed to the informal foreign affairs steering committee group.[59] Gaitskell also attempted to build bridges with other Bevanites, with Wilson becoming Shadow Chancellor and Bevan became deputy leader.

This improving relationship was further demonstrated when Gaitskell became Godfather to Crossman's first child, Patrick, who was born in 1957 at the end of the Labour Party conference. However, relations between Gaitskell and the Bevanites were not easy, and following the 1959 general election defeat, the situation became considerably more difficult. The 'Hampstead Set' which Gaitskell associated closely with included Douglas Jay and Tony Crosland.[60] This group was eager for the party to free itself from Clause IV, the clause in the party constitution which committed the party to nationalisation. In the opinion of this group, this was confusing to the electorate and electorally unsuccessful, as demonstrated by the recent election defeat.[61]

While Crossman and Wilson were not great supporters of Clause IV, they both concluded that it was not worth upsetting the party faithful over, particularly as it was not controversial or high in the electorate's consciousness. The issue was not particularly important to them but both Wilson and Crossman understood its importance to others. Crossman argued that 'Gaitskell is quite unrepentantly determined to get his way about dropping nationalisation and cares about nothing else. All our ideas of making the Party a more efficient fighting instrument are to him quite unimportant.'[62] Bevan was deeply opposed to the rewriting of Clause IV, and this conflict combined with other tensions led both Crossman and later Bevan to break free of the leader to express their personal views. Wilson, while not overtly rebelling, experienced increasingly difficult relations with Gaitskell, challenging him unsuccessfully for the leadership of the party in 1960. With Bevan's death in July 1960, Wilson began to develop into a much stronger candidate for the next party leader, though few believed that he would have the opportunity to achieve this quite as quickly as he did. Gaitskell's sudden death in January 1963 certainly enhanced the career prospects of both Wilson and Crossman. As Crossman stated in 1974, quoting Harold Laski, 'where there is death, there is hope' and with this change of leader came a change in Crossman's fortunes.[63]

Wilson as Party Leader

The leadership contest of 1963 was fought between George Brown, a committed Gaitskellite, James Callaghan and Harold Wilson, who was still being incorrectly labelled by some as a Bevanite or a left winger. Wilson was a skilled tactician and while he and Crossman had remained linked to the unofficial Bevanite group, they had both become more centre-left figures. His ambitions had encouraged him to seek support and acceptance from other groups within the party, not simply limiting himself to the left. While he was not universally liked within the party, he was generally respected as a capable politician. This coupled with Brown's reputation as an alcoholic with a difficult temperament ensured that Wilson became leader.[64] Crossman was almost immediately appointed as Shadow Minister for Science and Higher Education. When the general election date was announced, he assumed that he would take on a very similar role to that which he had adopted in the 1959 election campaign, where he had been recruited to help with the writing of the manifesto. Instead, Wilson decided to appoint an NEC sub-committee to do this job and he took personal control of large parts of the campaign, leaving Crossman feeling redundant. However, he was sure that if Wilson became the next Prime Minister, he would be appointed as Minister of Education in the new Labour government.

Crossman as Minister

When Labour won the 1964 general election with a majority of four, Crossman was made a minister but did not enter the department he had hoped for or expected. Instead, he became Minister of Housing and Local Government, a department which had been previously occupied by Keith Joseph, Duncan Sandys and Harold Macmillan. Crossman was fifty-six with nineteen years backbench experience but no experience of government or shadow cabinet. He threw himself into his new job, both as a minister and as a member of the cabinet, though he knew little about his new department and he found that the party had few manifesto pledges relating to it, and had done almost no research on it.[65] The cabinet itself reflected Wilson's need to keep his political opponents' faithful and his enemies closer than his friends. It included James Callaghan as Chancellor and George Brown as head of the DEA (Department of Economic Affairs) and deputy Prime Minister, with the later additions of Roy Jenkins and Anthony Crosland. Of his more left wing colleagues, Wilson included only Crossman and Barbara Castle as Minister for Overseas Development (Tony Benn was initially outside the cabinet as Postmaster General). The balance of his government was centre-right and Crossman noted that many ministers were preoccupied with their own departments. He concluded that this made intelligent policy making in cabinet impossible. Despite his concerns he also became very departmentalised, spending his time dealing with his departmental work.

While Crossman did not easily adapt to life in government, he seems to have enjoyed his time in his first department and believed he had adapted to his new life very well, though it was rather isolating. As early as November 1964 he wrote in his diary, 'for the first time since I became a minister I woke up out of my departmental seclusion and looked at the world around me...'[66] His relationships within his first department were not particularly good, but he concluded that by 1966 the department had achieved many things and he was personally proud of a number of these, including measures on coastal erosion, water supplies and the reshaping of boundaries within England and Wales. However, his initial Permanent Secretary at the Ministry of Housing and Local Government, Dame Evelyn Sharp, did not consider his tenure as minister particularly effective, describing Crossman as a bull in a china shop. 'He wanted to hear the china smashing.' Instead she considered Harold Macmillan to be her favourite minister, believing Crossman would be remembered for his diaries, not for his ministerial career.[67] He hoped to grapple with new projects now that he was fully acquainted with the workings of his new department and he had moved individuals into position he felt he could work well with.

During the 1966 election, he again adopted a very central position which brought him into close contact with Wilson. Every morning he would breakfast with Wilson, discussing policy and tactics, before communicating these discussions to Callaghan prior to his daily press conference. Just as Crossman was beginning to feel comfortable in his ministry, he was moved to another post, which he was not particularly excited about. In August 1966, perhaps because of their renewed political relationship, Wilson appointed Crossman as Leader of the House of Commons and Lord President of the Council. This involved the pomp and circumstance which he had shown a distinct dislike of while on the backbenches but also brought him into close regular contact with Wilson. His position was initially unclear in his mind, as he was not entirely sure what Wilson wanted him to do. Even before moving to his new job he wrote 'I shall always miss this [the Ministry of Housing and Local Government].'[68] The fundamental issue which he had to attend to was the organisation of the business of the House of Commons with the Chief Whip, John Silken. The demands of ministers had to be balanced with the workings of the House so the legislative programme of the government could be enacted. Additionally, Crossman also had to liase with the Queen and inform her of events in the House, travelling to whichever palace she was residing in. There were certain procedural reforms which had been agreed while Bert Bowden had been Leader of the House which Crossman was now required to implement regardless of his own views. These included morning sittings in the House of Commons and the televising of Parliament. Additionally, he had been calling for less secrecy and more accountability in government since 1939 and his new position allowed him to implement reform. One of his first reforms was the introduction, on a trial basis, of specialist committees, giving detailed consideration to the policies of certain departments. Crossman hoped that these committees would create more cohesive policies with fewer unexpected consequences, but they were initially unpopular and ministers were unhappy at having their work scrutinised by backbenchers. While they gradually became an accepted part of parliamentary life, they were not popular during Crossman's lifetime.

The most contentious reform which Crossman hoped to implement was reform of the House of Lords. He aimed to alter the composition of the House as well as the power, believing the two to be intertwined. He hoped to split the peers into two groups, speaking peers and voting peers. Hereditary peers would be allowed to speak in the chamber but not vote. The government of the day would be able to change the composition after an election to ensure they had a majority in the upper chamber. He hoped to create cross-party support for these reforms and was initially fairly successful. However, due to political disputes on other issues, and the determined opposition to reform of a small group, the deal collapsed and the bill was instead sent to the Commons. Crossman moved from Leader of the House to being Secretary of State for Health and Social Security in 1968, while the reform bill was still being written. His new position as minister of a mammoth government department diverted his attention and his move meant that he was not as involved with the bill as previously, with the process losing his driving force. Morgan argued that the situation became particularly difficult when Crossman moved departments and 'handed over the leaderships of the Commons to a successor who was less vigorously dedicated to parliamentary reform.'[69] In the House of Commons, a small and rather unusual group of MPs, containing those on both the left and the right wings of both parties, united to slow the bill's progress down. It became obvious that this opposition was very damaging and was disrupting the whole legislative programme. Additionally, many ministers were 'completely uninterested in reform of the House of Lords.'[70] Eventually the bill was dropped and Crossman's chance of reform was lost. He appears to have been resigned to its fate, and involved in his new department, leaving his difficult period as Leader of the House behind him.

In his final two years as a cabinet minister, Crossman focused on the work of his new department. He had been interested in the social security system since the mid-1950s and was eager to reform the National Health Service he had witnessed when Zita had lay dying, where assumptions of wealth had guaranteed her admittance to hospital rather than her illness. He was also concerned about the care of the mentally ill, due in large part to the report which had been produced by Geoffrey Howe on abuse at Ely Mental Health Hospital. Upon entering the department, Crossman was made aware that the department had been in conflict with Howe for several months over how much of the report to release, for fear of the political implications. He immediately instructed the department to release the full report, accept the consequences and learn the lessons which the report flagged up for attention.[71] Along with other day-to-day decisions, these activities took up much of his time and he tended to show the departmentalism which he had criticised, but understood, earlier in his ministerial career. He accepted that due to his increasing age and the lack of direction within the Wilson government, he would not be a minister again, even if the Labour Party won the 1970 general election. Instead he was appointed editor of the *New Statesman* in addition to remaining a constituency MP. His period as editor was not particularly successful and after a dispute with the board in 1972 following his initial diagnosis with cancer, Crossman was sacked from his position.

Life After Government

Crossman's increasing wealth and less demanding lifestyle meant that it became possible for him to focus on writing in his spare time, and he also began a BBC series called Crosstalk, a late-evening interview programme. He met each week with politicians, civil servants and journalists to discuss various political issues, continuing until his ill health began to take its toll on him in late 1973. He had signed a two-book deal with Jonathan Cape in 1965 and was now hoping to deliver these books. One of these would be an academic study on the procedures of Parliament, utilising the knowledge he had gathered while in government, and the other book would be his memoirs. Crossman insisted he wanted to write another Bagehot, writing a book which would demystify the British Constitution.[72] As it was, circumstances were to make the writing of these books impossible. He had additionally set about writing a biography of his great friend Chaim Weizmann, the first President of Israel but in 1973, when he was again diagnosed with the cancer which would kill him, he was forced to abandon this project. Instead he dedicated his time to working on his political diaries.

Crossman's diaries had been recorded on tape and transcribed by his secretary on a regular basis since the 1950s. He appears to have taken the decision in 1973 that these diaries should be edited and published to demystify government:

> It was not very long before I realized the interest of a diary which gave a daily picture of how a minister of the Wilson government spent his time, exactly what he did in his department, in cabinet committee and in cabinet itself, and how much time he spent outside his office visiting authorities under his control, and finally what he had left for his family at the weekend.[73]

He maintained that the diaries had not been written for publication but purely to provide raw material for his other books on government which he did not have time to write. This was not another Bagehot but it would certainly achieve its aims.[74] In order to get this work started as his health deteriorated, and also to ensure that details were not edited out of the diaries which would decrease their accuracy, Crossman employed Janet Morgan of Nuffield College. Morgan met him when she was writing her PhD thesis, later published, on the House of Lords reform which he had attempted while Leader of the House of Commons.[75] They began editing the volumes, starting with the period 1964 to 1966, while Crossman had been Minister for Housing and Local Government. While they managed to complete the editing of this book, with Crossman writing the introduction to this volume, he did not live to see it published, dying of his illness in April 1974. Morgan continued the editing of the diaries, completing the editing of another two volumes of the *Diaries of a Cabinet Minister* which covered the periods 1966 to 1968, 1968 to 1970 and his earlier backbench diaries which covered the period 1951 to 1963.[76]

When Crossman told Wilson of his intention to publish his diaries, Wilson asked him to delay until after the 1974 election, so as not to damage the chances of the party, which Crossman did. When the first volume of the diaries was serialised in the *Sunday Times* in January 1975, nine months after his death, the Wilson government immediately set up the Radcliffe Committee to consider the issue of ministers publishing memoirs or diaries.[77] When the book was ready for publication in June 1975, the Wilson government took the publishers to court and attempted to ban the publication of the diaries on the grounds that it broke the Common Law of Confidentiality. Crossman had appointed the executors of his will carefully, selecting Michael Foot to help his wife Anne. Foot and Anne Crossman, as executors of the will, joined forces with the publishers, Hamish Hamilton and Jonathan Cape, and the *Sunday Times* to fight this censorship, hoping to publish in full. After a lengthy legal dispute, the first volume of the diaries were published in 1975 and the controversy regarding publication can only have helped sales. Subsequent volumes were published and other ministers eventually published their own diaries, including Barbara Castle and Tony Benn's many volumes. In addition, many ministers from the Wilson cabinet published their memoirs, including Wilson himself.

Conclusion

Richard Crossman had a unique career. While not achieving any of the top three jobs in government he was, none the less, a very influential individual with an almost unprecedented political career. His 'bump of irreverence' caused him to have very rocky relations with two of the three leaders whom he served, but he was lucky enough, after nineteen years on the backbenches, to have one of his closest political friends become leader and then Prime Minister. While Wilson's impressions of their friendship may perhaps have varied from those of Crossman, they had a very close working relationship when this was appropriate, and Crossman indicated in his diaries that they were loyal friends.[78] He was undoubtedly an excellent teacher and a good journalist, but he was also a dedicated and hard-working cabinet minister, despite upsetting several high-ranking civil servants during his career, Dame Evelyn Sharp being perhaps the most injured. While his manner was blunt and direct, he was a dedicated husband and father, who inspired loyalty from his constituents, who loyally supported him from 1945 until his death in 1974. His ability to work through the night, to absorb information quickly and to make educated decisions under pressure made him a good departmental minister. This was countered by his ability to make monumental slip-ups when he wasn't thinking, such as when he left his cabinet papers under a chair in an expensive London restaurant, only for them to be returned to the police via the *Daily Mail*.[79] While tactically lacking in many respects, his career was, on the whole, very successful and he achieved high office, though did not necessarily enjoy the experience as much as he had hoped. His diaries, while being insightful and unique, were simply one element of this complex and unique individual, and by focusing solely on them, the reader can forget the other publications which he produced and his hard work in the Labour Party, on the NEC and as a member of the Wilson cabinet from 1964 to 1970. While not a leading minister, nor a leading thinker within the Labour movement, he was certainly not just another MP, but fulfilled a unique position within the party bringing to it a personality which people either loved or hated.

3

Crossman, Socialism and Social Democracy

The Labour Party experienced some of its fiercest internal wrangles between the late 1940s and the early 1960s. One of the key issues of this dispute was the development of socialism and the effects of the nationalisation programme of the Attlee government. While categorisations are never without exceptions, the dispute tended to be fiercest between those on the left and right wings of the party. Those on the left of the party tended to support 'traditional' socialism, favouring extensive and increasing nationalisation of industry. Thorpe argued that the left's 'lack of a coherent and distinctive ideology kept it marginalized.'[1] Those on the right favoured a re-evaluation of the party's aims, with a move away from socialism toward social democracy. These different ideologies have been labelled as socialism and social democracy, highlighted by their left and right wing supporters' labels as either Bevanite or Gaitskellite. Socialism and social democracy shared many similarities; both favoured equality, though they defined it differently, and alluded to some form of wealth redistribution within society, the key difference being over the nationalisation of industry. The 'traditional' definition of socialism, which was itself not a single definition, argued that nationalisation was essential to form a more equal society. The specific details of nationalisation programmes varied, but it was the central part of a socialist policy supported by those on the left. Jefferys noted that 'Bevan made much of the ideological clash over "party purpose", between "fundamentalists" wanting more nationalisation and "revisionists" who favoured a less traditional agenda.'[2] Those on the right of the party tended to question the continued necessity of nationalisation in the changing economic circumstances of post-war Britain.

The left-right separation was not as clear-cut as it may initially seem. Many within the party tended to be more central figures, often focusing on more practical issues, leaving the more theoretical arguments to the intellectuals or key individuals on both wings of the party. Even of those who could be categorised as being members of either the left or right wing, their opinions tended to evolve over time, meaning that their understanding of socialism very often adapted to both the changing economic circumstances and the changing dynamics of the party. Following the deaths of both Bevan and Gaitskell in the early 1960s, and the economic influence of a decade of Conservative rule, the dispute moved away from ideological differences instead focusing on the practical policy details. Jefferys argued that 'neither side had formulated a coherent programme to apply to domestic politics, and they shared more common ground than was apparent, particularly over the achievements of 1945-51. What this left in essence were differences of style and emphasis, compounded by a hardening of personal loyalties.'[3] Wilson's succession as leader in 1963, while not ending the conflict, united the party, many of whom were willing to bury difficulties over ideology in their desire for office. While Wilson had been a centre-left figure for much of his political career, his brief flirtation with the Bevanites in the early 1950s had left an indelible impression on his right wing colleagues, many of whom he included in his 1964 to 1966 cabinet in order to consolidate his position.

In order to contextualise Crossman's views on socialism, we will consider how his opinions compared with those of R.H. Tawney, Evan Durbin and Anthony Crosland. Durbin, who died in 1948, was an early thinker on how socialism could evolve and how it should develop in the future. His friend, Crosland, was a key thinker on the development of social democracy and the rethinking of socialism following the end of the Attlee government. Crossman noted that R.H. Tawney had been a huge influence on his own thinking, indicating in his diaries in 1960 that he considered Tawney to be one of the great 'socialists'. He concluded that others in the Labour Party were less enthusiastic, merely paying lip service to his views, 'they admitted that Tawney's our greatest socialist fighter. But why bother about reading books?'[4] While these individuals were all intellectuals, and they often dominated the debate, reflecting the intellectual influx into the Labour Party, particularly in 1945, there were key individuals within the debate who had alternative backgrounds. Aneurin Bevan was undoubtedly the most prominent non-intellectual within the debate, reflecting his working-class background and support for nationalisation. He seems to have gathered his supporters due to his personality and charisma, developing almost a 'cult of personality'. However, many MPs did not take an active role in the debate, instead focusing their attention on more practical matters. Thorpe argued that Bevan was surrounded by an intellectual circle of associates who seem to have encouraged him to consider more ideological issues, though he seems to have required little encouragement, probably egged on by his personal animosity for many of those on the right and his deeply held left wing views. 'Bevan was not anti-intellectual: far from it. In the sense of having a questioning and open mind, looking for new solutions and being receptive to new ideas, he was more of an intellectual than Gaitskell himself.'[5]

Michael Freeden has considered in *Ideologies and Political Theory* the confusion which can arise when terms are utilised without being fully explained.[6] The meaning of individual terms and labels can be interpreted differently by different groups, within different geographical locations and over different eras. 'Ideologies are distinctive configurations of political concepts and …they create specific conceptual patterns from a pool of indeterminate and unlimited combinations.'[7]

This lack of clarity can lead to conflict where, with greater explanation, there would be only minimal disagreement. An example of this can be found in Harold Wilson's views on the future of socialism. Wilson's views on socialism can be categorised as being centre-left. He was not a devotee of nationalisation and this often led him into conflict with those on the left, who do not seem to have ever accepted Wilson as a Bevanite, despite his labelling by others in the party. In reality, Wilson's views on socialism were fairly similar to those of the Gaitskellites, with the main difference seeming to be one of presentation rather than policy.[8] However, the possibility of Wilson being categorised as, or labelling himself, as a member of the centre-right was impeded by the personal animosity which many on the right felt towards him. Freeden noted that 'socialism entails a massive leap of faith and imagination, an emotional as well as an intellectual effort to claim that what has never been, or what belongs to a conjectural history, is nevertheless normal and proper to human beings and their societies.'[9]

As Wilson began to associate less with those on the left, they also began to feel animosity towards him. Ian Mikardo indicated that Crossman and Wilson were considered to be a more centre-left sub-grouping by the late-1950s with their own methods and aims. '...Neither Dick nor Harold ever suffered the perils of spontaneity, or ever made a move without first thinking it out very carefully; I found it ironical that they were precisely the left-wing equivalents of the two men they had knocked off the NEC, Morrison and Dalton.'[10] To say Crossman always thought carefully before acting or was never spontaneous does seem misleading considering some of the awkward situations he placed himself in due to a lack of planning. Additionally, Mikardo's description of Wilson and Crossman as 'operators' or 'wire-pullers' seems ironic considering that Mikardo was considered by many to be rather an operator himself.[11] However, it is useful to see the distance which Mikardo perceived between the Wilson-Crossman alliance and the other Bevanites by the late-1950s. The personal animosity which many on the right felt towards Wilson encouraged him to seek support initially from the left, but he also attempted to gain support from more central figures.

The conflict between the Gaitskellites and the Bevanites was based on more than confusion and a lack of understanding. There were real ideological differences between the two sides, but very often personality clashes seem to have played an equally important part. Bevan's irritation at Gaitskell's promotion to Chancellor of the Exchequer in October 1950 seems to have contributed to his resignation from the cabinet in April 1951, and much of Wilson's hostility to the Gaitskellites while he was Prime Minister was focused on Crosland, limiting his career and his economic influence over the rest of the cabinet. Often, circumstance played its part in the conflict, such as the 1959 election defeat re-igniting the debate once again over nationalisation, with Clause IV becoming the new battleground.

The Attlee Government

The Labour Party had been in existence for over forty years when Attlee became Prime Minister in 1945. The party had been established primarily to provide Trade Unions with a political voice, reflecting the needs of both their leaders and their members. The future of socialism was generally viewed as being of secondary importance to more practical motivations, such as the establishment of greater equality within society:

> The principles of socialism were not invented by the founders of the party. They inherited them from a long succession of Radicals who fought against tyranny and privilege, and from those Christians who always know that their faith must include a struggle against social injustice.[12]

While the party members generally accepted socialism of one type or another, it was very rarely considered to be as important as practical legislation to help the working classes. While the 1918 party constitution committed Labour to public ownership, the Labour governments of 1924 and 1929-31 did not enact this, demonstrating that the constitution was not a guarantee of nationalisation. These minority governments were hamstrung by circumstance, with their weakness making any radical reform impossible. As Thorpe noted, the infamous Clause IV was not included in the constitution due to a deep-seated belief in socialism within the party. It was to 'sweeten the pill for committed socialists of a constitution which gave more power than ever to the unions.'[13]

When Attlee became Prime Minister, the circumstances were somewhat different to those of the previous Labour governments. While the party had been out of power in the 1930s, they had considered numerous different policy areas, creating general policy outlines for many. This meant that in many areas, including nationalisation, the party could be guided by existing plans, though this was often fairly problematic in practice. Jefferys noted as an example that 'Dalton spearheaded a move towards a form of democratic socialism which combined demand management with physical control economic planning.'[14] In addition, the government was far stronger than the Labour governments under MacDonald had been, with a majority of 159 in the Commons and experience of government during the Second World War. The wartime conditions in Britain had led certain controls to be introduced on industry which would have previously been almost unthinkable, including a central control of labour by Bevin as Minister of Labour.[15] The success of these measures and the desire for a new approach to government which the Labour Party had outlined, gathered public support to the party and nationalisation began to feature seriously on the political agenda. 'Attlee's party, it seemed, offered both immediate redress for a war-weary population and a long-term commitment to a reconstructed "welfare state."'[16] While nationalisation was an important part of the government's plans, it was not universally supported by all members of the party, as many limited their support to implementation in failing industries, demonstrated by the battle over steel nationalisation in the late 1940s.

Crossman, Wilson and the Bevanites

While Crossman spent his early parliamentary career focusing on foreign policy (see chapter 4), he was, by 1947, already a member of left wing groupings within the party, considering both foreign and domestic policy. In 1947, Crossman teamed up with Michael Foot and Ian Mikardo to write Keep Left, a pamphlet considering domestic and foreign policy, representing the response of the wider *Keep Left* group to the actions of the Attlee government. The first half of the pamphlet focused on domestic policy and while it appears that Crossman did not write this section (Mikardo claimed the section was based on a series of papers he had written) he seems to have supported all of its recommendations.[17] 'In its final form it [the pamphlet] has been written by only three of us – Dick Crossman, Michael Foot and Ian Mikardo – and they take responsibility for the detail and form of its arguments. But, nevertheless, this book is a joint production of all of us.'[18]

The pamphlet praised the nationalisation programme of the Attlee government as far as it went. It argued that the programme needed to maintain momentum with other industries requiring nationalisation, including chemicals and electrical components:

> This nationalisation programme has been carried out vigorously, and needs to be continued to embrace every industry which has a hold over our national economy or those which cannot be made efficient in private hands. The former group includes heavy chemicals and some non-banking forms of finance, such as insurance, and the latter include the iron and steel industries and the manufacture of some things, like motor-vehicles and certain electrical components, which need much more design-standardisation than they will ever get under multiple ownership.[19]

Additionally, the pamphlet criticised the speed of the programme, insisting that in future it should be implemented far more quickly, and the lack of modernisation within industry needed to be remedied immediately. 'The main theme running through this book is that we need, in all our planning, a greater sense of *urgency* than has been shown over the last couple of years, and a realisation that the economic struggle we've got on our hands can't be waged with the leisureliness of a phoney war.'[20]

However, the pamphlet provided very little practical detail on how these proposals should be implemented, how business should be modernised or even on what basis certain industries had been earmarked for nationalisation. This gave the proposals a sense of arbitrary selection, with no discussion of the criteria on which these industries were selected. There was little consideration of whether the industries which had been nationalised were accountable to Parliament, an issue which Crossman was to return to later repeatedly in his own writing. The only suggestion which was put forward in this pamphlet regarding increasing accountability was the proposal to extend Joint Production Committees which had been set up during the war.[21]

Crossman's first serious 'solo' attempt to consider domestic socialism and its future came in 1952, when the *New Fabian Essays* were published.[22] These were an updated version of the original *Fabian Essays in Socialism* which had been published in 1889.[23] As well as editing the essays, he also contributed an essay entitled "Towards a Philosophy of Socialism". In this he argued that the Labour Party had lost its way after 1950. Much of the legislation which had been planned before the Second World War had been implemented and the party was now unsure of how to proceed. He concluded that there was a lack of theoretical research within the party and that socialism was often based on general understanding and even hunches. 'The Labour Party has lost its way not only because it lacks a map of the new country it is crossing, but because it thinks maps unnecessary for experienced travellers.'[24] He demanded that more research be done, upon which future legislation could be based. However, Crossman also argued that centralisation and a planned economy were not necessarily part of a socialist programme anymore. Instead, concentrations of power, whether they be in the public or private sector, should be prevented and more accountability introduced into the system.[25] This was his first consideration of accountability in terms of domestic policy, though he had previously considered how unaccountable the constitutional arrangements were in Britain.[26] In this essay, Crossman did not consider nationalisation and did not comment on the future of this policy, though this was an issue which he would consider less than four years later.

Crossman's most complete individual study on socialism came in his 1956 Fabian pamphlet *Socialism and the New Despotism.*[27] This publication really demonstrated how far his opinions had moved away from those of the Bevanites. He argued that many socialists had concluded that capitalism would simply collapse due to its inherent immorality, which would simply not happen. Instead Britain was living in a situation which was worse than that existing in either the USSR or the USA, due to falling between the two stools of 'full socialist planning and a modern American Keynsianism.'[28] He argued that to remedy this, the Labour Party needed to appreciate that socialism should not be based on any specific economic policy. Socialism was instead a moral protest against social injustice and that required all concentrations of power to be challenged, a point Crossman had made in his 1952 essay.[29] He argued that all nationalised industries should be made fully responsible to Parliament.[30] Additionally, he argued that worker participation within management might encourage more accountability, though this was not easy to achieve. While he recognised that he did not have any specific proposals for the implementation of this, Crossman argued that Britain might be able to learn from the German style of workers participation (Mitbestimmungsrecht), and that this should be studied to see if any common ground could be found.[31]

While socialism was to be a moral protest, Crossman argued that nationalisation was not a blanket policy, though it was still an important tool, similar to Crosland's argument that nationalisation was a method, not a goal in its own right. Crossman therefore did not provide a list of industries which should be taken over by the state, suggesting instead that industries should only be nationalised if non-socialists could be convinced of the benefits. 'We would be prudent, therefore, to select industries where even the non-socialist can be convinced that it is desirable.'[32] In practice, this would mean that many industries would escape nationalisation and this policy would only really be instituted in failing industries, particularly those which were fundamentally important to the country, such as coal nationalisation had been in 1947. However, he also argued that certain municipal policies which impacted on the public might fall into this category, such as housing rent, or even the creation of municipal theatres and cinemas.[33]

Socialism and the New Despotism was split into two parts, with the first section considering the economic future of socialism and how concentrations of power could be avoided. The second section concentrated on the accountability of government, an aspect of socialism which Crossman felt was particularly important. He was able to provide more detailed plans in this pamphlet, suggesting the establishment of specialist parliamentary committees and changes to the recruitment of the civil service. These constitutional reforms are considered in chapter 5 because, while accountability was a key element of Crossman's personal form of socialism, his views on constitutional reform were so wide-ranging and detailed that they need separate analysis. This pamphlet is particularly worthy of note as it shows how Crossman's luke-warm enthusiasm for nationalisation had decreased even further by late-1955. Additionally, it shows him focusing on issues which particularly interested him, with his consideration of the development of socialism focused on accountability and constitutional reform, while his discussion of economic restructuring or reform is really very slight in comparison to, for example, Crosland's study published in the same year.[34]

Crossman's last publication specifically on socialism and nationalisation, *Labour in the Affluent Society*, was somewhat different to his other pamphlets and chapters.[35] This pamphlet had a rather abrasive style and was quite contradictory to his earlier publications, particularly *Socialism and the New Despotism*. Crossman argued that the west was being increasingly dwarfed by the economic strength of the USSR. He then proceeded to make some projections about what would happen to the USSR, the vast majority of which were later proved completely inaccurate. For example, he stated that 'the Kremlin is sure that, in the course of the next twenty years, the North Atlantic area will become a prosperous backwater ... Recent history supports their confidence.'[36] Crossman argued that Britain would be negatively affected by the European Common Market and that the only answer to this combination of factors was a gigantic transfer of power from private industry to the government, though no specific industries were named. He stated that this process would not be without problems, noting that 'there would be dangers to freedom in this process of subjecting irresponsible economic power to public control.'[37] Crossman concluded that Crosland's proposals for influencing the behaviour of industry through taxation and other economic incentives, were unworkable and that it was impossible to control private industry.

Labour in the Affluent Society is far more positive about the implementation and effects of nationalisation than any of his other writing and it seems likely that this was a reaction to Crossman's fall out with Gaitskell and his response to the 1959 debate over the rewriting of Clause IV. Crossman commented on the influence on his work of Thomas Balogh, who became an economic adviser to Wilson, and how he far preferred his work to Crosland's restatement of socialism, reflecting the important of personalities within the dispute.[38] None of Crossman's other writing is as defeatist about the threat of the USSR and as positive about the advantages of nationalisation, so this pamphlet needs to be viewed in terms of the external events which it seems to have been a reaction to. While it called for a huge nationalisation programme, Crossman never returned to this theme again, and his enthusiasm for nationalisation had never previously been particularly strong. Had Crossman remained on good terms with Gaitskell it seems likely that this pamphlet, which was so critical of the Gaitskellites, would not have been published.

Following his 1960 pamphlet, Crossman did not write anything else on either socialism generally or nationalisation more specifically.[39] He was already spending much of his time concentrating on issues he found more interesting and his career as a part-time journalist. From 1963 onwards, he was preoccupied with his role within Wilson's opposition front bench and later his government. However, it should not be assumed that his views on socialism remained static. Instead, the development of his views which had begun in the mid-1950s continued. Crossman was gradually becoming a member of the establishment, which he was both pleased with and critical of. He objected to the pomp and circumstance of the establishment, complaining repeatedly about his need to wear a morning suit or bow to the Queen when he became a member of the Privy Council in 1964.[40] Despite this rejection of the establishment and his support for individual freedom, he gradually became less accepting of individual protest, something which was completely at odds with his earlier views. This increasing conservatism can be seen in his reaction to the student riot in Oxford in 1967, describing it as similar to 'the atmosphere of a Weimar Republic meeting...'[41] While Crossman objected to the views of the young, which were very much at odds with his own, he never made any plans to introduce any measures which would have limited the right of people to demonstrate or limited their individual freedom. While his private views as expressed in the diaries were changing and becoming far less radical, his public political doctrine remained fairly constant, seeking accountability from government and protecting the rights of the individual.

While his increasing age and time in government undoubtedly influenced Crossman's views on socialism and personal freedom, I would argue that his lifestyle seems to have been the decisive factor in his changing personal views.

When he married his third wife Anne McDougall, they moved into Anne's father's home, Prescote Manor, a 360-acre farm in Oxfordshire. His increasingly affluent lifestyle is noted in his diaries, where he wrote about his new swimming pool and his happiness in this haven. 'Now I can have my regular swim of 500 yards each day before breakfast and another 500 yards before supper. Heavens, the difference it makes to my general health and sense of strength and well-being.'[42] He considered in his diaries whether his increasingly wealthy lifestyle had affected his political views, often concluding, with rather typical self-deception, that his life at Prescote had not particularly affected his opinions. However, his increasing wealth and his lifestyle at Prescote added to his increasingly conservative attitude to issues relating to socialism, such as taxation and personal freedom. 'You may laugh, but from this farm responsibility I have learnt about growth, about investment and about tax. It's a business with a £30,000 turnover, and I have learned a tremendous lot about business management.'[43] His radicalism, which Crossman had held so dear, was waning and his support for socialism, while never particularly strong, was weakening. 'Does this wealth blunt our socialism? The answer, I'm afraid, is that of course it does.'[44]

While Crossman's commitment to both the left wing and nationalisation was never particularly strong, his commitment reduced dramatically in the early 1950s, so that by 1955 he was more accurately identified as being on the centre-left of the party. Rather than being a Bevanite by instinct, Crossman was a Wilsonite. He was one of Wilson's most loyal allies, and as time passed and their careers diverged, with Wilson reaching greater and greater career heights, Crossman began to focus his energy on aiding Wilson. His views, particularly on socialism, were very closely linked to those of Wilson. However, despite this developing relationship, he did not completely break away from the Bevanites. Bevanite meetings were still held on occasion in the sitting room of 9 Vincent Square, Crossman's London home, throughout the 1950s and he was a regular attendee. Pimlott argued that Wilson failed to join the Gaitskellites due to personality clashes with other members, 'we should not over-simplify the barrier that divided Wilson from such people [Gaitskell and Jay], whose intellectual leadership counted for so much in the Labour Party.'[45] It seems probable that Crossman continued to attend Bevanite meetings for the social benefits.

The Bevanites combined a cult of personality which seems to have existed around Bevan, with a more traditional definition of socialism, with nationalisation at its very core. It could not easily be argued that Wilson possessed the same type of magnetism as Bevan who, like Crossman, appears to have revelled in his reputation as a rebel. The public personas of Bevan and Wilson were also very different. However, Wilson was capable of being dynamic and cultivating close professional friendships, such as that he shared with Crossman, and in many respects he was a far better leader than Bevan would ever have been. His skills in people management were put to good use while he was Prime Minister, controlling difficult individuals, like George Brown.[46] Wilson was not particularly enthusiastic about nationalisation, believing instead that economic planning and the use of management techniques were very useful tools for a government. As Crossman himself pointed out in 1952, differences within the right and left wing of the party were more limited in domestic policies than may be assumed. 'Douglas Jay and Harold Wilson really wanted the same economic policy and that between Nye and Hugh Gaitskell there were really only differences of emphasis, temperament and will as regards domestic policy...'[47]

The term 'Wilsonite' can only be used to describe a very limited number of individuals, of which Crossman was one. He was completely loyal to Wilson and his more centrist position, and while their views were not always in tune with each other, they tended to share commonalities, such as their lack of enthusiasm for nationalisation. As Crossman rather arrogantly stated, 'I think he [Wilson] really does rely on me personally and is probably the only member of the Parliamentary Labour Party who is not afraid of my brutal brain power.'[48] Wilson was very important in his life, filling a variety of different roles – friend, mentor, ally, political superior, intellectual equal. The developing opinions of Crossman can often be linked to those of Wilson, indicating that, in some respects, he was to Wilson as Crosland was to Gaitskell, an intellectual (and friend) who supported another in spite of, or perhaps partly because of, their own aspirations. As Pimlott indicated, Crossman's support may have strengthened over time due to his realisation that he would never be leader of the Labour Party:

> Some time before Gaitskell's death, he [Crossman] had come to the conclusion that Wilson was the political professional, while he himself was only a gentleman amateur. He had decided, on this basis, to feed ideas and schemes to Wilson's computer–like brain for efficient, detached processing.[49]

Marcia Williams argued that 'they are both close friends and old rivals. In the inner recesses of Dick's mind must lurk the thought that he himself might have been the leader of the Labour Party.'[50] This surely must have been an over-exaggeration of the situation, as many within the Labour Party would have sincerely hoped.

While Pimlott argued that Crossman was feeding Wilson ideas, it seems likely that Wilson only adopted ideas which fitted in with his general philosophy. It also seems probable that this transfer of ideas was not simply one-way. While Crossman might provide him with certain ideas, Wilson allowed Crossman the forum in which to formulate these, by appointing him to certain committees and government departments. In Wilson, he had a friend who had a good chance of becoming Party Leader were events to take a turn in his favour, as they did in 1963. By courting and cultivating their working relationship, Crossman might be able to find an alternative way to the front bench, to act as a loyal lieutenant to a possible future leader. As he wrote in 1963, following Wilson's appointment as Leader of the Labour party, '... of all the 249 Members of the Parliamentary Labour Party, Harold is the one person closest to me, the one I get on best with, the one whose relationships with me have been tested over twelve years by some fairly trying times.'[51]

Wilson and Crossman's views, while not identical, did share many similarities. Their political ideologies were, by 1954/5, very similar, leading to them sharing a number of policy views and a common outlook. However, as Pimlott noted, Wilson's views were very difficult to firmly establish. 'Wilson's actual views were hard to pin down. Since his cleverness and knowledge made it possible for him to argue every position, and he frequently shifted ground, critics wondered whether he had any.'[52] This criticism was often levelled at Crossman. Denis Healey accused him of the very same fault when considering a disagreement they had once had. 'Like a Greek sophist, Dick was always more interested in the process of argument than its conclusion.'[53] While Wilson rarely argued with his colleagues as Crossman did, probably due to his political skills and differing style, they were both viewed with suspicion by much of the rest of the party, and as their friendship and political alliance deepened, this suspicion increased. This convergence of personalities and ideas can be demonstrated by looking at some of the key ideological issues which Crossman considered and were of importance to the wider discussion of socialism.

This close professional relationship between Crossman and Wilson culminated in Crossman's appointment as Minister of Housing and Local Government in Wilson's first cabinet. His three positions within Wilson's government were not within the economic sphere, undoubtedly due to his lack of knowledge and Crossman did not focus on socialism again, instead focusing predominantly on departmental issues. However, his diaries show his developing views on socialism, which gradually became less radical and reflected his absorption into the establishment. His changing circumstances seem to have affected his views on socialism. His lifestyle at Prescote, his Oxfordshire manor house, also seems to have affected his views, with his diaries mentioning the building of his swimming pool and his concerns over tax rises, hardly the comments of a devoted socialist. This gradual change in his views seems to have been a continual process which had begun in the early 1950s, being reflected in his essay in the *New Fabian Essays,* which was uncommital about nationalisation and economic planning.[54] This gradual change reflected the unsteady foundations on which Crossman's version of socialism was built, that of rebellion and controversial opinion. Healey noted that Crossman believed that the duty of a socialist was to 'automatically ... oppose anything which was being proposed', a situation he thought was intolerable.[55] While objecting to the establishment and the staid views of those members of it, Crossman gradually became part of it and his views became less radical as he grew older. His views were not, even in the early 1950s, in line with those on the left wing of the party and by the late 1960s, his views on socialism were uncontroversial and represented only a very small part of his wider ideological views. Instead, he focused on constitutional reform, Israel and the legislation which his various departments introduced.

The Revisionists

For many on the left, nationalisation was an end as well as a means, as discussed above. For Crossman, nationalised industries were merely a useful mechanism for creating a planned and dynamic economy within Britain. As his thinking developed during the 1950s, nationalisation seems to have become less important to him, but the overall aim of an equal and freer society remained the same. While his thinking was gradually changing, becoming less left wing during the early 1950s, the right wing of the party were also reconsidering their aims. Following the reforms of the Attlee government from 1945 to 1950, many of the key policies which had been worked out in opposition had been implemented and by 1950 the government had run out of steam with several of its key members severely ill, including Bevin and Cripps. In 1933, Morrison had argued that

> The function of Labour governments in the future will rather be to secure the socialisation of industry after industry under a management which can, broadly, be relied upon to go on with its work. And having done one good deed the minister can let the people put in charge carry on with the work thus done, whilst he immediately sets about the other good deeds of socialisation which await his attention.[56]

This continual nationalisation did not occur, but once the key industries had been taken into public control, the government began to focus on the consolidation of this process. This was completely unacceptable to those on the left and it provided only a temporary answer. In the longer term, the right wing of the party needed a new programme, and this would provide an opportunity for some within the party to reach new conclusions, which would sideline nationalisation in favour of less interventionist policies.

This re-evaluation of the aims of the party had begun in 1940 when Evan Durbin published *The Politics of Democratic Socialism*.[57] This book did not have an immediate or explosive impact, mainly due to its publication during wartime when many, including Durbin himself, were focused on Britain's survival. However, it was an early indication of the future discussions within the party over the development of socialism. In this book, he accepted some of the party's traditional aims, arguing that nationalisation was very important and should be instituted regardless of other considerations. In other policy areas, his views were more progressive, re-evaluating the party's means and ends. He favoured formal economic planning, with vigorous competition within industries, the preservation of liberty and he heavily criticised the USSR's human rights record.

The work of Durbin was continued and developed in new directions after his death in 1948 by Anthony Crosland, his close friend, culminating in his 1956 publication *The Future of Socialism*.[58] This book was the culmination of the revisionist movement's thinking on socialism:

Traditional socialism was largely concerned with the evils of traditional capitalism, and with the need for its overthrow. But to-day traditional capitalism has been reformed and modified almost out of existence, and it is with a quite different form of society that socialists must now concern themselves.[59]

Unlike Durbin, Crosland argued that nationalisation was redundant in the new economic circumstances of post-war Britain. 'No longer could it be supposed that the conversion of private into public ownership of the means of production was sufficient to make redundant any concern with the political organization of freedom.'[60] Instead of spending millions of pounds of taxpayers' money on compensating share-holders in industries ear-marked for nationalisation, a fraction of that amount could be used as an incentive to encourage industry to adopt certain measures or locate in certain areas. In Crosland's opinion, this was a more economical and practical economic strategy for the party to adopt. He argued that nationalisation was not central to socialism and instead 'a more promising path would seem to be that offered by attempts to define socialist values (such as equality and fairness) and then to give effect to these values in terms of structures and procedures (such as equality and fairness).'[61] However, he did not dismiss nationalisation, aiming instead to make it less of a blanket policy, using it only when necessary for a specific industry. 'We no doubt want more nationalisation than we now have. But I at least do not want a steadily extending chain of state monopolies, believing this to be bad for liberty, and wholly irrelevant to socialism as defined in this book.'[62]

In 1959, Douglas Jay argued that the Labour Party's commitment to nationalisation was having a negative impact on Labour's electoral prospects. He 'wanted to abandon, not just nationalization, but also the unions and even the name 'the Labour Party' and to work for a pact with the Liberals.'[63] He convinced Gaitskell that Clause IV of the party's 1918 constitution, which committed the party to nationalisation, was unpopular amongst the electorate, though Gaitskell was not enthusiastic about nationalisation anyway. By re-writing Clause IV and removing this commitment, Jay and Gaitskell believed that the party would be more electorally successful, possibly even seen as modernising and moving with the times, driving the party in a different direction. 'In diverting the attention of socialists from questions of class power, Jay pointed to a definition of socialism which had more in common with the New Liberalism at the turn of the century.'[64] While nationalisation was not as popular within the party as it had been in the 1930s, 40s and early-50s, it was still a touchstone of the party and viewed as being part of the party's heritage and tradition.[65] While those on the left were obviously outraged by Gaitskell's proposals, they were not viewed any more sympathetically by those in the ideological centre of the party. Many believed that Jay's theory was completely false, and that this proposal was being forwarded in order to provide an excuse for the 1959 election defeat.[66] Pimlott argued that Wilson believed that 'changing the constitution in order to remove or adapt Clause IV, which formally committed the party to nationalization, seemed to him particularly absurd.'[67]

Crossman was not particularly interested in Clause IV either, as he believed it was fairly irrelevant. 'I don't care a fig about Clause IV, more particularly as I hear from Michael Foot that Gaitskell has got a very good redraft of the whole clause, which with a bit of amendment should be perfectly O. K. If that is so, I will give it to him. But I care really about nuclear weapons.'[68] However, he understood how important a symbol Clause IV was to some within the party and he concluded that Gaitskell's attempt to have Clause IV rewritten was an unnecessary process. The attempt to re-write the clause was unsuccessful, being defeated by the party conference but the battle was vicious and threatened to re-open old ideological wounds. The revisionist movement was not eradicated, either by this conference failure or by the unexpected death of Gaitskell in 1963, which robbed them of their leader and replaced him with the much-disliked but most acceptable candidate, Wilson. The dominant position which social democracy occupied within the Labour Party and the move away from socialism could be seen when Tony Blair pointed out in 1996, '...it is not and never was satisfactory to define socialism by state ownership and centralized planning.'[69]

Economic Planning

The measures which had been introduced during the Second World War to control consumption and direct industry had been very successful and relatively easily accepted by the public and industry bosses. While the circumstances of the Second World War had obviously created a new set of priorities, these were utilised by the Attlee government after 1945. Many of the controls were maintained well into the late 1940s, leading Wilson, in his role as President of the Board of Trade, to conduct his 'bonfire of controls' between November 1948 and February 1949. The Labour Party and the wider electorate did not see these as being contradictory to individual liberty. As Tudor Jones explained, 'it [central planning] had been legitimized ... by technical arguments, advanced by a number of investigative and advisory committees.'[70] The success of economic controls in Britain, though not long lasting, did pave the way for the discussion of economic planning. The Labour governments' legislation appeared to its supporters as 'a realization of long-standing commitments of principle and policy and hence as a partial fulfilment of deep-seated aspirations.'[71] Additionally, as will be considered later, the example which the USSR was setting in its adoption of the five-year economic plans, which were viewed by many as being extremely successful in the short term, was looked on with envy by many left wing members of the party in the early and mid-1950s, including Crossman.[72]

Economic planning, which had traditionally been viewed as important to socialism, was also an important element of social democracy and Tawney, Durbin, Crosland and Crossman all considered the relevance of this and whether it was beneficial in the changing circumstances of post-war Britain.[73] The main purpose of this planning was to encourage a levelling-up of society rather than a levelling down to create equality. Durbin believed, like Tawney, that this levelling up of society should be executed primarily by overall economic growth:

> The need to reduce incomes could ... be removed by new investment, which would allow general wealth to grow rather than redistributing the existing wealth. It was not an attack on the ruling class that was needed, but a concerted policy to increase the general wealth.[74]

Practical measures on how to introduce economic planning were fairly difficult to formulate due to the changing economic circumstances in Britain. Tawney, Durbin, Crosland and Crossman all supported some form of economic planning, but their plans were distinct, and in many cases, lacking in detail. Durbin suggested the creation of a Supreme Economic Authority, which might well have been like the Department of Economic Affairs (DEA) which Wilson established in 1964. This Supreme Economic Authority would plan the economy with its main focus being on the nationalised industries, but Durbin's plans were not particularly detailed, again due to the difficulty of detailed future planning in the changing circumstances of the 1940s. 'I should like to state at this point my conviction that it will be highly desirable to set up at an early stage some central control, or Supreme Economic Authority, for the "socialised sector" of industry.'[75] Tawney, Crosland and Crossman did not support the creation of such a body, with Crosland instead recommending a less interventionist approach to state direction.[76] When Wilson established the DEA, Crossman was dismissive of the plan and Wilson's motives for implementing it. Writing in 1965, Crossman noted that 'though George Brown is a great success, the division of power between the Treasury and the DEA is a development for which we are having to pay a heavy price in divided authority and dissension in central planning.'[77] Tawney and Crossman both supported some form of economic control and the establishment of an economic plan, but they were both very hazy on the details, with Crossman offering no suggestions on how this should be instituted. While various schemes existed on how practically to plan the economy, they tended to be unclear and patchy, with very little detailed thinking on the proposals, the focus instead being the general policy outline. However, it seems likely that for individuals such as Tawney and Durbin, the problem was in predicting the future state of Britain's economy rather than a lack of will to produce a plan of action.

The issue of planning led to a debate over what was an acceptable level of governmental bureaucracy and control, as it was concluded that too much control from the centre might be damaging to the economy. Again, the intellectuals had rather undefined and conflicting ideas. Tawney, Durbin and Crosland all agreed that too much government interference and bureaucracy would be harmful to business, which made economic plans more difficult to formulate. Tawney argued that 'public control and criticism are indispensable. But they should not be too detailed, or they defeat themselves.'[78] Crosland went further and indicated that state direction of industry was made more difficult by a lack of will by government ministers:

> If socialists want bolder planning, they must simply choose bolder ministers and – just as important – themselves accept a greater degree of self-restraint when the results of planning impinge unpleasantly, as they often will, on their constituents or their pet spheres of influence.[79]

However, none of these individuals actually outlined which specific forms of direction were acceptable or unacceptable. Crossman failed to give any consideration to how bureaucracy would impact on economic planning, though he did insist that accountability to Parliament was paramount, particularly in nationalised industries:

> For the socialist, as much as for the liberal, the state leviathan is a necessary evil; and the fact that part of the civil service now administers a welfare state does not remove the threat to freedom which the twentieth-century concentration of power has produced.[80]

In Crossman's case, this lack of analysis seems to have been due to him having no economic training or knowledge, as demonstrated in 1966 when he asked Michael Stewart, a fellow cabinet minister, to give him a 'severe tutorial' on the effects of various economic policies.[81] While he knew generally what he was interested in and what he wanted to be achieved in this field, he did not have the specialist knowledge to actually plan any of it out in detail. Anthony Crosland noted Crossman's lack of expertise and credibility within economic circles when criticising his position on the development of the Russian economy, 'in such an uncertain field, with so much not properly understood, nothing can be stated with the "mathematical certainty" which Mr Crossman, a non-economist, apparently feels.'[82]

The recurring feature in the writing of our four intellectuals was an accepted level of generality, with almost no detailed planning. Instead the broad policy area was of paramount importance, with detail being overlooked or unattainable. Many of the plans which Tawney, Durbin, Crosland and Crossman advocated in terms of economic planning in Britain shared some similarities. They all supported some form of planning, though the specific details or level of participation in business by government were not outlined in any detail. While Tawney, Durbin and Crosland did attempt to generate detailed plans on other issues, they failed to do so in terms of economic planning. Crossman did not have the practical expertise or knowledge to provide any detailed plans, and socialism and economic planning were not areas in which he expressed a prolonged interest.

Nationalisation

An important element of economic planning, nationalisation, was at the very heart of the dispute between the Gaitskellites and the Bevanites. As has been previously noted, the left favoured nationalisation, believing that it was a key element to create a more equal society. The Bevanites believed that when key industries were nationalised, a more equal society would simply happen, very little else was needed. The right believed that, while nationalisation might be useful within certain industries, competition was essential to create a successful economy, with excessive central governmental control impeding these market forces. Those on the right, such as Crosland, argued that private ownership was 'compatible with a high degree of equality, while state ownership, as the Russian experience has demonstrated, may be used to support a high degree of inequality.'[83] While there were raging battles within the party over the future of socialism and the necessity of nationalisation as a policy to create equality, there was much common ground, with conflict existing in only limited areas. As Tawney noted, in reference to the disputes in the 1920s and 30s,

> much eloquence and some heat have been engendered in recent years by the supposed division of the movement into a left wing and a right. Whatever the source of such suggestions, nine-tenths of them are nonsense. The differences are not what they are supposed to be, nor, in so far as they exist, have they the importance ascribed to them.[84]

The conflict reached its height in 1959 during the Clause IV debate. As has been previously discussed, while this conflict raised questions about the party's heritage and its own image, its future plans were at the very centre of the debate. Individuals such as Bevan and Foot believed that nationalisation was not simply a tool for creating a more equal society, it was something which was desirable in its own right. Bevan argued that 'for the socialist, Parliamentary power is to be used progressively until the main streams of economic activity are brought under public control.'[85] Crosland opposed extensive nationalisation or a blanket policy, while Tawney and Durbin were generally in favour. Crossman's views changed during the period 1945-55, but he had never been particularly enthusiastic about nationalisation, and he gradually became less in favour of the implementation of this policy on a large-scale.

Tawney, Durbin and Crossman (at least until 1956) were in favour of some form of programme of nationalisation, while Crosland believed that nationalisation was an ineffective way of directing many industries, though it could work in certain unspecified industries. Durbin is often associated with the revisionist movement, and he was in broad agreement with Crosland on many economic issues, but he supported nationalisation of industry regardless of any other considerations. As Geoffrey Foote indicated, 'Durbin was a major forerunner of revisionist thought in political ideas, but his belief in a centrally planned economy prevented him from breaking out of corporate socialism.'[86] He was so dedicated to nationalisation that he even went so far as to suggest that social security payments should be cut to pay the compensation to shareholders of nationalised industries:.

> It is not wise in the long run to expect to live upon golden eggs and slowly to strangle the goose that lays them. At a certain point economic power must be placed before social betterment if social betterment is to be secured.[87]

While this would undoubtedly produce short term hardship, he believed that the increasing production of industry would eventually lead to higher tax payments, which would allow social security payments to gradually rise again. Durbin's plans for nationalisation were more extreme that those suggested by either Tawney or Crossman, who both agreed with Durbin on the broad outlines of policy, though not on the blanket policy of nationalisation which he supported. It seems possible that had Durbin lived longer and seen the implementation of much of the Attlee government's nationalisation programme, his views might have been affected by their impact, though it is impossible to guess how they would have changed. Perhaps, like Crosland, he would have looked for other alternatives to nationalisation after the experiences of the post-war Labour government.

Tawney, Crosland and Crossman suggested that a blanket policy of nationalisation should not be instituted, with industries or businesses being considered individually instead. Crosland additionally looked to other methods of influencing industry. Tawney indicted that 'whether control should take the form of regulation, or of their acquisition by the State and management by a public body, is a question of expediency, to be answered differently in different cases.'[88] While Crossman did mention certain industries that could be nationalised in his diaries, he did not outline why he had picked these specific industries. In 1951 he wrote in his diaries that a new Bevanite pamphlet, which he would have been associated with had it come to fruition, would 'probably include a demand for a wide extension of public ownership, including the nationalization of oil and chemicals as essential if we are to have sufficient power over the private sector to be really able to plan.'[89] However, as previously discussed, his views changed during his career so that by the mid-1950s, he was less accepting of nationalisation. Tawney was somewhat more reasoned, noting that certain industries and resources were so important to the national economy that they needed to be under the control of the state:

> There are certain natural resources, certain kinds of property, certain types of economic organization, on the use of which the mass of mankind depend for their well being. The masters of these resources, therefore, are in a position, in the absence of countervailing measures, to secure exceptionally favourable terms for themselves, and to exercise an unusual degree of control over the lives of their fellows.[90]

Crosland believed that in the changing circumstances of post-war Britain, it was not crucially important who owned certain key industries, as they tended to be run by professional managers who were seeking the same outcomes as business owners. These managers, '(like the capitalists before them) pursue the goals of growth, profits and personal wealth.'[91] While nationalisation was not completely dismissed by Crosland, he considered it to be only one solution among many. In 1956 he argued that many socialists were no longer in favour of nationalisation on the scale which had been seen previously. 'Do we simply go on, and in our next period of office take over the next five largest industries, and so on *ad infinitum*? Not many socialists would now definitely answer yes.'[92] When nationalisation was to be introduced in an industry, Crosland argued that it should be carefully evaluated to discover whether it was the most useful or relevant solution and if a better, simpler solution couldn't be found.

While Durbin and Crosland were at odds over whether individual industries should be selected for nationalisation or a more widespread policy implemented, they both agreed that the economy should not be radically restructured, and that any form of nationalisation should not extinguish competition. As Durbin noted, 'little good will be done, and the purposes of planning will not be served, if we merely replace a growing number of State organized rentier monopolies by a larger number of autonomous "socialized" monopolistic Corporations.'[93] Competition was an important element of a capitalist economy, forcing businesses to explore new areas and take informed, and sometimes radical, decisions. The idea of competition or the retention of the capitalist economy was not considered at all by Crossman, with his preferred method of accountability focusing on parliamentary investigation. Tawney seems to have concluded that a mixed economy was inevitable, as he did not advocate wholesale economic reform. The maintenance of capitalism in at least some sectors of the economy was necessary to Tawney's vision of a socialist society to ensure irresponsible monopolies did not develop, although he was not unrealistic and believed that competition, as it already existed, was not as prevalent as some would argue. 'The choice before him [the consumer], to an increasing extent, is not between competition and monopoly, but between a monopoly which is irresponsible and private and a monopoly which is responsible and public.'[94] He did not support radical change or upheaval, and even his preferred form of taxation was designed to minimise costs and conflict. Tawney argued that by raising the overall level of industrial production, the state would be able to accumulate wealth through the taxation system. When the owners of specific industries of great importance to the country died, the company could then be taxed again via the inheritance tax system.[95]

Another area where there was a real lack of detail and understanding was on the participation of workers in the management and control of the nationalised industries. The belief that certain members of staff within a nationalised industry should take an active role within the management of that industry was a traditionally accepted element of socialism for some within the party, though it was very rarely thoroughly planned and was difficult to implement. Many Trade Unions did not favour this policy, being adamant that a distinction must be maintained between 'managerial responsibilities and prerogatives on the one hand, and trade union functions and workers' tasks on the other.'[96] Morrison had indicated in his 1933 publication *Socialisation and Transport* that the nationalisation blueprint which had been created by the Labour Party, and was subsequently implemented by the Attlee government, was workable and should be used in future. This blueprint had, as an integral, if minimal element, the role of the worker in the management of the industry:

> The new order of things will fail if the administrative and operative workers in the industry, however humble their grade may be, do not have thrown open to them wide avenues of higher industrial education and of industrial self-government, wherever practicable and sound in the public interest.[97]

The problem with worker participation was that it had not been developed into a workable framework due to the problematic nature of actually implementing and defining it. Crosland indicated in *The Future of Socialism* that while this policy was an accepted element of social democracy, it had been superseded by changes in industry. This meant that even if such a scheme were designed, it would not necessarily be effective:

> The workers' moral (and logical) claim to such representation is, I believe, incontrovertible. The trouble is first that they seem to have little desire to exercise it, and secondly that such reform, besides being subject to severe practical difficulties, cannot be guaranteed to produce any real benefit.[98]

Tawney and Durbin did not consider worker participation within industry, perhaps because it was such a difficult and complex issue, but it seems rather unusual that they would overlook such an integral part of the socialist ideology. Crossman indicated that the participation of staff in the management of the nationalised industries was still a key element of socialism but then he simply did not consider how such a scheme would work.[99] He did not indicate, as Crosland had, that this issue was particularly thorny and while perhaps advantageous would be difficult to implement. He simply failed to produce any detailed plans, suggesting instead that the German example might have some useful elements, and paying mere lip service to this important part of the ideology.

Nationalisation was often the battleground between the different wings of the party, but as has been demonstrated, the views of specific individuals were far more complex than they at first appear. Durbin's views on nationalisation seem to have much in common with Tawney's more traditionally socialist views, both agreeing that nationalisation was essential in certain industries. Crossman and Crosland, rather unexpectedly given their reputations, both concluded in the mid-

1950s that nationalisation was only one of many different solutions to Britain's economic problems, and that it should not be accepted in every industry. While there continued to be a gulf between Crosland and Crossman, their views shared many commonalties from the late 1950s. The main difference between their writing was Crosland's economic detail and expertise with Crossman providing a more general outline. This difference in accuracy and detail was coupled with their accepted, if inaccurate, categorisations as Gaitskellite and Bevanite. However, Crossman was not an expert in this field, a fact he was well aware of, and he therefore was not in a strong position within the debate, something he seems to have resented. 'I am not an economist and I am not here concerned with the strictly economic controversy. What matters to me are the basic assumptions about the nature of Western society which a socialist should accept.'[100] Instead each industry had to be considered on an individual basis, and a case built to support its adoption.

Liberty and Personal Freedom

Socialism and the 1945 Labour Party's policies on economic planning and controls had some rather unfortunate connotations in the post-war world. Churchill highlighted these impressions during the 1945 election insisting, in a BBC radio broadcast, that Attlee 'would have to fall back on some form of Gestapo' to complete his socialist reforms.[101] Governmental control had, in the aftermath of the Second World War, gained overtones of totalitarianism from Nazi Germany and particularly the USSR, which would be hugely damaging to the Labour Party were the electorate to believe they would implement a policy of this nature. The increasingly totalitarian regime in the USSR, which had labelled itself 'socialist', also gave the party cause for concern. As news of oppression began to filter out of the USSR, the Labour Party was at great pains to point out that this aggression and control was not part and parcel of a socialist state. Instead they insisted the opposite was true. Writing in 1952, Bevan noted that 'Soviet communism and socialism are not yet sufficiently distinguished in many minds.'[102] The retention of democracy and the freedom of the individual, which was associated with this, was a key part of the party's ideology.[103] The redistribution of wealth and the levelling up of society was not seen as being contradictory to personal freedom, in fact freedom seems to have been a factor which the Labour government wanted to preserve and expand within society. All of our intellectuals supported the encouragement and protection of liberty within Britain and many more members of the party were at great pains to highlight this liberal philosophy.

There seem to have been two areas of consideration in regard to liberty and personal freedom. Firstly, many individuals primarily focused on the role of Parliament, and how government and government-control industries could be made accountable to it. Crossman falls into this group, as his discussion of individual liberty was considerably less detailed than his writing on parliamentary control. The second group focused on the protection of the individual, and the laws which controlled people's lives. Crosland falls into this category, as he tended to focus on this issue far more than on the ability of Parliament to scrutinise legislation. Durbin, Crosland and Crossman all agreed that the two-party system of democracy was a useful and important check on government and that it needed to be maintained. As Crossman argued, 'as democrats, [we] must get a rough-and-ready knowledge of how government works. If we want to use the state for the achievement of our ideals, we must understand its machinery.'[104]

Tawney similarly believed that parliamentary democracy was of paramount importance and that socialism was not inherently anti-democratic. He also concluded that it was important that the public were aware of the democratic tradition within British socialism, arguing that 'if the public, and particularly the working-class public, is confronted with the choice between capitalist democracy, with all its nauseous insincerities, and undemocratic socialism, it will choose the former every time.'[105] Uniquely amongst our four intellectuals, Tawney believed that certain individual liberties could be sacrificed as long as parliamentary democracy was maintained to protect the masses. Crossman went further than Tawney, suggesting that the current system of accountability needed to be much stronger and that Parliament was not providing, in its existing state, a rigorous enough check on government. The issue of which reforms were required is covered in chapter 5, but for our purposes here, it is enough to focus on Crossman's calls for accountability.

Durbin, Crosland and Crossman believed that individual freedom was just as important as parliamentary democracy, perhaps even more so, and that the two were not mutually exclusive. Crossman believed that individual freedom, government accountability and a strengthened legislative system were all part of the same package, and that each component was equally important.[106] Durbin argued that 'the only conceivable route to a better social order lies in the pathway of democracy, and that the political method of democratic government is an essential principle, not an accidental accompaniment, of any just society.'[107] Crosland argued that individuals needed more freedom than they currently had, pointing out that 'morally driven legislation' such as that governing abortion and homosexuality, should be repealed. He called for these moral restrictions to be repealed to extend personal liberty, in addition to his call for parliamentary democracy to be preserved. 'Many of these are intolerable, and should be highly offensive to socialists, in whose blood there should always run a trace of the anarchist and the libertarian, and not too much of the prig and the prude.'[108] Durbin and Crossman did not write about these types of legislation, though Crossman was in favour of these reforms when they travelled through the House of Commons.[109]

Durbin, Crosland and Crossman saw no contradiction between collective and personal freedom, so both could and should be protected. Crossman focused on equality and parliamentary accountability in his writing on socialism, perhaps because he felt most confident in this area, due to his lack of economic training:

Since our socialism is based on the moral demand for greater equality and an enlargement of freedom, and postulates that irresponsible power corrupts, the socialist must be courageous enough to admit that the evils of oligopoly are not limited to the private sector of the economy. Public corporations and departments of state can also exhibit managerialist tendencies, favour inequality and become a threat to freedom.'[110]

He supported accountability in all political fields, and this meant that Parliament needed to be reformed. This would ensure that the government was accountable to the people, and that individual freedom could be protected against the worst excesses of the state. Individual liberty and freedom were at the very heart of thinking about socialism and social democracy.

Tawney's strongly held Christian beliefs influenced his views on personal freedom, making them slightly different to those of Durbin, Crosland and Crossman. He believed that with freedom came responsibility and were basic Christian values to be widely accepted, they would ensure that basic freedoms were protected. Additionally, his views on the supremacy of collective freedom made the preservation of personal freedom less important to him, 'equality implies the deliberate acceptance of social restraints upon individual expansion.'[111] Had Tawney been writing at the same time as Crosland his views on personal freedom might have been different, perhaps impacted upon by the experience of the Second World War.

The Impact of the USSR

As has been previously mentioned, the USSR had a huge impact on the Labour Party and the campaigning of their opponents. The atrocities and totalitarian dictatorship of the Soviet Union did not sit well with a party which considered personal freedom and liberty to be an integral part of its brand of socialism. The socialist label which the Soviet Union had given itself led to questions from the opposition and certain sectors of the electorate as to the 'true' nature of a Labour government. While all of our intellectuals supported the general maintenance of liberty, it was Crossman who criticised the Soviet regime the least. While Tawney, Durbin and Crosland criticised the USSR and qualified any praise of its economic miracle, Crossman tended to overlook these issues, focusing on the supposed economic phenomenon which the USSR had experienced.

While many believed that the USSR had undergone an economic transformation during the first five-year economic plan, its human rights record led many within the Labour Party to conclude that its economic record was sullied. Tawney, Durbin and Crosland all noted the practices of the Soviet government and criticised the regime, indicating that the abuses of power which had been seen in the USSR made their economic success irrelevant. Tawney argued that the terror was a product of the country's Tsarist history. 'In those countries where democracy was non-existent, as in Russia, or where, as in Italy and post-war Germany, it was an exotic plant, the collision was violent, and the denouement trenchant.'[112] Durbin wrote a very compelling and graphic description of the atrocities which the country had seen, arguing that the human cost which had been paid was too high and was not justified by the economic growth of the nation:

> I have tried to show why I so profoundly believe that we cannot proceed by the Communist road to a better social order. Strong and violent men have always believed that they could build a new heaven and a new earth, if only they were allowed to override and destroy those who disagreed with them. Monotonously and horribly the victims will continue to tramp down to death, their shoulders bowed by suffering, their eyes glazed with hatred and fear. [113]

Additionally, he argued that, as parliamentary democracy was an essential part of a healthy, equal society, the USSR was not the utopian state which some observers had suggested. Crosland also condemned the gulags in the region and was quick to point out the key differences between socialism and communism, arguing that the USSR was a communist country. Crosland, like Tawney and Durbin, argued that the USSR had not been a good model and that Britain should not follow their example. The human rights violations which had occurred in the region were reason in itself to discredit the Soviet model. In reference to the USSR, Crosland argued that 'economic decisions impinge on the social, political and cultural spheres; and they cannot be judged as good or bad unless their consequences in these spheres are taken into account.'[114]

Crossman, who had been the most vocal of our individuals in calls for the defence of personal freedom and liberty, was the least vocal on the carnage which occurred in the USSR. While he was aware of the situation in the USSR, he failed to ever condemn the Soviet Union, instead focusing on his own limited experience of the region. While he failed to condemn the totalitarian state in the USSR, he did mention that the Cold War was driving them to 'adopt more and more brutal methods.'[115] When he visited Moscow in 1958, he was shielded from the harsher realities of life within a totalitarian state by government authorities. 'This fortnight in Moscow was frustrating, partly because the weather was foul, partly because I arrived on the wrong sort of passport, partly because the Russians are extremely defensive.'[116] Wilson, on the other hand, had more experience of the USSR, although again, little on the practicalities of living in a communist state. Following his resignation from the Attlee government in 1951, he was employed part-time by Montague L. Meyer as an economic consultant. This gave him the opportunity to visit the USSR on numerous occasions, allowing him to talk with some perceived authority on the USSR. As Pimlott pointed out, 'Soon, Wilson was developing a man-of-the-world line which went down well on platforms, especially left-wing ones. "We have got to learn to live with this new Soviet Union" he was wont to say, speaking with the authority of a hardened explorer.'[117]

It seems likely that Crossman was not particularly interested in the situation in the USSR. While he focused on foreign affairs for much of his early career, he was generally only interested in Britain's role, maintaining no interest in circumstances in other unrelated countries. He barely touched on the Soviet regime's practices and instead focused on the success of the first five-year plan, arguing that this kind of plan could be successfully instituted in Britain. However, he did note that the introduction of a similar policy to that of the USSR would be less successful in Britain due to the freer state of the country and the ease with which a totalitarian state can control its population. He did not seem to think that the experiences of the USSR had been devalued by the horrors which had been seen:

> Communism is still an inferior way of life compared with that of the Affluent Societies of the West. But this does not alter the fact that, *in terms of military power, of industrial development, of technological advance, of mass literacy and eventually, of mass consumption too, the planned socialist economy, as exemplified in the communist states, is proving its capacity to outpace and overtake the wealthy and comfortable Western economies.*[118]

It can only be concluded that Crossman was aware of the situation in the USSR but did not want to give it serious consideration, and this led him to limit himself to discussion of the economic situation, ignoring the human cost.

With the notable exception of Crossman, the other individuals considered here all criticised the Soviet model of government, where people were sacrificed in the pursuit of the economic miracle. Regardless of the great strides forward which the USSR might be experiencing, the fact that it was built on human misery allowed Tawney, Durbin and Crosland to criticise the Soviet model repeatedly and heavily. Crossman's stance on the issue seems to have been due to his general lack of interest in the internal circumstances of the USSR. This lack of interest can be shown in his failure to act on any human rights violations overseas, coupled with his enthusiasm for what he saw as a great economic development in the region, which he almost unquestioningly accepted and supported. While Crossman believed that lessons could be learnt from the USSR, his failure to criticise the regime, even to a limited extent, made his work on the subject partial and incomplete. However, he did suggest that the west was unable to co-operate with the USSR in light of its humanitarian record, at least acknowledging the situation in the region:

> We can co-operate with the Americans as allies, influencing their policies despite their superior strength. It would be folly to expect such a relationship with the Soviet Union. Co-existence, yes. Mutually beneficial agreements, yes. But never co-operation.[119]

The 'White Heat' of Technology

When Wilson came to power in 1964, his party was no longer viewed as being a throw back to an earlier time. Instead, it was viewed as a dynamic party, looking to modernise and liberalise Britain, characterised by Wilson's focus on science and technology and his enthusiasm for the 'white heat of technology'. 'It was a mark of Wilson's seriousness about science that he gave Crossman, who might have expected something better, the science portfolio. When Crossman expressed disappointment, the new Leader declared that it was now a major job, linked to "advanced socialist planning."'[120] This reputation was due, in no small part, to Wilson's 1963 conference speech in which he discussed the 'white heat of technology'. Technology was seen as a way in which Britain's reputation for decline could be halted. Additionally, this policy was a way of defusing the left-right disputes which the party had experienced over nationalisation. Instead of focusing on nationalisation or the different types of economic plans which could be introduced, the party could unite behind the modernisation of industry. A lack of technical expertise was, Crossman believed, hindering government modernisation and so external experts needed to be introduced, a policy which he implemented while a minister, though this was not an original idea. Experts and specialists were required in all fields, and Crossman included Whitehall in this:

> Scientists and technologists are deliberately kept out of all key positions which are reserved overwhelmingly for professional administrators with a non-scientific (or an anti-scientific) bias; and even in ministries where scientists are employed, they are segregated and treated as technical experts with no direct access to the minister.[121]

Crosland also believed that experts were required in government, and he was able to introduce specialists into his various departments while he was a government minister, often to the horror of his civil servants.[122]

Crossman, as Shadow Minister for Science and Higher Education, was required to develop the initial policy of modernisation and 'white heat' into a tangible series of recommendations. As he had had no real experience of this policy area, he set up a group of individuals to consider how to formulate advantageous policies, named the 'Crossman group'. It consisted of various scientists and MPs, including Patrick Blackett [Nobel Peace Prize Winner for Physics in 1948], Judith Hart [Labour MP for Lanark], Tam Dalyell [Crossman's close friend and PPS] and Terry Pitt [member of Transport House]. 'The agenda of the Crossman Group was the creation of policies based on the "new case for socialist planning", but in terms which would appeal to the broadest constituency within the party.'[123]

While technology had played a role in Crossman's thinking on socialism, with him praising the developments of the USSR in this field, he was never able to implement any of his plans. Instead he became Minister of Housing and Local Government and the 'white heat' of technology remained a slogan rather than a policy initiative. However, various ministers, most notably Crossman, Crosland, and to a lesser extent, Wilson, all introduced specialists into their various departments, and while this was far less than the rhetoric of the 'white heat of technology' speech had promised, it was, none the less, a step in the right direction.

Conclusion

While conflict existed between the Gaitskellites and the Bevanites, it is often assumed that easy divisions existed between the left and right wings of the party. However, the situation in the Labour Party between 1945 and the mid-1960s was certainly not this clear-cut. The views of individuals inevitably developed over the period leading to a more fluid definition of ideologies, coupled with the knowledge that the vast majority of Labour Party members belonged to neither the left nor right wing. Socialism, as interpreted by the left wing, was considered by some, particularly those on the right wing of the party, to be out-dated and no longer relevant. While the views of other individuals evolved and developed over time, there is a perception that Crossman's views did not so much evolve as change completely, leading Marquand to label Crossman as a 'gadfly'.[124] While Crossman's writing on socialism does suggest that he lost his previous enthusiasm for nationalisation, this would be incorrect, as he had never been particularly enthusiastic about this policy. The revisionists considered nationalisation to be less relevant than it had been in the 1940s because of changing economic circumstances. However, their attempt to amend Clause IV was extremely unpopular within the party and the wider Labour movement. As Crossman indicated in 1957 'the two most important emotions of the Labour Party are a doctrinaire faith in nationalization, without knowing what it means, and a doctrine faith in pacifism, without facing its consequences.'[125]

It seems likely that Crossman's writing on the benefits of nationalisation, in *Keep Left* and *New Fabian Essays*, was influenced by the views of his Bevanite colleagues and friends. Nationalisation was a central policy to the Bevanites and while Crossman was not particularly enthusiastic about this policy, he seems to have accepted it in order to fit in with the group. As he gradually moved away from the group and instead supported Wilson, whose own support for nationalisation was, at best, lukewarm, he began to support nationalisation less and less. By as early as 1956, he was arguing that nationalisation should only be instituted in industries where non-socialists could see the benefits, namely failing industries. This was a noticeably different position to his position in 1951, when he had argued that the chemical and oil industries should be nationalised. When Crossman was interested and enthusiastic about an issue, he either wrote about the issue or gave it plenty of consideration privately, which can then be identified in his diaries. However, the issue of socialism was not one which he gave a great deal of consideration to in either his diaries or his writing after 1955. In Crossman's diaries from 1964 to 1966, there are virtually no references to socialism and only seven mentions of nationalisation, all referring to steel.[126]

Crossman's views can be very difficult to pin down. He is considered by many to be a gadfly, a man who in Marcia Williams' view was an 'intellectual gymnast', an opinion which many would have agreed with.[127] As will be demonstrated throughout this biography, Crossman thoroughly enjoyed argument and considered it a tool to develop views and policies. He utilised his experiences as a Don to develop discussions and arguments on policies believing, in a very Socratic way, that the truth could be reached through disagreement and argument. However, while this approach led to him being considered unprincipled and 'gadfly-esque', changing his views repeatedly, his methods should not be confused with his views and guiding principles. He had hinted in his earlier career that he would write a larger-scale book on socialism, but Tony Benn wrote that this had not been written 'because if he did he thought he would discover he wasn't a socialist.'[128] This lack of publication, or a firm basis for his brand of socialism, did not prevent Crossman from noting in his own diaries in 1967 that 'he [Crosland], Roy [Jenkins] and I are the only serious socialist intellectuals in the government, and he's [Crosland] written the only thorough and thoughtful book on modern British socialism.'[129]

Individual freedom and liberty were vital to Crossman's ideological views. He maintained his views on the importance of freedom for his entire political career. One of his most deeply held beliefs was that accountability in government was absolutely essential. It was imperative that government should be accountable to both Parliament and the public. This could be achieved in numerous different ways. As is considered in chapter 5, constitutional reform was required to hold government to account in Parliament. In terms of nationalised industries, Crossman argued that specialist committees should be set up to monitor the activities of each individual industry, ensuring that the managers were serving the public interests rather than their own. Additionally, and perhaps more generally, individual freedom and liberty for all should be maintained at all costs and strengthened if possible. These safeguards, though vague in some areas, were vital to Crossman's version of socialism and he pursued them in various ways for much of his career. While the protection of individual liberty was important to many socialists and supporters of social democracy, Crossman's active interest in this issue was quite unusual amongst Labour MPs. He was also aware of the danger of government bureaucracy. As William Gwyn argued 'many socialists who value liberty highly have failed to see a threat in administrative activity because of their belief in the great merit of the British Constitution.'[130] This made his lack of condemnation of the USSR in relation to its authoritarian techniques even more surprising.

Bearing Crossman's wider ideological framework in mind when considering his response to events in the USSR, his actions or lack of them seem unbelievable. He was not particularly interested in events abroad which did not involve Britain, and only very rarely spoke out about humanitarian disasters or conflicts overseas, being far more interested in the actions of Britain and its citizens. While he was impressed by the economic successes he perceived in the USSR, he failed to comment on the horror of the gulags or the totalitarian regime. His only trip to the country had shielded him deliberately from the realities of life on the eastern side of the iron curtain, and he seems to have been slightly overwhelmed by the perceived economic success of the Soviet bloc.[131] Wilson's positive views on Russia also seem to have influenced Crossman, perhaps even convincing him of the positive economic effects of a totalitarian state, though he would never have advocated their use in Britain. His attitude seems to have been one where external events were really of no concern to him, only Britain mattered.

While Crossman was a Bevanite early in his parliamentary career, by 1955 he was a Wilson man, becoming one of his loyalist lieutenants. Even as late as 1969, Crossman felt his loyalty was primarily to Wilson, not the Labour Party. 'I am still rated, and rightly, as an absolute solid Harold man, never dreaming of challenging his authority.'[132] Wilson was far more tactically minded than Crossman, maintaining numerous political friendships, but Crossman felt their friendship was more important than many others. Wilson, he believed, could trust him entirely to be loyal to him. Although they obviously disagreed from time to time on specific policies, most notably Wilson's decision not to devalue the pound in either 1964 or 1966, Crossman's views often shared many features with Wilson's own thinking. Writing in 1966, he noted that

> Harold is nearer to me as a person than anybody else I have mentioned. But Harold is very much separated from me now, first by his position and second by his suspicion that anyone who stands up to him is intriguing against him, maybe wanting power.[133]

Indeed, Wilson and Crossman seem to have drifted away from the Bevanites during the early 1950s together, seeming to loosely link their views together. While Wilson was undoubtedly dominant within their relationship, Crossman was a useful friend to have and they tended to utilise each other. Wilson did not approve of some of his activities, but this does not seem to have affected their personal friendship, as can be seen in the warm and glowing speech which Wilson gave at Crossman's memorial service in 1974.[134] While both were very clever and able, Crossman's writing on numerous issues marked him out as an intellectual, while Wilson had a more practical approach to politics. Crossman's image as a flighty and unreliable individual seem unfair – a case of style over content. His most deeply held views, on socialism and other issues which will be considered in subsequent chapters, were very constant and he was very committed to them.

4

Crossman and Foreign Policy

Richard Crossman concentrated on one field of governmental policy for much of his early parliamentary career – foreign policy. He was interested in a variety of foreign policy areas, with the issues being raised over Germany's post-war future of particular interest when he entered the Commons in 1945. This interest appears to have been encouraged by Crossman's wartime occupation, when he was a self-proclaimed 'psychological warrior' producing propaganda for the allies. Germany seems to have been an issue which he concentrated on due to the expertise he had gained both before and during the war, making him more knowledgeable on this issue than on others initially.[1] However, within a short period, he began to focus on other foreign policy issues, including the implications of the Cold War, probably because of his increasing knowledge and growing confidence.

The most important post-war issue for Crossman was the development of Israel and the problems within the Middle East. He had almost no knowledge of Palestine or the Zionist calls for a Homeland when Ernest Bevin appointed him to the Anglo-American Commission in 1945.[2] During his time on the Commission, Crossman became a loyal supporter of Zionism and later a devoted friend of Israel. Hector McNeil, Bevin's Parliamentary Private Secretary (PPS), told Crossman in 1945 that his lack of public pronouncements on Palestine had been a key factor in his selection for the Commission.[3] While initially being unsure about joining the commission, he eventually accepted and he approached the problem the commission faced in accordance with his own socialist beliefs and his views on liberty and individual freedom. Following his time on the Commission, he became committed to the Zionist movement and particularly to Chaim Weizmann, who became the first President of Israel in 1948. He was also a member of the Labour Friends of Israel group. He was one of many Labour MPs who fought very hard for Britain to adopt a more pro-Israeli policy, participating in debates in the House of Commons and writing articles on Israel for various publications. In 1972 after bring sacked from the *New Statesman*, Crossman began work on a biography of Weizmann. However, due to his terminal illness, which was first diagnosed in 1972, the project was abandoned before completion.

An example of Crossman's growing confidence on foreign affairs was his pivotal involvement in the production of *Keep Left* in 1947.[4] Written by Crossman, Michael Foot and Ian Mikardo, the pamphlet covered both domestic and foreign policy issues. While the section on domestic policy supported many of the government's policies and simply suggested a more rapid change of pace, the foreign policy section was far less favourable. It called for a socialist foreign policy, criticising the policies of Ernest Bevin and the Labour government, implying that they would be detrimental to Britain. Despite the term socialist foreign policy being utilised, no definition was provided in the pamphlet. Crossman himself did not produce a definition of the term at any point in his career, though it seems to have rested heavily on some form of co-operation with a loose European grouping and a more balanced relationship with the USSR, encouraged by a more distant relationship with the USA.

In the years immediately after the end of the Second World War, it became clear that while Britain had won the war, she might not economically survive the peace which she had fought so hard to establish. Economic instability in Britain and increasing nationalism within the colonies contributed to undermine Britain's position as an imperial power. This was further exacerbated by the growing importance of the USSR and the USA – the Superpowers. It was very difficult for Britain's political establishment, and the population generally, to accept the change in Britain's status. The inability of Britain to have complete control over her foreign policies, due to the actions and influence of other nations, was equally difficult to accept, and often led to demands for action which were unrealistic in the circumstances. This was a dilemma that the Keep Left group said it was aware of, though the actions of the group and of some of the individual members did not support this statement.[5] This issue was very difficult for Britain to face and the group appear to have downplayed this problem when writing their pamphlet. Instead they cast Europe, with Britain as a key player, in the role of a conciliator which, due to its great international standing, was able to defuse conflict between others and was of equal standing to the Superpowers.[6]

Some very important issues will not be considered here, not because of lack of importance either internationally or even internally within the Labour Party, but because of Crossman's lack of participation or interest, both publicly and privately. One such example was the Suez crisis in 1956. Crossman was ill and confined to bed and then was overseas for much of the crisis, and his discussion of the situation and influence on events was very limited. He also showed a lack of interest in issues such as the Vietnam War and the racial difficulties in South Africa, though problems arising from minority rule in Rhodesia are reported in his diaries due to the activities of the Wilson government on this issue and his membership of the Rhodesia X committee. Between 1964 and 1970 as a member of the Wilson cabinet, he was privy to some very difficult and controversial foreign policy discussions, but his interest seems to have been fairly limited. This was at least partially due to departmentalism, which he described as limiting his time and interest in issues not directly linked to his own departmental work.[7] As this chapter will demonstrate, Crossman's interest in and commitment to the discussion of foreign policy issues gradually decreased between the years 1955/6 and 1970 and he never regained the enthusiasm and dedication which he exhibited during the years 1945 to 1954/5. This initial decrease in his activities on foreign affairs issues was a direct result of Gaitskell's succession to the leadership of the Labour Party. While the increasing influence and eventual succession as leader of Gaitskell in 1955/6 seems to have led him to focus more on domestic and defence issues than previously, with less time being spent on overseas issues, this does not explain why he failed to recapture his interest in foreign affairs. While he was undoubtedly occupied fully by his departmental work from 1964 to 1970, he was a member of the Defence and Overseas Policy Committee (OPD) from 1966 to 1970, indicating that he had not completely lost interest in foreign affairs. In 1966, he commented that 'the value of my sitting at OPD is that at these meetings I shall be provided with the ammunition which I can use at the critical moment when the great foreign policy decision is no longer avoidable.'[8] Crossman never got his chance but his comment explains why his diary entries on OPD meetings are generally a report of events, rather than an outline of his own views, being episodic in nature rather than indicating a sustained interest. He considered himself a reporter in these meetings, not an active member of the committee. Certain key issues, such as Crossman's commitment to the defence of the state of Israel were maintained, but these were not indicative of a wider interest in foreign policy after 1955/6.

Labour Party Approaches to Foreign Policy

There appears not to have been a single Labour Party approach to the issues and conflicts which arose within foreign policy, with a variety of approaches being adopted within the party dependent on interests or concerns. The approach taken by the party leader and the Foreign Secretary did not always provide a lead which all members of the party followed, although some obviously supported the leadership. There were strands of opinion within the party, particularly on the left wing, which were strongly in favour of pacifism and even appeasement, these elements dating back to the birth of the party at the turn of the twentieth century. Of the individuals who did not support these policies, the range of opinion was still very broad.

A socialist foreign policy had been a traditional Labour aim since the 1930s. The aim of its supporters was to address problems abroad by using the same tools as were intended to be used at home to combat social divisions. However, these aims were never explicitly outlined by their supporters, appearing to rely on a rather loose set of proposals and suggestions to gain support. The overall detail must be pieced together by studying various articles, though it does not produce a complete explanation. In addition, there were differing strands of opinion between those on the left, leaving the impression that a socialist foreign policy was a label which covered a multitude of differing opinions and maintained unity amongst those on the left of the party for much of the 1940s due to its ambiguous nature.

Writing in 1969, Michael Gordon outlined four main principles of a socialist foreign policy – internationalism, international working-class solidarity, anti-capitalism and anti-militarism.[9] However, Gordon's analysis is based on the predominant themes of a number of different left wing publications, not simply those within the party seeking a socialist foreign policy in this period, and, as Rhiannon Vickers pointed out, the party did not offer 'a radically alternative view in terms of providing a socialist foreign policy. Indeed, it has never been self-evident as to what such a policy would look like.'[10] Writing in 1974, Eric Shaw separated the left wing of the party into two main groupings, labelled as Social Democratic Marxists and Radical Democrats.[11] Shaw determined that the key distinction between these two groups was in their priorities. He noted that Social Democratic Marxists were 'drawn largely from the Marxist tradition [and] subscribed to liberal democratic values and accepted the parliamentary road to socialism.'[12] The key determining factor was that Social Democratic Marxists were ruled by national self-interest. 'In the sphere of international politics this means that the primary aim of policy-makers was the preservation and furtherance of the interests of the social order of the country they represented.'[13]

Radical Democracy, Shaw argued, was the predominant theme within the party pre-1945 'and supplied the basis for Labour's critique of traditional foreign policy.'[14] Radical Democrats believed that national self-interest was at the root of many international disputes and conflicts and that national interests needed to be put aside on occasion to achieve peace.[15] Shaw's definition can be utilised to highlight a shift in Crossman's thinking though his views are not easily or neatly categorised and Shaw did not attempt to do this. The Keep Left group, while not being ruled solely by national self-interest, did exhibit some characteristics of the Social Democratic Marxist thinking – pursuing better relations with Europe and the USSR, primarily for British benefit. While Crossman's later thinking did not abandon British needs and aspirations, it was much more in the Radical Democratic tradition, which many in the party subscribed to. Shaw described the Radical Democratic approach as 'the socialist orthodoxy which the [Attlee] Labour government, in affirming continuity, repudiated.'[16] In 1948, this division was deepened over Britain's membership of NATO, with the Radical Democrats favouring continued membership, while the Social Democrats called for Britain to leave NATO and concentrate on relations with the USSR.[17] Crossman's views on Israel, for example, reflect a Radical Democratic view which containing an element of national self-interest. However, his support for British membership of NATO demonstrates that as early as 1948, his thinking on foreign policy was developing, and he was not easily categorised in this early period.

Linked to this undefined socialist foreign policy was the third force philosophy. This idea was somewhat more comprehensively outlined by the left, and was an idea which was endorsed by the Keep Left group in 1947, of which Crossman was a prominent member. The philosophy called for a level of co-operation between socialist governments, leading to a socialist European grouping, which would be led by Britain.[18] This group would then rival the USSR and the USA in international relations, hopefully defusing the increasing conflict between them. Crossman noted that 'we socialists dreamed that somehow between capitalist America and communist Russia, democratic socialist Europe could act as a mediator, a third force between them.'[19] It was not a European community as envisaged in the 1950 Schuman Plan, but followed on logically from the aim of international working-class solidarity, which Gordon identified as one of the key aims of a socialist foreign policy. Crossman and the wider left wing groupings in the party spent much of the period 1945-47 outlining their differing set of values to the government and attempting to persuade them to follow this hazy ideal. As Vickers pointed out, while elements in the party called for a socialist foreign policy 'it never really explained how it would be possible to implement a policy based on socialist ideology in a world where the existing nation-states were capitalist nation-states.'[20]

The call for a third force and a socialist foreign policy was overtaken by events. As relations between the four-powers (the USA, USSR, Britain and France) began to fragment into an East-West conflict, the left wing of the party called for more understanding of the USSR and ever greater efforts from Britain to ease their fears. Shaw argued that 'the Social Democratic Marxist left felt, the behaviour of the American and UK government provided little cause for Russia to modify her suspicious outlook.'[21] However, as relations deteriorated further and more information became available demonstrating the intransigence of the USSR, coupled with the positively friendly actions of the USA, such as Marshall Aid and the joint establishment of NATO, the left wing groups began to rethink their views. Shaw argued that the perceived softening of the attitude of the American government and their package for Europe encouraged the left's changing attitude, though their initial views had been unrealistic:

> There was no reason to assume (as the left did) that America, with the great leverage supplied by Marshall Aid, would acquiesce in the formation of a 'Third Force', following economic and foreign policies she was bound to dislike, in place of a western bloc organised along lines she could, to an extent, determine.[22]

Henry Pelling argued that the third force was overtaken by events, including 'the formation of conservative governments in France and Italy and …the generous offer of economic help for all European countries which was made by General Marshall…'[23]

By 1949/50, the left wing of the party had experienced a change in its viewpoint. While some continued to believe in pacifism, or the ability of 'left to speak to left' many, including Crossman, began to rethink their opinion of America and the aim of a socialist foreign policy. This was partly due to the changing international environment, but in Crossman's case, his opinions seem to have been influenced by his views on Israel and the pro-Israeli stance of America which he sympathised with. The increasingly unrealistic nature of a pro-Russian policy is highlighted by Crossman's move away from calls for a socialist foreign policy which were not repeated again in any of his pamphlets or publications after 1947.

Israel and Palestine

The Zionist movement became increasingly vocal and strong during the inter-war period, particularly in the United States. The movement demanded a Jewish homeland, although the exact location of this was a cause of division. The accepted location of this homeland was considered by many Zionists to be in the pre-war country of Palestine in the Middle East. Palestine in 1939 was a predominantly Islamic area, although immigration, predominantly of European Jews, was an ever-increasing problem for the state. Britain had been granted colonial rights over Palestine at the end of First World War after the disintegration of the Ottoman Empire and was therefore protectorate of the state, a difficult position to be in.[24] Following the end of the Second World War and the awareness of Nazi atrocities, the calls for a Jewish homeland began to receive a more favourable response from politicians, particularly in the US. Displaced European Jews began to travel to Palestine to resettle in their 'homeland' and the governing authority – Britain – had difficulty responding to the issues involved.[25] The British government traditionally held a fairly pro-Arab stance, primarily due to the vitally important oil trade which existed between Britain and the Arab states and the proximity of many current and former British colonies to the Middle East. Britain, as a colonial power, had had many dealings with the Middle Eastern authorities.[26]

Due to the resistance within the Middle East to increasing Jewish immigration, British foreign policy had generally resisted this measure as much as possible, instead favouring European resettlement. This policy was undermined for several reasons. The first reason was the pressure which was put on the British forces in Palestine. As displaced European Jews began to enter Palestine, often illegally, the demands for equal rights and an independent Jewish-governed homeland became harder to ignore.[27] Secondly, the USA, now Britain's main ally and a Superpower, had a large and very powerful domestic Jewish population which demanded nothing less than a Jewish homeland in Palestine at the earliest opportunity. This internal pressure on the American government meant that Britain could expect near constant pressure from the American administration concerning the future of Palestine.[28] To add further confusion to the situation, different British announcements had promised different results. The Balfour declaration had committed Britain to establishing a Jewish homeland, while the 1939 white paper on Palestine had firmly supported the status quo in the region.[29] This was the uncomfortable situation which the Labour government found itself in when it entered power in 1945.

The Labour Party, prior to gaining power had pledged its support to increasing Jewish immigration into Palestine, inevitably leading to a Jewish state within the Middle East. A number of members of the Attlee cabinet had supported the establishment of such a state, including Herbert Morrison, Stafford Cripps, Hugh Dalton, Hugh Gaitskell and Aneurin Bevan. There seems to have been two predominant solutions forwarded by these individuals. The first group, including Morrison, supported a bi-national state, made up of Palestinians and Jews with a multi-national force keeping the peace. The second group, which included Bevan and, from 1945 onwards, Crossman, argued that Palestine needed to be partitioned into two separate countries, as the two sides would not be able to co-habit peacefully.[30] However, upon entering government, it became clear that this policy would cause severe upset within the Middle East at a time when Britain could not afford to alienate allies. Ernest Bevin, the Foreign Secretary, concluded that by drawing America into consultation on the issue of Palestine, this might force the American administration into taking a more realistic stance.[31] As Crossman himself pointed out in 1946, Bevin 'had been determined to drag the Americans off the side-line on which they have been "rooting" for twenty years.'[32] After consultation, Truman agreed in 1945 to a joint Anglo-American Commission to consider the granting of 100,000 certificates to European Jews to enter Palestine, essentially the first step towards a Jewish state. The figure of 100,000 does not appear to have had any particular significance, although some surveys had placed the figure of displaced European Jews at 100,000 while other surveys had placed the figure much higher. William Roger Louis argued that 'the British intended to demonstrate [during the Anglo-American Commission] to the Americans that the refugee problem was so great that its solution could not be found in Palestine alone, but rather in the acceptance of Jewish displaced persons in other countries, not least the United States.'[33]

The conflict in Palestine did not come to Crossman's attention until 1945, when Bevin instructed him to join the Anglo-American Commission. Hector McNeil, Bevin's Parliamentary Private Secretary (PPS), indicated to Crossman that he had been chosen for the commission due to his lack of public statements on the future of Palestine.[34] It could be argued that Bevin gave Crossman this role in order to test his abilities, perhaps with a future governmental position in mind.[35] While he proved himself intellectually capable, he did not prove himself loyal, a fact which damaged his career prospects immeasurably.

After travelling with the Anglo-American Commission for much of 1946, Crossman found himself in a difficult position. If he had been placed on the Commission to represent the British pro-Arab stance, he was a bitter disappointment for the British government. As he wrote to Attlee following the publication of he commission's report,

when we were appointed, no indication was given to us whatsoever that you desired us to push responsibility on to America. If I had been told that this was your wish, I would of course have declined to serve on the committee unless the British government had persuaded the American government <u>in advance</u> to promise to help carry out the report if unanimity were achieved.[36]

Crossman was seeking an answer to the problem, not a convenient solution for the British Government or the Labour Party, and he believed an essential component of that was to establish peace in the region, allowing British troops to return home. In accordance with his personal views, he suggested to the Anglo-American Commission that not only should the 100,000 entry certificates be issued to displaced Jews, the partitioning of Palestine and the creation of a Jewish state should also be recommended. The majority of the Commission members did not accept this view, and instead Crossman concurred with the majority recommending the issuing of the 100,000 certificates but falling short of advocating a Jewish state in the region.

Crossman believed that before he set out for the overseas Commission hearings, Bevin had promised the group that a unanimous report would be implemented and its recommendations accepted by the British government.[37] By using all of his skills to establish a unanimous report, and by personally supporting partition, he believed that Weizmann would be able to control the Zionist movement, leading them down a moderate path, ending any violence or extremism. The British government would be able to begin bringing troops home in the near future, once the new arrangements were in place. Michael Cohen argued that Crossman was very naïve about Zionism, believing he had found a solution in Chaim Weizmann.[38] His optimism was misplaced. When Bevin received the report and learnt of its contents, he concluded that he simply could not accept its recommendations, but instead announced he would use it as a basis for discussion, 'perhaps a timetable, in return for concessions from the Jews toward the Arabs.'[39] The stumbling block was not primarily over the entry certificates. The issue which the British government was deeply concerned about was armed terrorists in Palestine, particularly the Jewish armed groups, such as the Irgun. The Attlee government wanted these groups disarming before the issuing of immigration certificates was agreed, while the report did not make this a pre-requisite.[40]

The Labour government's lukewarm response to the commission's proposals was compounded by Truman's almost immediate call for the British government to implement the recommendations of the commission, going even further and recommending the establishment of a Jewish state in the near future. Without the disarming of the Jewish terrorist groups, the Attlee government refused to agree to the issuing of the 100,000 entry certificates. This left the situation in stalemate, with the work of the Commission being largely divisive and not providing the peaceful solution that had been hoped for.

As well as the issues over peace in the region, Bevin appears to have been concerned about the defence capabilities in the region. The Labour government believed that it was essential to have a military base in the Middle Eastern territory, and with rocky Anglo-Egyptian relations over the renegotiation of their 1936 Treaty, Palestine was a possible location for an alternative base. This additional factor simply muddied the waters of the Middle East even more, making decisive, clear decision making even more difficult and unlikely.

This division between the Labour government's position and the views of the Zionist supporters in the party put the government in a very difficult position. Bevin's motives have been widely viewed as anti-Semitic, but there appears to be little evidence of this and Bullock insisted that Bevin was very keen for a peaceful solution to be found to the problems within the Middle East, particularly in Palestine. As Bullock explained 'British policy is not to be explained in personal terms of an "implacable hatred" of the Jews on Bevin's part which, despite his angry reproaches at Jewish hostility towards the British, there is no reason to believe he felt.'[41] Crossman indicated that the Colonial Office was standing in the way of a solution, arguing that the plans of the British government were 'a Colonial Office concoction designed in the true tradition of that office to avoid finality. It retains all the keys of power in British hands and even if the Jews and Arabs were prepared to work, it maintains that uneasy equilibrium between that two communities.'[42] Crossman's membership of the Anglo-American commission and his criticism of the government's response to its report essentially established his credentials within the Zionist community and he became one of a fairly large group within the Labour Party who supported the Zionist movement and the state of Israel after its creation.

In this period, Crossman's views were not particularly radical or rebellious. He was, in fact, supporting the policy which the Labour Party had previously adopted concerning Palestine and the Zionist calls for a Jewish homeland in the Middle East prior to 1945, a solution which was supported by many other Labour MPs. Crossman referred to this in a letter to Attlee, noting that 'the Labour government, which has consistently supported Zionism and denounced the white paper, cannot go back on its word in the face of this unanimous report without causing the very bloodshed you are so anxious to avoid, and also performing what must be a deeply dishonourable action.'[43] Crossman's reputation as something of a troublemaker was due, in large part, to his blatant unwillingness to toe the party line, even if that party line had moved since the entry of the party into power and his own entry into the Commons. As he himself noted in 1954 in a conversation with Frank Soskice 'you seem to have forgotten that Clement Attlee and Ernest Bevin plotted to destroy the Jews in Palestine and then encouraged the Arabs to murder the lot. I fought them as murderers.'[44] Even bearing in mind the effect of time and the degeneration of relations between Crossman, Attlee and Bevin, this remark indicates that time did not lessen Crossman's feelings of betrayal.

The situation may have been compounded by the fact that Bevin had very little knowledge of foreign policy when he became Foreign Secretary in 1945, having being Minister of Labour in the coalition government during the Second World War.[45] This meant that he did not necessarily know or accept the policies which, as the Labour government's Foreign Secretary, he and the party were committed to.[46] This led to a gradual re-thinking of certain policy areas between himself and Attlee, leaving the party and its previously accepted foreign policies behind, some of which had already become invalid in light of developments after the Second World War while others were surrendered less easily.

This inevitably led to difficulties between the backbenchers and the Labour front bench, and Crossman, particularly in foreign affairs, does not seem to have shied away from this conflict. In fact, he appears to have relished it. It may be that in bringing himself into conflict with the front bench and Bevin in particular, he was earning himself a reputation which he desired – that of a principled rebel who was not afraid to fight his own party if necessary. In reality, Crossman was beginning to look like something of a traitor and a double-crosser to certain elements of the party. Not for nothing did he gradually begin to be known as "Double Crossman". In a letter to Attlee, Bevin stated that 'nothing I can say will make him [Crossman] alter his ideas about Palestine which derive from his lack of judgement and his intellectual arrogance.'[47] At the 1947 Labour Party Conference in Margate, Bevin's reference to being 'stabbed in the back' was firmly directed at Crossman. In 1967, Attlee commented 'Oh, Crossman! He was up to anything, I think. There is always that lunatic fringe.'[48] In a similar vein eight years later, Wilson noted that 'Dick died as he lived, a bloody juvenile delinquent.'[49]

British foreign policy in Palestine was heavily influenced by Bevin's personal views. While he does not appear to have been anti-Semitic, as discussed above, he concluded that Zionism was a religious sect, as opposed to a developing nation. Many supporters of Zionism, including Crossman believed this interpretation was incorrect and potentially dangerous. In 1961, he recounted on American television a conversation he had with Bevin concerning the definition of Zionist. He stated that Bevin had told him that the Jews were a religious group, not a nation:

> "Mr Bevin, you may well tell me this, but these people are going to fight like a nation." "Well," he said to me "then they aren't Jews." I replied; "You'll find out in the end, Mr Bevin, that if you treat them merely as a religion and mistake their nationhood, they will throw you out." And they didn't behave just like a religion.[50]

This difference of opinion on the nature of Zionism and Judaism may have been at the root of the difficulties within the party over the future of Palestine and the displaced European Jewish population.

In 1947 the situation in Palestine was referred to the United Nations. This appears to have been done for a number of reasons, the most obvious reason being that the British government felt that they could not agree with the decisions which the Anglo-American Commission had reached despite pressure from the USA and increasing violence in Palestine. The British government had tried and failed to find a solution which would be satisfactory to all and now the problem was to be referred to the council of countries within the UN. However, Crossman believed that this referral to the UN was simply the first step in the process. 'Even more important, he [Bevin] should state that, whatever UNO [United Nations Organisation] decides, British officials, policemen and troops will be withdrawn *by a definite date.*'[51] This UN referral had the benefit of forcing countries that had made difficult and often unrealistic demands of the British government, particularly the United States, to become involved on a more practical level with the situation. It was hoped by the Government that this would highlight Britain's difficulties and that a more realistic policy could be drawn up. Even after the issue had been referred to the UN in 1947, Crossman was still calling in the *New Statesman* for Bevin to '(1) decide, (2) act, and (3) get out.'[52] While Crossman favoured the creation of a Jewish state, his first priority seems to have been the safety of British troops.

The UN Commission eventually concluded that mass Jewish immigration into Palestine was to begin immediately and that a Jewish homeland should be created as soon as feasibly possible, leaving Britain in a very difficult position. As the occupying force Britain would have to implement a policy which she did not support, and in doing so would almost certainly have incurred the anger and hostility of the Arab states which she had tried so hard to satisfy. However, it was unthinkable for Britain to stand in the way of the implementation of the UN resolution. Bevin and the wider British government were deeply committed to the UN organisation, being one of the founder members, and such resistance would have been very damaging, perhaps even fatal, for the fledgling organisation. Bevin in particular was eager to avoid the UN becoming a 'talking shop' as the League of Nations had been in the inter-war period. Bullock indicated that Bevin had not viewed the League of Nations 'as a complete failure, and [he] now thought they could advance to world government at a single step' via the United Nations.[53]

This dilemma led Britain to take an unusual decision. Bevin and Attlee concluded that by removing British troops from Palestine, the British could not be held responsible by the Arab nations for the creation of a Jewish homeland. Additionally, this removal of troops would allow the creation of a Jewish homeland, if the Jewish population were militarily strong enough to resist the Arab invasions which would inevitable occur when the British forces were removed. Very few individuals in Britain believed that Israel would ever be created as it was assumed that the Arab forces would overpower them even before the state had been established. Crossman indicated that this false belief had led Britain and the Labour government to make bad decisions in the region. 'Starting from the fatal illusion that the Arab armies could easily overwhelm the Jews, our Palestine policy has been based on the foundation of a myth, buttressed by prejudice which now threatens to destroy our whole Middle East position.'[54] Therefore, while Britain did not actively encourage the creation of Israel and took action to make its creation more difficult, it could not be accused of actively resisting such action.

With the removal of British troops the immediate dilemma in Britain was no longer over whether the state of Israel should be allowed to develop. The embryonic Israeli forces were forced to fight almost as soon as the state of Israel came into being in 1948. However, these forces were not overrun as anticipated and Israel survived this initial test of strength. Crossman, writing in 1949 stated that even the people of Israel were surprised by their success but still wary of the future. 'They still feel it is a miracle that they have won, and can conceive no desire but peace. But Egyptian, Iraqi and Syrian armies still stand on the soil allocated to Israel by UNO [United Nations Organisation]. In this tiny country, one feels the presence of the invader everywhere, hemming in.'[55] From this point onwards, the key issue in Britain was concerning arms sales to the region. The arms industry in Britain was and is a very important industry which generates large amounts of revenue. In the economic situation of the late 1940s Britain did not really have an economy which could stand the refusal of lucrative arms deals, almost regardless of where these came from, particularly when these orders were placed by states which had generally remained friendly to Britain. When the Arab states placed large arms orders to fight the Israelis, whom the United States armed, Britain accepted these orders, driving another wedge between itself and Israel.

From 1948 to 1960 Crossman appears to have written less prolifically about Israel than he had during the period 1946 to 1948. While he supported the rights of Jews to have their own homeland, his primary concern was how this affected Britain. When British troops were withdrawn from the region and the Israeli state was established, his writing on the issue decreased, though he remained committed to Weizmann's legacy, following his death in 1952, and interested in the state's future. From 1948 onwards Crossman wrote about the future of Israel on occasion, usually combining this with a detailed explanation of the history which had proceeded this. An example of this can be found in the *New Statesman* in 1951, when he wrote a series of four articles on various aspects of the relationship between Jordan and Israel. He urged that Britain should take the opportunity to fulfil its duty and create the conditions for peace between the two sides by firstly helping Jordan to resolve their refugee problem.[56] His first article in the series outlined Bevin's approach to Palestine and the relationship with Jordan, insinuating that Britain was at least partially responsible for the difficulties in the region and that it was Britain's <u>duty</u> to aid both sides in the pursuit of peace.[57] Crossman continued to write these articles on a sporadic basis for much of the 1950s.[58]

In 1960 Crossman took part in a series of lectures in Israel. The three lectures considered the contribution of Weizmann and the birth of Israel, Ernest Bevin and the view of the post-war Labour government to the difficulties in Palestine, and finally the future for the newly created Israel. This was the most complete and comprehensive writing which Crossman had done on the issue of Israel since his activities on the Anglo-American commission. This, coupled with his continued commitment to local Zionist groups for much of the 1950s, exhibited his devotion to the state of Israel. In the Crossman Papers there are numerous invitations asking him to attend and speak at a variety of Zionist meetings and gatherings. In his 1960 series of lectures, he spent much of his time examining the past and discussing the birth of Israel. It was only in his last lecture where he considered the future of Israel. He indicated that Israel was similar to how he had envisioned it before its creation in 1948. He also outlined that while the new state had features which he had not anticipated, these were almost wholly positive. Using militarism as an example, he explained that neutrality was 'unsuited to the Israeli temper'.[59] Unsurprisingly, bearing in mind the speaker and his audience, the final lecture on the future of Israel was overwhelmingly positive and, even bearing his environment in mind, this lecture shows that he held the state of Israel generally, and Weizmann more specifically, in very high esteem.

Between 1961 and 1974 Crossman wrote very little concerning Israel or the issues which were raised by, for example, the Palestinian refugees or the militarism of Israel which he had accepted as part of the Israeli temperament. This is probably because he was using his time and energy on other policies which became more pressing to him during this period, as outlined later in this chapter. Defence considerations, nuclear weapons and more domestic issues began to occupy Crossman's time. This was coupled with the fact that once Israel had been created, and had not been overrun by its Arab neighbours, he believed that his main objective had been achieved and Israel could now function as a nation, turning itself to the problems and concerns which face other, more established, nations.[60] During this period, Crossman appears to have been less preoccupied with Israel than he had been during the period 1946 to 1948. Between 1961 and 1972, he did not even find the time to write articles on Israel as he had done during the 1950s, although this is almost certainly due to his party and governmental responsibilities. However, Crossman did become President of the Labour Friends of Israel, according to Hayim Pinner.[61] In 1972, he began to research a biography on Weizmann which would have utilised his knowledge of his friend and the birth of Israel. However, due to his ill health, he was forced to abandon this project and between 1973 and his death in 1974, he was preoccupied with the editing of his diaries, with the issue of Israel became much less prominent.

The Cold War and the Third Force

When the Labour Party entered government in 1945, they carried with them the expectations of a nation eager for change. While many Labour MPs were particularly keen to push through socialist domestic policies, such as the creation of the NHS and the nationalisation of key industries, some wanted to see socialist thinking continued into areas of foreign policy. Ernest Bevin, Foreign Secretary from 1945 to 1951 had never served as a backbench MP, and Bullock indicated that foreign policy during this period was based largely on the personal views of Bevin and Attlee as opposed to prior policy documentation.[62] Due to the international circumstances in which the Labour Party entered government, some cross over of policy was inevitable, and a consistent attitude was necessary when dealing with the USA and the USSR. The actual hand over of government took place in the middle of the Potsdam conference in 1945 and it meant that information had to be passed from Churchill to Attlee and from Eden to Bevin. This was helped by the working relationships which these individuals had fostered during the life of the wartime coalition government. Bullock described the experiences of those involved in the coalition as an opportunity for the Labour Party's leading figures 'to exercise power and share in real decisions ... an experience of government at its peak, uncomplicated by parliamentary manoeuvring or party rivalry.'[63] Attlee and Bevin appear to have concluded that while domestic policy should be adapted in line with the party's socialist policies, foreign affairs were in too fragile a state for party politics to dominate and ideologies to take precedence. As Bullock indicated, Bevin 'saw himself in a national not a party role...'[64] In order to maintain a consistent attitude to foreign affairs, he had discussions with Eden, the shadow Foreign Secretary, concerning key events.[65]

In addition to this almost bi-partisan approach to foreign affairs, Britain was in a very difficult situation internationally, which further limited her freedom of movement. While Britain had been a victor of the Second World War, economically she was shattered. The termination of American Lease-Lend coming so quickly after the end of the war left Britain in dire straits, and it was obvious that the only country economically able or willing to help Britain was the United States. This dependence, coupled with the close wartime collaboration between the UK and the USA, meant that America's policy concerns were vitally important to Britain. This reliance on the USA additionally meant that Britain could not act as an independent nation in all circumstances. Writing in 1947 the same year that *Keep Left* was published, Crossman indicated that 'the need for dollars makes satellites of us all.'[66] However, in the face of these difficulties, the Labour government and Bevin personally managed to secure American support for some of the long-standing achievements of the era, such as the creation of NATO and the introduction of Marshall Aid. These developments were of crucial importance to Britain and Western Europe and were encouraged and often based on the ideas of Bevin and the Labour government. In such delicate circumstances, the idea of Britain mediating between the USSR and the USA was riddled with difficulties and was viewed by many as unrealistic and fanciful.

This consistency of policy between the front benches on foreign affairs was unacceptable to some Labour backbenchers, who felt that a socialist government should be adopting a more socialist foreign policy. One of the most important areas of concern was the developing tension between the USSR and the USA. As mentioned above, many, particularly left wing MPs, believed that a British socialist government could act as a mediator for the two superpowers, helping to bridge ideological differences. Bullock indicated that Bevin had applied the phrase 'left understands left, but the right does not' to post-war France, but many on the left applied it to the Soviet Union.[67] This was due to socialism being considered by some as mid-point ideologically between communism and capitalism. Writing in 1951, with the benefit of hindsight, Crossman directly challenged this assumption, as he believed that the idea of an ideological bridge was unrealistic.[68] However, during the mid to late 1950s he was committed to a socialist foreign policy. With the creation of the Keep Left group in approximately 1946 or early 1947 (there appears not to have been an official commencement date), the call for a socialist foreign policy began to focus around a small group of Labour MPs keen to turn this label into a more coherent policy. The *Keep Left* pamphlet, which was published in 1947, demanded a socialist foreign policy and the adoption of the third force ideal.[69] It is important to note that the Keep Left group did not include all left wing MPs or all those who would later form the Bevanites. Until 1951, Bevan himself was a member of Attlee's cabinet and therefore committed to Bevin's policies due to collective cabinet responsibility.[70]

The third force was based upon a more unified Europe. This grouping, with socialist Britain at its heart and likely to take a leading role, would act as another superpower, encouraging the USA and the USSR into closer relations. Europe would act as an independent force between the two powers, eradicating misunderstanding and division. Crossman indicated that the decision which the British government would have to make on her favoured allies was dependent on the outcome which the Labour government was seeking:

> Britain has to choose between a special partnership with America and a special partnership with France and our other European neighbours. If the Labour government regards Russian aggression as the one threat to British security, it must choose the first. If it still believes in the possibility of an understanding with Russia, and of world government developing slowly through the United Nations, it will choose the second.[71]

However, in order to achieve this, Britain and Europe would need to be seen as a neutral, united force, which seemed highly unlikely in the light of internal European divisions and American economic support. Crossman's hopes for a unity of purpose in Europe did not extend to any sort of formal grouping, such as that created in the 1950s firstly as the European Coal and Steel Community (ECSC), then later as the European Economic Community (EEC). Instead he seems to have favoured a much looser grouping with a unity of purpose. *Keep Left* indicated that Britain was becoming an American subordinate while instead, in conjunction with Europe, Britain should be maintaining an independent central position between the USA and the USSR. Good relations, it argued, were vital with both superpower states, not simply with the USA, as Britain could not heal the world breach 'if we ourselves have taken sides.'[72] The pamphlet indicated that Russia was suspicious of the motives of the Western states, and with some justification. If Britain, at the heart of a united Europe, were to act as a mediator or third force between the two superpowers, disaster could be avoided and the separation of

Europe and Germany could be averted. As Crossman argued, 'the security of each and of all of us depends on preventing the division of Europe into exclusive spheres of influence.'[73]

The *Keep Left* pamphlet was based on the assumption that the USSR was willing to co-operate and work with the Western powers and that a reasonable compromise could be found which would be acceptable to both East and West, particularly as 'the USSR has no ... economic motives for expansion.' Instead the USSR had for many years attempted 'to avoid war and concentrate at home.'[74] This premise became questionable almost as soon as the pamphlet was published. The actions of both sides in negotiations, particularly those of the USSR, began to become public knowledge in 1947-8 culminating in the Soviet blockade of West Berlin. While events had made the idea of a European third force unrealistic, prior to 1947 the idea, while being very optimistic, does not appear to have been overly idealistic in origin. Crossman indicated in 1953 that his hopes for a thawing out of the Cold War and the removal of external superpowers from Europe was no longer realistic in the current circumstances. 'Is that vision utopian and fantastic? Certainly it looks so today.'[75] In 1947, many MPs were unaware of the difficulties which Bevin was experiencing with Molotov and the difficulties which were being faced by the government. While Bevin had made some attempt in 1946 to outline difficulties between East and West, it appears that many Labour MPs concluded that 'a better case could be made for Soviet suspicion' and many continued to believe that their actions could be viewed as the result of fear of the Western powers.[76] The pamphlet highlighted the uncertainty with which Britain faced a post-Second World War world. All possible allegiances were questionable and uncertain, but it was clear that Britain would find it very hard to stand alone.

Crossman's views on the Cold War and Britain's relationships with the superpowers evolved over time in the light of international events. Following the Berlin blockade and the response of the Soviet states to Marshall Aid, his views began to move away from the idea of a third force, and instead he attempted to view the Anglo-American relationship in conjunction with other important issues. For example, in 1950 Crossman indicated that while a break with America would be very damaging for both parties, this should not be interpreted, as he believed Churchill had interpreted it, as a reason to bend to American demands regardless of the consequences:

> The right of the [Labour] party shares Mr Churchill's view that, in the last resort, we should stand by the USA right or wrong, because otherwise the world is wide open to communist domination. The left of the party, while fully agreeing about the dangers of an Anglo-American rift has, on the other hand, seen more clearly the dangers of a partnership in which Britain, in the last resort, always gives in.[77]

Crossman was again calling for the independence of Britain from many formal and even informal pacts, particularly with America, though he continued to support Britain's role in the UN and NATO. This was a theme which was to run through much of his thinking on British foreign policy, a belief that Britain should be allowed, as he perceived other nations were, to make decisions based on her own national interest without following the lead of the United States or any other power. 'What we cannot afford to accept is a two-bloc world and a divided Europe. That is why we must have an independent British policy.'[78]

Another factor which limited Britain's decision making was the extent of her overseas commitments and the resources which were required to maintain these. An overhang from the days of empire, Britain retained troops in numerous territories as well as having a large number in Germany. If these were to be withdrawn there was real concern as to what would happen in these countries and whether communism would replace fragile democracies. Crossman argued that withdrawal would lead to other interest groups making significant gains in popularity:

> But it is certainly true that, if British troops were suddenly withdrawn without replacement, this would strengthen neutralist and nationalist tendencies among the Arabs and probably lead to explosions in Iraq and Saudi Arabia similar to those in Persia.[79]

Communism was viewed as a very negative ideology which bore no resemblance to socialism and this meant that Britain was forced to divert resources from other vital areas to pay for troops overseas. The USA was the only other country practically which Britain could hand these commitments over to in the short term, but she was, for much of the period, unwilling to pick up these commitments. Crossman called for a reduction in these commitments sporadically during the period 1945 to 1964, but when Britain's commitment to forces East of Suez was raised in a cabinet meeting in December 1966, he indicated that the method of withdrawal was important as well as the longer-term aim.[80] The removal of troops by the British was an issue which could and would have brought Britain into conflict with the US and it may well have damaged Anglo-American relations.

Crossman, from 1949 until the mid-1950s appears to have rather optimistically believed that a reduction in British overseas commitments would have no damaging effect upon Anglo-American relations. Indeed, he believed that were Britain to show that she was not simply going to acquiesce to all American demands, the relationship would develop into a more equal partnership than currently existed. This would require Britain to have closer ties with European countries, 'if we could make it clear that we regard our relations with them [European countries] and with our dominions as our first and major pre-occupation, and that we are determined to avoid exclusive commitments to either the Americans or the Russians the way would be open to a genuine European solution of the German problem.'[81] However, Crossman's views on a European grouping, while not idealistic, were never particularly realistic, due to his lack of consideration of the internal situation in countries such as France, Italy or the Benelux countries. He additionally overlooked Franco's dictatorship in Spain, purely focusing his attention on Germany. Due to the economic support which the Americans gave to Britain during the period, this independence of policy seems to have rather an unrealistic basis, but this was coupled with a realistic evaluation of Britain's overseas commitments, an evaluation which many MPs simply did not want to face. This desire to remove British troops, particularly East of Suez hinted at a loss of status which many within Parliament were unwilling to accept.

Germany and Europe

Germany was a country in which Crossman had a deep personal interest. He had visited Germany during the time of the Weimer Republic, spoke German fluently and was deeply concerned about the future of the country after the end of the Second World War and how this reviled nation would fit in and co-operate with other European States. As he argued in 1954,

> if we give the West Germans sovereignty and encourage them to revive their national ambitions, can we be sure they will remain our faithful partners when they realise, as some of them are already realising, that the Russians have far more to offer them than we do?[82]

This apprehension was deepened by Britain's role as an occupying force in Germany and the developing threat of communism in Eastern Europe. This was also coupled with concern as to the fate of the Jewish community within Europe. As the most central city of Europe, as well as being occupied by both Eastern and Western forces, the fate of Berlin was closely bound up with the wider future of Europe and the development of the Cold War. Initially following the end of the Second World War, Europe was divided over how Germany should be allowed to develop to avoid another terrible war. As Germany became divided into East and West during the late 1940s and the Cold War began to become a reality, the future of Germany became bound up with the future of Europe. The Labour Party, in common with the Conservative Party, had internal divisions as to how Europe should develop in the post-war period.

Crossman's views on Europe also seem to have developed and changed over the period 1945-70. This may well have been due to the changing circumstances in Europe and the lessening sense of fear which many felt from Germany after its separation into East and West. This was a very gradual process which had been developing since the end of the Second World War. France, which had been occupied during the Second World War, was particularly worried in the late 1940s that a united Germany would have military desires on her territory and therefore a European group of nations might be beneficial. It must also be noted that

Crossman's definition of a European group or third force in 1947 was not an identical concept to the European Community as envisaged during the signing of the Treaty of Rome in 1957. This section will consider whether Crossman's views on Britain's membership of a European Union did change between 1945 and 1970, what the definition of a European group was during the period and how this developed. Also, this section will consider the role of Germany within Europe and how Crossman and the wider Labour Party changed and developed their views on Germany and Europe during this period.

Following Germany's defeat in 1945, the country and its capital Berlin were split between the occupying powers – the USSR, the USA, Britain and France. Four-power talks were devised to ensure that decisions about Germany's future could be made in unison, thereby guaranteeing it a unified future. The four-power talks were very difficult almost from the beginning, leading Bevin to eventually abandon any realistic belief in a four-power resolution to the issue of Germany's future. Writing of the Paris Peace Conference in 1947, Bullock explained how the public and politicians responded to reports of difficulties between the East and West blocs. 'The headlines and daily reports from Paris drove home, for the first time for millions of newspaper readers, even to a minister as well-informed as Dalton, how serious and far-reaching was the dispute between the Soviet bloc and the West.'[83] The Keep Left group, for the period 1946- 47 were calling for these four-power talks to be continued and for Bevin to ensure British independence from America with the aim of a more united Europe. The *Keep Left* pamphlet called for the government to do 'everything possible to reduce our economic dependence on the New World so that we can co-operate with the USA on free and equal terms.'[84]

The Keep Left group believed that any Soviet intransigence during the negotiations was due to the Soviets being suspicious of western actions which could be overcome by better communications between East and West. There was an underlying belief within the members of the Keep Left group of the good intentions and political stability of the communist government in the USSR. There seems to have been a belief that while socialism and communism had considerable divisions, they shared many of the same ideological goals, while capitalist America was lacking in these humanitarian, social aims. Crossman indicated this ideological common ground was the key to understanding and co-operation in Europe, stating in 1945 that 'only if Britain and Russia can achieve a real understanding with regard to the social problems in Europe will co-operation be possible.'[85] The pamphlet argued that America was so obsessed by fears of a communist Germany that 'they prefer to keep Germany and Europe divided in order to check Russian expansion.'[86] At this point, the Keep Left group viewed the USSR as an ally, a country which supported the aims of socialism though it implemented them in different ways from Western countries.

This view of the USSR began to be undermined in late 1947 and 1948, culminating in the Berlin blockade. Berlin was situated in the Soviet-controlled section of Germany but as the capital city, it had been split into four zones, each controlled by one of the four-power countries. The Soviets began to prevent the movement of food and other essential goods through their zone in March 1948, meaning that large numbers of people in the Western controlled areas of Berlin would starve to death in the winter of 1948 if rapid action were not taken. The USSR implemented the blockade as she was not achieving her demands at the negotiating table. Stalin was particularly incensed at the British and American attempts to combine their quarters of Germany so they could begin to increase German industrial output, thereby reducing the economic drain on their domestic economy.[87] The British and Americans decided to use air transportation to overcome the blockade and feed the Berliners in the Western quarters, a policy which was highly successful and broke the blockade, which ended in failure in 1949. Crossman, in light of the information which was reaching Britain of the USSR's perceived hostility to negotiation and preference for demanding concessions from the Western powers, began to change his views on the future of Germany and the role of the USSR.

By 1950, the questions over Germany's future were beginning to change. Germany was now a more overtly divided country, and the Soviets were retreating into their own sphere of influence behind the iron curtain. The two main questions which Crossman and the wider Labour Party were beginning to face were questions of vital importance to the future of Europe. The first key question was should West Germany be re-armed? The defence costs in Germany were a drain on the British economy and the Americans and many within the Labour Party, as well as many Conservatives, were keen for Germany to provide some of her own troops to defend herself on the new front of the Cold War. However, this obviously raised questions over whether Western Germany could be trusted to be militarised again. Crossman asked in 1954 'would it really benefit either the USA or France or Britain if a Greater German Reich were once again created?'[88] Along with much of the left wing of the Labour Party, he was deeply opposed to the idea of German rearmament, feeling that it would have negligible positive effects in the current situation while the possible consequences could be disastrous. 'In short, the principle of German rearmament was adopted as a desperate measure to meet what some considered to be a desperate situation. No one now claims that the same desperate situation exists.'[89]

Along with many who had vivid memories of the horror of the Second World War, the prospect of arming the old enemy was not particularly palatable. Germany was also viewed as a violent country with an aggressive national temperament which made rearmament a very disturbing prospect. Crossman argued that 'at the very least it must be admitted that the effort to add German military strength of the Western Alliance is fraught with danger.'[90] This view ignored the economic situation in Britain at this time, when it was essential to make savings on overseas troops. Were Germany to have her own troops, this would mean an initial drop in Britain's income, as Western Germany paid for Britain to provide troops for her defence. However, supporters of German rearmament argued that after this short-term effect, Britain would economically gain from not having to provide as many troops for German defence. Additionally, the troops in Germany would be members of NATO, and would not be so great in number as to be of any great risk or capable of effective, long-term aggressive action. These assurances did not persuade individuals such as Crossman, and many of the Bevanites, who continued to believe that German rearmament was very dangerous. He was not in favour of indefinite neutralisation of Germany, but in 1953 he called for neutralisation to remain in place in for the immediate future and for more talks with Russia concerning the reunification of Germany.[91] Crossman and much of the left wing of the party continued to call for German reunification, and therefore, indirectly, for continued talks with Russia.

By August 1952, Crossman was beginning to accept that the permanent dividing of Europe was a reality and in light of this he called for Germany to become involved in the European Defence Council (EDC). This act would not increase western security but was primarily 'to get over French fears of Germany; but no-one is going to tell me that the creation of the EDC has made it any easier from a military point of view to organize European defenses.'[92] This policy had several advantages. Firstly, the parts of Germany which the Western powers controlled would become bound into a Western alliance, meaning that infiltration by communist elements would be much less likely. Secondly, the creation of this alliance would make France far less afraid of German intentions in the future.[93] Thirdly, Britain and America were linked in their aim to maintain a free and democratic Europe, making American isolationism seem less likely, and providing stability for Britain. While in 1949, there is little evidence to suggest that Crossman was in favour of close Anglo-American relations, by accepting the entry of Germany into an Atlantic pact with, amongst others, the USA and Britain, he was calling for a measure which would inevitably strengthen NATO and Anglo-American relations. This is an indication that his views were changing in the light of international events.

The second crucial question which the Labour Party and Britain generally was having to give more thought to from 1950 onwards was the future of Europe. The Schuman plan published in 1950 opened the debate over a united or even federal Europe. The plan called for an iron and steel community between European countries and Schuman appeared to be organising the beginnings of a political union in Europe. This plan was particularly difficult for Britain to participate in. Edmund Dell indicated that the British people and the government were ambivalent about Europe. 'Twice in a lifetime the protection of British independence and European liberty had imposed a heavy price in lives and treasure. The temptation ... was to retreat behind the moat.'[94] The union raised wider questions over Britain's relations with Europe and the rest of the world. Britain and America had maintained a very close relationship after the end of the Second World War, which Britain considered to be closer than any other political relationship either had with other countries. While America was keen for Britain to join in any new European communities hoping she would provide a powerful, democratic lead, Britain was not eager to sacrifice her special relationship with America.[95] Additionally, Britain had her Empire links to consider, and entry into a European community would impact on the Commonwealth nations. Preferential trading links existed within the Sterling area of the Commonwealth, which linked many countries to Britain which had been Dominions previously. These links were vital to Britain as they made up a large percentage of her overseas trade. Britain also had close political links to many of these countries which until fairly recently she had been governing, such as India and New Zealand. Were Britain to enter a new European trading bloc, how would this impact on relations, and trade with Commonwealth countries? Dell noted that 'the Foreign Office was worried that any form of membership, even partial membership [of an economic group] could cause problems in Britain's relationship with the Commonwealth.'[96] The situation was exacerbated by Britain's view that 'nothing important could happen in Europe without British involvement.'[97] For all these reasons, Britain refused the offer to join the iron and steel community in 1950.

Crossman, as we have seen, had been calling for Britain to be less reliant on America since the end of the Second World War. The initial form that he had called for this independence to take was for Britain and Europe to form a third force. However, by 1948 this idea was outdated and unrealistic due to divisions within Europe and concerns over the actions of the superpowers. With the Schuman Plan in 1950 and signs of a more united Europe, Crossman began to support Britain's entry into this group. The beginnings of a European grouping would hopefully allow Britain the independence from the superpowers which he had been calling for since 1946. Additionally, as a victor from the Second World War and a previous great power, Britain would be the strongest nation in a European grouping, providing a lead to other nations and creating a union in its preferred form, as opposed to following the blueprint of another nation, such as France. In 1948 Crossman briefly called on Bevin to accept the fact that 'Western Union is coming.' He indicated that he was aware of the dangers of entering into this union, but continued 'the only question is whether Britain's Labour government takes the lead in building it on a sound plan or whether we are dragged into it by the Americans and the French on their terms.'[98] However, he was not in favour of Britain abandoning or forgetting about her Commonwealth links which he considered very important. Instead he was calling for the British Commonwealth to be included in a European union, with preferential trading links being preserved. He indicated that the issue of trading links would be a decisive one for the UK, later stating in 1962 that 'the decision whether Britain enters or not will be made in the last resort in terms of a single problem, the entry to Europe of the temperate zones food-stuffs from Canada, Australia and New Zealand.'[99]

This idea of extending the European group to include Commonwealth countries was not unique to Crossman, but it did lead him to the conclusion that a federal Europe was a mistake and that the removal of national governments must be avoided.[100] Instead he was specifically calling for a European grouping with a united Germany included if at all possible, where member states would have preferential trade agreements, a forum for discussion and agreement and a common defence force, but would not have a federal framework. By 1956 Crossman was calling for a United States of Europe, but this appears to have been a soundbite, as opposed to a call for a federalised Europe.[101]

The events of the 1950s, especially the signing of the Treaty of Rome in 1957 and the creation of the European Economic Community (EEC), began to affect the views of many in Britain, including Crossman. Britain had not participated in the beginnings of the European Community, a decision which would come back to haunt the Wilson government in 1967. By 1962 Crossman's previous enthusiasm for a loose European grouping was fading and instead he was being more guarded and wary of entry into the European Economic Community in its current form. He was now insistent that Britain should not be bound by any measures which might disadvantage a Labour government, such as legislation which might limit socialist policies. He specifically criticised any restrictions which would limit the British government's actions. 'We socialists, for example, are keenly concerned to ensure that the kind of full employment and nationalisation measures that a Labour government would like to introduce are not likely to be forbidden by the High Commission.'[102] He again called for the entry of the remaining British Empire to be given consideration, but the entry of Commonwealth countries to the EEC seems to have been effectively dropped by Crossman, probably due to the framework which had been established by the Treaty of Rome. This meant in practice that a deal would need to be reached between the EEC and Britain which provided the Commonwealth countries with preferential trading links with the EEC in order for Britain to join. This would probably have included, for example, New Zealand butter, which was included in the Conservative negotiations, prior to Britain's entry to the EEC in 1973. By 1973, Crossman was deeply opposed to Britain becoming a member of the EEC and indicated that he was very unhappy about the decision to join as well as the terms of entry. [103] His preferred European grouping appears to have been very different to the reality of the EEC.

De Gaulle's veto of British entry into the EEC in 1963 dented the enthusiasm of many pro-European MPs in both the Conservative and Labour Parties. It also signalled an end to the discussion over European entry at least in the short term. By 1967 when the Wilson government was discussing a possible bid for entry into the European Community, Crossman was very much in favour of avoiding entry all together. He described his aim to be for Britain to be an 'offshore island.'[104] While the cabinet was split, he concluded that there was little point in Britain beginning talks on entry into the EEC while de Gaulle remained President of France.[105] He appears to have been more perceptive than some of his cabinet colleagues. At heart, by 1967, he was very much against Britain's entry into the EEC and this was a view which he maintained until the end of his life. He concluded that the European Community would not be beneficial for Britain, and he also questioned the effect upon Commonwealth trade links. He had become a 'little Englander', which was a world away from his views in 1947 of Europe becoming a third force with Britain at the heart of a community of like-minded nations.[106]

Crossman's views on Europe and Germany were deeply influenced by the events of his lifetime. While he retained some optimistic elements in his thinking, he seems to have recognised these as overly optimistic and perhaps even slightly idealistic, describing them as 'in the present state utopian.'[107] These were objectives to be aimed at, not necessarily achieved. As the EEC developed and the Cold War deepened with the separation of Germany becoming a more fixed reality, his views developed. By 1962, he was calling for Britain to remain outside the EEC and the Common Market if Britain could not achieve all of her aims in negotiation. This realism was confirmed when he predicted in 1967 that de Gaulle would veto Britain's entry into the EEC, an event which Wilson had hoped would not materialise. He was equally realistic if optimistic about Germany for much of the period. Again, until the late 1950s he called for a United Germany if at all possible, and called repeatedly for talks between East and West to prevent Germany drifting into separation.

Once the separation of Germany had been confirmed and the Cold War had escalated, his views on Germany became more realistic. By 1971, Crossman was a member of the Committee for the Recognition of the German Democratic Republic (GDR). Crossman hoped that by recognising the GDR, European security would be increased and the chances of misunderstanding and hostility through ignorance would be reduced. He identified the specific aims as being 'to break down the existing barriers resulting from non-recognition which seriously interfere with the growth of trade between the two countries and with the exchange of ideas, knowledge and pleasure in the whole field of cultural relations.'[108] By recognising the GDR and even inviting them, along with the Federal Deutschland Republic (FDR), to join the UN, he believed that the lines of communication between East and West would be re-opened and Britain could achieve a more realistic view of East Germany and the wider situation in Europe and cultivate working relationships if possible. Crossman also believed that Britain would benefit economically through recognising the GDR, something he believed the French had already achieved. [109] As can be seen, his views on Europe and Germany were very realistic, tinged with optimism for the future. He hoped for better relations with Europe and a united Germany, but does not appear to have believed that these could be achieved easily. Indeed, he indicated that many hard decisions lay in front of a British government, whether that be a Conservative or a Labour government. He stated that if the EEC could not be transformed into a world organisation, then Britain would 'regretfully but firmly stay outside.'[110] Socialism was, by the mid-1950s not necessarily the bonding force which Crossman had believed it to be in 1947. Even as early as 1949 he was indicating that Europe would need American financial backing for the foreseeable future and that America should be the ally who Britain and Europe looked to for continued economic help.[111] Concerning Germany, he was advocating a more realistic worldview and was not suggesting that Britain should work alone to re-open lines of communication with the GDR. Instead he was insisting that Britain should not miss out on the opportunities afforded by recognition of the East German state. His views on Europe and Germany seem to have become more realistic as time progressed, partly due to the developments in Europe and partly no doubt due to his developing views on foreign affairs, and developing experience of political negotiations.[112]

Nuclear Weapons

The issue of nuclear weapons was a very taxing and difficult issue for the Labour Party to deal with, and with developments within the nuclear research field continuing at a rapid pace, these decisions needed to be regularly re-evaluated and re-considered. Nuclear power and weaponry was a new issue which became more important and relevant after 1945. Nuclear weapons had been developed in great secrecy between the Americans, the British and the Canadians during the Second World War. Few Labour MPs were aware of issues surrounding nuclear weapons or even their existence until the Americans dropped a nuclear bomb on Hiroshima in 1945. Even after this incident, nuclear weapons and the actions of the British government were shrouded in mystery, making relevant and intelligent discussion very difficult.[113]

An additional problem which the Labour Party faced when considering nuclear weapons was the composition of the party. Far more than the Conservative Party, the Labour Party contained a wide variety of opinions varying from some relatively central views to those on the left, some of whom had communist sympathies or were described as fellow-travellers and pacifists. This variety of viewpoints made it very difficult for the Parliamentary Labour Party leadership to formulate a policy which the entire party could support.[114] This difficulty was compounded by the actions of the post-war Attlee government. Unknown to his party and even much of his cabinet, Attlee encouraged nuclear research and authorised the hugely expensive development of a British independent atomic bomb, co-ordinated by the GEN 75 cabinet committee.[115] Following Churchill's announcement in 1955 of the actions of the Attlee government, the party was divided on both past and future policy. The variety of viewpoints was exacerbated by the range of issues which were covered by the umbrella term of 'nuclear research'. Following the dropping of atomic bombs in Japan, some MPs were deeply concerned about the health effects of exposure to nuclear material. Others were concerned specifically with the use of nuclear weapons, whether these new and devastating weapons should be used, and if so which countries should have access to them. Crossman, for example, was opposed to Germany controlling nuclear weapons.[116] This also led to discussion of how to encourage nuclear countries to destroy their weapons, and how such actions and weapons would impact on more conventional defence systems. The issue was episodically divisive within the Labour Party until approximately 1963 when Wilson became leader when, because of a number of uniting factors, the party's internal factions became less vocal. This section will consider the debates within the Labour Party concerning nuclear weapons, Crossman's views on nuclear weapons, his views on how best to inform the electorate, and how he influenced the views of the wider party.

Nuclear weaponry was an issue which certain individuals devoted themselves to for their entire career, in a similar way to Crossman's interest in Israel. However, for many MPs, including Crossman, it was one of a number of issues which they had to consider, and for these individuals there were two particularly volatile periods within the nuclear weapons debate. While in government between 1945 and 1951, Attlee had kept the issue of nuclear weapons and development within a very small circle of ministers, comprising of Ernie Bevin (Foreign Secretary), Herbert Morrison (Lord President), A.V. Alexander (Minister of Defence), Lord Addison (Dominions Secretary) and John Wilmot (Minister of Supply).[117] However, upon leaving power Attlee was in a vulnerable position as his actions could be revealed at any time. In 1955, during a defence debate, Churchill informed the House of Commons that the Attlee government had authorised research and development of an independent British nuclear deterrent force. Writing in early 1955, when Crossman like many of the members of the party was attempting to discover what Britain's nuclear status was in the light of Churchill's announcement, his uncertainty was clear. He concluded that while socialist backbenchers 'were seeking to insert into the Atlantic Energy Bill a clause forbidding the government to make the H-bomb without parliamentary consent, production had already begun.'[118] This information on the Labour government's activities, which came as a surprise to many within the party, was coupled with the announcement by the Conservative government in February 1955 that Britain was to begin manufacturing the hydrogen bomb.

Many, particularly those on the left wing of the Labour Party, were opposed to the manufacture of nuclear weapons for a variety of reasons. There were, of course, those within the party who opposed the use and production of all weapons. Of those in the party who were not pacifists or fellow travellers, there were a variety of differing reasons why individuals objected specifically to an independent British nuclear deterrent. Such a deterrent raised questions and fears over Britain's world role and its comparable position within the world order. Highlighting Britain's weakness without nuclear weapons, Crossman noted that 'if we promised in no circumstances to use the atom bomb, the Red Army could occupy Europe and the Middle East without serious resistance.'[119] How could Britain afford such an expensive deterrent, particularly when Britain was still counting the cost of the Second World War, as pointed out by Crossman in the House of Commons in 1953?[120] If this expense was too great, how would Britain maintain her nuclear status in the ever-developing field of research and would this be economically viable? Putting cost to one side, how would a nuclear Britain co-operate or compete with other nuclear nations? Crossman argued in 1949 that 'the knowledge that we made atom bombs here would expose us to aggression. Moreover, we simply cannot afford to enter the atom armament race. We should be far wiser to invest what limited resources we can afford in the peaceful development of atomic energy.'[121] In the immediate post-war period, Truman had ensured that nuclear secrets which should have been shared by America with Britain and Canada under the terms of the Quebec agreement were kept exclusively in America and not shared with other nations. There appears to be little evidence to suggest that the USA was specifically opposed to Britain becoming a nuclear power pre-1948, though it seems likely that the American administration was keen to maintain the exclusivity of its nuclear position.[122] However, after the USSR detonated its first nuclear bomb in 1948, there seems to have been less resistance in America to Britain becoming a nuclear nation, although there were still questions left unanswered as to who would control and essentially own the weapons on British soil.[123]

During the mid-1950s, Crossman's views on nuclear weapons were fairly clear. He had for much of his parliamentary career, questioned successive governments on their defence policies, costs and the length of conscription. He had been in favour, certainly since the end of the Second World War when the post-war situation was becoming more clear, of a re-evaluation of Britain's overseas defence programme and a more general review of how Britain's new world position following the Second World War should affect its overseas commitments. While Crossman was seeking this re-evaluation, he does not appear to have concluded that Britain was a declining power after 1945. He believed that while Britain could not claim to be a Superpower alongside the United States and the Soviet Union, Britain was still a great power and had the ability to be highly influential in international relations. Writing in 1947, he indicated that Britain was 'a balancing factor; without us, neither America or Russia can make war on one another.'[124] Writing in 1949 about the possibility of nuclear weapons being manufactured and based in Britain, he argued that instead of increasing British security they might instead make Britain a target.[125]

Crossman was concerned that if nuclear weapons were adopted without a re-evaluation of conventional forces, it would create an overwhelming burden which Britain could not carry.[126] With the beginning of the deconstruction of the British Empire, most visible with the granting of independence for India in 1947 and its entry into the Commonwealth, he concluded that many of Britain's previous military obligations and overseas bases were unnecessary, and involved too high a cost in terms of manpower and international relations as well as monetarily. Instead he indicated that Britain might be 'wiser to invest what we can afford in the peaceful development of atomic energy' instead of entering into an expensive, unsustainable arms race with the USA and the USSR.[127] He concluded that in the new nuclear age, if Britain were to adopt a nuclear deterrent policy, it should lead to a more general review of Britain's conventional forces. These forces would become far less important in a nuclear age, and should be reduced in line with this.

Additionally, the cost of nuclear weapons research and development would make spending on conventional forces unfeasible and unnecessary. As early as 1947 Crossman and George Wigg were writing about how Britain's defence burden needed to be reduced, but by 1955, in light of the developments in nuclear weapons, their views on defence were incorporating this new factor. They highlighted the situation and asked 'what do we gain by keeping 4½ divisions and a tactical air force in Europe if the only defence of these islands is, as the white paper states, the deterrent threat of the H-bomb?'[128]

When Hugh Gaitskell became leader of the Labour Party in 1955, relations between himself and Crossman were more amicable than at almost any other time. Philip Williams indicated in his biography of Gaitskell that upon becoming leader, he decided to concentrate more of his efforts on foreign policy issues.[129] It seems likely that by providing Crossman with an alternative policy focus, Gaitskell was hoping to reduce the likely areas of conflict between them. He needed to find domestic issues which Crossman could concentrate on, and these issues included a rethink of the pension scheme and some limited defence issues. Perhaps because of Crossman's work with Wigg on nuclear weapons in 1955, he appointed him to a party advisory committee on nuclear weapons in 1958. Howard concluded that this was an unusual appointment due to Crossman's rather contradictory views on nuclear weapons, but there seems little evidence to support such a statement.[130] While being a member of this committee, Crossman's attendance seems to have been rather lacking in comparison to other members.[131] In 1955, Crossman had concluded that Britain should remain a member of NATO and while having a long-term aim of disarmament, should have control of a nuclear weapons programme for the foreseeable future.[132] This was a view which was held by Gaitskell and many within the PLP and was not particularly unconventional. Williams concluded that Crossman, along with Wilson was, in 1958, a 'fudger' allowing their true views to be hidden behind inaccuracy and uncertainty, instead of speaking out clearly.[133] It seems unfair to pinpoint Crossman for criticism for not providing the public with a detailed discussion of this very complex issue, when very few MPs communicated detailed arguments or outlines of their opinions on this issue. In *The Future Labour Offers You*, a pamphlet published in November 1958 which was Crossman's brain child, no detailed discussion of any policy appears, as this was meant to be a very accessible document for the public, and not a closely argued academic work.[134]

During the period 1958 to 1960, the relationship between Gaitskell and Crossman crumbled and this coincided with a particularly difficult period in Gaitskell's leadership. Coupled with the issue of Clause IV that was raised following the 1959 election defeat, and is covered in chapter 3, was the issue of nuclear weapons. This period of conflict could be viewed as slightly unexpected due to Gaitskell's willingness to set up a group to consider the whole issue of nuclear weapons and Britain's role in a nuclear world, with the aim of finding a policy that could unite the party. However, as previously mentioned, the Labour

Party contained a variety of individuals with differing opinions on nuclear weapons and wider defence policy, so agreement on this issue was unlikely and hard to achieve. The issue of British nuclear weapons was re-opened in early 1960 when the Macmillan government decided to abandon the British nuclear programme, Blue Streak, and instead decided to order the American Skybolt nuclear weapons system. The pre-cursor to the dispute had displayed itself early in the year when on 1st March 1960, forty-three MPs had opposed an official Labour defence motion in the debate on the government's defence white paper. Williams identified the leaders of the revolt as George Wigg, Manny Shinwell and Richard Crossman.[135] The issue came to a head at the 1960 Labour Party Conference, the same conference at which the policy on the renunciation of Clause IV was defeated. The government had announced the abandonment of Blue Streak and now, as well as the traditional issues involved in the debate, the issue of American reliance came into the argument again. Many who were not traditionally opposed to nuclear weapons or to Britain possessing them were deeply concerned about American nuclear weapons being located at British bases, and this raised a variety of questions. Who would control these weapons? Would having these weapons on British soil make Britain a target for invasion during the Cold War? What was the longer-term aim of nuclear policy? Would this affect Britain's relationship with the USA? Crossman did not speak on this issue at the 1960 party conference but writing in 1957, he indicated that Britain did not simply have to acquiesce in American views on nuclear weapons and should maintain her own independence and initiative.[136]

Due to the cancellation of Blue Streak, the Labour Party needed to rethink its own policy on nuclear weapons. Up to this point the Labour Party had supported Britain retaining independent nuclear weapons while the USSR retained them, with a longer term aim of multi-lateral disarmament. While this policy was being re-evaluated, it became increasingly obvious that it would be difficult to find a suitable accommodation for all. There was a group within the Labour Party which was calling for Britain to unilaterally disarm, some of whom, like Frank Cousins leader of the T&GWU, supported Britain's membership of NATO (essentially Britain being defended by American nuclear weapons while occupying the peaceful higher moral ground herself). This was a policy which Crossman discouraged and described as being advantageous only 'in terms of narrow, national self-interests.'[137] While Cousins does not appear to have been an appointed leader for the dissenters, due to his position and his union's sympathies for unilateralism, he appears to have been viewed as a leading dissenter. Crossman, George Brown and Morgan Phillips wrote a draft defence policy in 1960 as a compromise document which Cousins seems to have accepted. However, Gaitskell concluded that the compromises were too one-sided and he renounced the document, much to Crossman's annoyance. However, some reworking was done and Gaitskell accepted the draft, at which point Cousins rejected it without amendments. As can be seen, it was a very difficult drafting process which was not particularly successful. Williams, almost certainly correctly, casts Crossman in the role of a negotiator whose aim was not to eradicate differences of opinion but merely to blur the differences so the situation became acceptable to all.[138]

Crossman had placed himself in a very contradictory position, partly because of his insistence that he could find a compromise. In substance, his views on nuclear policy were very similar to those of Gaitskell. He concluded that a British nuclear weapons programme would be beneficial and should lead to an overall re-evaluation of conventional forces, something he and Wigg had supported as early as 1955. He also favoured, like Gaitskell, Britain remaining a nuclear member of NATO, feeling it would be hypocritical for Britain to renounce her own nuclear weapons while sheltering under the nuclear protection of America and NATO. The main difference between Crossman and Gaitskell on the issue of nuclear weapons was a differing style of presentation and approach to relations within the party. Williams indicated that Gaitskell had adapted his approach and instead of seeking to compromise, he wanted to stamp his authority on his party.[139] Crossman viewed this as intransigence and stubbornness on the part of Gaitskell, while he was seeking compromise and conciliation.[140]

In reality, there is no evidence to suggest that in 1960 Crossman was seeking to find conciliation in order to ease Gaitskell's position as leader. The compromise that he was seeking could have improved his standing in the party if it had been successful, possibly leading to a place in the shadow cabinet and better relations with Gaitskell. Much of this is speculation due to the failure of the compromise and his ever worsening relationship with Gaitskell, but there is no evidence to suggest he was attempting to aid Gaitskell as he made no other attempt to do this. The compromise might well have ended the row over nuclear weapons in the short term but such a compromise could easily have disintegrated at a later point. In this matter it seems clear that Crossman was attempting to be an intermediary between the main warring parties and find a compromise, but his motives for doing so are impossible to outline with any certainty.

At the 1960 Labour Party Conference, the delegates were faced with an array of defence resolutions upon which to vote. These votes had the added confusion of being held at the same conference as a debate concerning the future of Clause IV, an issue which caused great hostility and anger to be directed primarily at Gaitskell from many of the delegates. Eventually the official policy was rejected but by only a small number of votes, while the AEU's unilateralist motion was endorsed. At the 1961 Labour Party Conference, the policy was reversed, much to Gaitskell's relief. After the conference the issue of nuclear weapons within the party, particularly the PLP, began to carry less significance and Crossman failed to concentrate his attention on the issue of nuclear weapons specifically again. Following Gaitskell's death in 1963 and Wilson's succession as leader the issue was not particularly divisive and does not appear to have been considered particularly important.

Between 1958 and 1961, the issue of nuclear weapons was of great importance to the Labour Party and the subject of some fierce exchanges. However, it was not a key issue in Crossman's life. While he was interested and obviously concerned about Britain's nuclear status and the role of NATO, he was more concerned with the overall defence strategy of Britain of which nuclear force was a key component. It was an issue which he had been concerned about since he had entered Parliament in 1945, but he could never claim to be as knowledgeable or influential as figures such as George Wigg or Denis Healey. Upon entering the cabinet in 1964, he did not take a particularly large role in cabinet discussions over defence policy and it was not an issue which pre-occupied him. From 1955/6 when Crossman's writing and activity on foreign affairs flagged until 1961, nuclear weapons appears to have been an issue which Crossman was intermittently interested in, and an area where Gaitskell appears to have allowed him to be involved at a policy-making level, not necessarily with the desired effects.

Conclusion

Crossman's early thinking on foreign policy, in regard to Israel and the broad ideology of Britain's foreign policy appears to have followed a path not dissimilar to that of much of the left wing of the Labour Party. While not being idealistic, his views were tinged with optimism, such as hopes for a European third force, with Europe being a superpower along with the USA and the USSR. However, while he pushed for these policies to be adopted, often in association with other MPs of a similar persuasion such as the Keep Left group or the Bevanites, he seems to have adapted his thinking to wider developments. For example, the opinions of some members of the Keep Left group and the Bevanites evolved after the publication of *Keep Left* in 1947, so that by the late 1950s Crossman was accepting a divided Germany and by 1960 Bevan was rejecting unilateral nuclear disarmament, unthinkable even a few years before. This shows that Crossman was developing and evolving his ideas even in such a short period. As can be seen when considering the issue of Europe, his views on Britain joining or establishing a European Community changed gradually over the period 1945 to 1974, moving from occupying a pro-European position prior to 1950 to questioning the relevance to Britain of a European community in 1962. It must be pointed out that the EEC was not the same organisation which Crossman had himself envisaged, perhaps explaining his hostility. Eventually by 1967, he was proclaiming himself a 'Little Englander', being anti-European and unconvinced of the benefits for Britain of being a member of the EEC or the Common Market.[141]

Crossman appears to have become gradually more pro-American during the period 1945 to 1974, a development which seems to have been reflected in many left wing MPs, although some particularly hard-line left wing MPs continually maintained their dislike of close Anglo-American relations. Following the end of the Second World War, many within the Labour Party hoped for good relations between the USSR and the Labour government in the UK. However, as this relationship became less likely, and the USSR began to retreat into its own sphere of influence, many Labour MPs, including Crossman, began to seek alternatives with many gradually accepting a close Anglo-American relationship, no doubt influenced by the economic difficulties of Britain and the support provided by America, particularly through Marshall Aid. During the period 1949 to 1974, Crossman appears to have become gradually more pro-American, although he was always more keen for Britain to be independent of all external powers than for Britain to become reliant on the USA. Writing in 1952, he stated that he saw the British Commonwealth as a second axis of Western civilisation along with America. 'I think that the British Commonwealth as such has a role to play as important as the USA.'[142] He appears to have concluded by 1952 when he published the *New Fabian Essays* that while co-existence could exist between the UK and the USSR, co-operation was not possible, a position which was very different to that he had adopted in 1947 in *Keep Left*.[143] This development in his thinking on foreign policy seems to be mirrored by his gradual movement ideologically from being on the left wing of the Labour Party to occupying a more central role, although his perceived position appears to have been generally accepted as left wing.

5

Crossman and the Constitution

While having a reputation for radicalism, the party has not always lived up to these expectations while in government. On certain constitutional issues, the party showed a distinctly conservative attitude, particularly the leaders and prominent party members. Socialist parties on the continent have on occasion advocated unconstitutional action, even revolution, to achieve their aims. The British Labour Party has not supported these views, preferring minimal constitutional reform instead. While certain individuals within the party called for quasi-revolutionary action, particularly in the 1930s, such as Stafford Cripps, these views were not widely supported within the party and were generally abandoned fairly quickly. Theakston argued that 'despite all their excitable talk about "executive dictatorship", emergency powers and so on … they [the left wing] did not in practice seem to envisage sweeping away the existing institutional landscape of British government (save for abolition of the House of Lords) so much as adopting it to serve socialist purposes more efficiently…'[1] This usage of the existing political system to achieve change was supported widely within the party, with the leadership rejecting more radical calls for reform. It is important to stress that the views of many individuals were not static and that while the party leadership generally rejected radical action, many within the party favoured more radical reform, even if fleetingly. Individuals such as Crossman developed their views during their political careers, for a variety of reasons.

The issue of constitutional reform was further complicated by the differing reforms which could be enacted, each viewed as a panacea to the range of problems which existed. This variety of solutions was due to the diversity of problems which were highlighted. John Mackintosh criticised the role of civil servants and the style of government which had developed since the First World War. Crossman focused on the role of the minister at the heart of a department and his need for more information, in addition to greater levels of accountability within government. Those on the left of the party tended to be interested in reducing the power of the House of Lords with MPs such as Michael Foot looking to reduce the power of the second chamber, or even to remove it completely. For Crossman, the aim of reform was not necessarily to reduce the power of the Lords,

but instead to form a second chamber which could actively scrutinise the
legislation which was sent from the Commons.[2] Individuals like Crossman, tended
to be seeking more accountability to Parliament, perhaps leading to a more
powerful House of Lords, which was the exact opposite of what many others
wanted. Right wing Conservative members of the Commons, such as Enoch
Powell, believed reform was not needed and that the current constitution worked
well in its current state.

One important issue which Crossman never discussed during his time in
government, in either his diaries or in any public speeches, was electoral reform or
the benefits of any electoral system. Indeed, before 1964, he had only considered
the issue twice before, very briefly. In his 1939 book, *How Britain is Governed*,
Crossman noted that the electoral system in Britain created a 'temporary
dictatorship' between elections.[3] He indicated that this was a useful tool for
governing, as having more than two main parties tended to lead to weaker
governments:

> For this reason proportional representation in parliamentary elections would
> be a national disaster. It would of course make the strength of the Parties in
> the House reflect more accurately the division of opinion in the country; but
> in so doing it would ensure the survival of the third party and encourage the
> formation of a fourth and fifth.[4]

This weakening of government, he concluded, would be disastrous for the Labour
Party and the working classes, as change and reform would be impossible. In 1963,
he again argued that 'wherever proportional representation has been tried, it has
fulfilled his [Bagehot's] prediction that it would undermine the independence of the
MP and increase the powers of the party managers who control the electoral lists.'[5]
He never considered electoral reform again, but his lack of action on the issue
suggests that he remained very sceptical about the benefits of electoral reform
generally, and proportional representation specifically.

Another important issue for the party was the concentration of government in
Westminster and Whitehall, leading to calls for decentralisation to bring change to
the working classes which were under-represented in the traditional citadels of
power. This would give more freedom to local areas, replicating in some ways the
Trade Union system, which tended to have powerful local branches which made
local decisions within a looser national framework. This decentralisation of power
reached further than the reform of local government, and began to incorporate
elements of nationalism within it. Attlee writing in 1937 argued that

> There is one great danger that must be avoided – over-centralisation. I
> conceive that under socialism there will be a wide regional decentralisation,
> and a deliberate endeavour to allow for each area the individuality of the

people. In particular there must, of course, be decentralisation in Scotland and Wales.[6]

It should be noted that decentralisation of power is not the same as devolution. While Crossman was not particularly interested in devolution or local government reform prior to entering government, two factors increased his interest. Firstly, through his PPS, Tam Dalyell, he was kept informed of the devolution issue. Dalyell, who lived periodically at Vincent Square with Crossman and was a close friend, was a passionate anti-devolution Scottish MP. Secondly, his time as Minister of Housing and Local Government between 1964 and 1966 brought him into contact with many local councils and local organisations. While not having exclusively good relations with local government organisations or advocating decentralisation to the regions, he did believe that the Ministry of Housing and Local Government was an overly centralised department, something which Crossman indicated Wilson wanted to extend.[7] His time at the Ministry of Housing and Local Government confirmed his views on how centralisation could stifle the freedom of individuals and lead to stagnation.

Labour Party Thinking on Constitutional Reform

The Labour Party has a tradition of considering constitutional reform and of it being an issue which generates conflict, although a debate now exists as to whether the party has ever taken it very seriously. Vernon Bogdanor, writing in 1997, commented on how different the views of the Labour Party in Britain were to the views which socialist parties held on the continent in regard to constitutional reform. While left wing parties on the continent faced 'considerable hostility from their capitalist opponents, in Britain, Labour was able to make its way within the existing constitutional structure, with the active assistance indeed of one of the "capitalist" parties.'[8] While other socialist parties were aiming seriously to reform, or even destroy, the existing parliamentary system, the Labour Party was seeking to work within it to win elections and become its master. Bogdanor argued that the British Labour Party was not a radical party in regard to constitutional reform, but was instead a 'constitutionally conservative party', with reform not taken particularly seriously when the party gained power.[9] Additionally, leading figures were not keen to see a strengthening of the parliamentary system, reducing their individual or collective power once in government. As Bogdanor indicated, a reformed and strengthened House of Lords 'could prove a far more effective barrier to a government of the left than the present House of Lords. Indeed any attempt to provide the Lords with democratic legitimacy would encourage it to use its powers to the full...'[10]

Miles Taylor, writing in 2000, provided a critique of the reforming nature of the Labour Party up to and including the reforms of the Blair government. He argued that while 'it remains fashionable to see it [the party] as constitutionally conservative, its record on parliamentary reform speaks for itself.'[11] In this statement he was not simply focusing on the latter day Labour Party. As he correctly pointed out 'two Lord Presidents – Morrison and Crossman – probably did more to overhaul the ordinary procedure of the Commons than any politician since Gladstone.'[12] Taylor was undoubtedly correct, but his viewpoint should not be seen as being in conflict with that of Bogdanor. Bogdanor used as his basis of explanation the issue of House of Lords reform, which was undoubtedly an area where the Labour Party has shown considerable restraint and a lack of will to reform. Taylor considered the day-to-day procedure of the House of Commons as a whole which was adapted and changed by various Labour governments, leading these two academics to different conclusions on the reforming nature of the Party. It is clear that in certain areas, particularly those which required reform for purely ideological reasons, the party has been unwilling to introduce genuine reform, while in other less ideologically driven, less divisive areas of constitutional reform, they have been willing and able to implement effective change.

Taylor indicated that electoral reform and the overhaul of local government were 'closer to the party's heart' than other reforms which the Attlee government instituted.[13] Morrison, as Leader of the House of Commons from 1945 to 1951, the position that Crossman would hold from 1966 to 1968, made some elements of constitutional reform his top priority, adopting a more practical approach to legislation. He pursued reform that was necessary to implement other Labour legislation, not that based on an ideological framework. The 1949 Parliament Act was implemented primarily to ensure that the Nationalisation of Steel Bill would be passed in a shorter period of time than was allowed under the 1911 Parliament Act in light of the forthcoming general election. Taylor argued that while constitutional reform may have been important to the rank and file of the party, the leadership tended to be much slower to adopt some of these ideas, highlighting an inherent conservatism within the leadership on certain constitutional issues. He noted that the Wilson government adopted a similar unhurried approach much as the Attlee government had, suggesting this conservative attitude prevailed within the leadership.[14]

The Attlee government of 1945-51, while containing some radical left wing members, did not have any enthusiasm for revolution or radical reform. Bevan, one of the most influential left wing rebels, who remained a member of the Attlee cabinet until 1951, was not a supporter of violent revolution, instead favouring change through the constitutional channels, and even Cripps appears to have lost his earlier, more radical views, utilising the Houses of Parliament to institute change. Theakston argued that left wing MPs were not in practice seeking wide-ranging constitutional reform.[15] This supports the view of Bogdanor that the Labour Party was, by 1940, seeking to utilise the existing parliamentary system to its advantage as opposed to dismantling it. One of the reasons for this lack of constitutional reform by the Attlee government was that its members had been heavily influenced by their experiences in the wartime coalition. Theakston argued that the Labour ministers were 'pragmatic insiders.'[16] While this experience of government, prior to the 1945 election, was undoubtedly advantageous to the Labour Party in a variety of ways, there is little evidence to suggest this time in office stifled revolutionary zeal. This zeal does not appear to have been particularly prevalent within the party by 1940.

The position of Clement Attlee is important to clarify here. As Prime Minister from 1945 to 1951 his views on constitutional reform were of great importance, and during his time within the party, these developed. Kevin Theakston pointed out that 'mostly, it has to be said, Prime Ministers – like most other politicians – operate within and work the system of government rather than thinking about the institutions and processes that make up that system.'[17] Writing in 1937, Attlee highlighted his support and commitment to democratic methods of reform:

> I am well aware how slight a hold the principles of democracy have on some of our opponents, but I believe that the vast majority of the people of this country reject such methods, and that an attempt of this kind would be defeated by the loyalty of the mass of the people to the government.[18]

He also indicated that it was essential to provide freedom for the individual, stating that 'British socialists have never made an idol of the state, demanding that individuals should be sacrificed to it.'[19] Here Attlee was deliberately distancing himself and the Labour Party from the experiences of the USSR, and also perhaps the more hard-line socialist parties on the continent. Attlee argued that the constitution did not require fundamental change, a view he maintained for his entire political career. Indeed he argued that 'with this machinery, we can bring about the fundamental changes which we desire, provided that we continue in this country to respect the will of the majority and to practise the principles of democracy.'[20] His call for decentralisation of government, made in 1937, was however an issue which his government did not act on and for much of the life of the government, Britain was particularly centralised, retaining many wartime controls for much of the late 1940s. The revolutionary zeal which Cripps exhibited in the 1930s appears to have also been calmed by the experience of the Second World War, as he served in Attlee's government between 1945 and 1951, with only very occasional outbursts. The experience of the Second World War was vital, not only for Attlee and Cripps, but for many Labour MPs, especially those who were members of the war cabinet, as it exposed them to government in a way that many had not experienced before, leading some to abandon their previously held conceptions of government and others to confirm their beliefs. Attlee concluded that he preferred a 'revolution without tears; it was more effective than the other kind' a view which he held from the 1930s onwards.[21]

While the Wilson government was in favour of modernisation generally, this did not extend to constitutional reform. Wilson highlighted the 'white heat of technology' as a remedy to Britain's flagging fortunes, but this electoral theme was not extended to constitutional reform. Theakston argued that parliamentary reform became an important issue in the 1960s as part of the 'What's wrong with Britain' debate.[22] Wilson seems to have concluded that constitutional reform was not a vote-winner and this issue was therefore less important than others. Crossman, however, continued to press for constitutional reform, which he had advocated for much of his parliamentary career, beginning in 1939. While he was in favour of modernising and reforming the constitution, many of his cabinet colleagues did not share his enthusiasm, appearing to loose any interest in reforming the system upon entering government.[23] His enthusiasm was utilised by his appointment as Leader of the House of Commons in 1966 with a remit to reform the House of Lords and streamline the workings of the House of Commons for the benefit of the government, a policy which fitted in well with Wilson's reforming image. However, Wilson does not appear to have been a staunch supporter of reform, and this reforming remit may have been Crossman's own invention rather than Wilson's. However, by 1968 the reforms, while having some success particularly in the Commons, were not viewed as overly successful and his Parliament (No. 2) Bill, dealing with the composition and power of the House of Lords, was abandoned in 1968. Wilson did not attempt further reform between 1968 and 1970 instead focusing on more 'practical' issues such as industrial relations.

William Gwyn, writing in 1971, identified the different approaches to constitutional reform which were adopted by those on the left and right wings of the party. Harold Laski had referred to these briefly in the late 1930s.[24] Firstly, Gwyn pointed out that many socialists were 'stirred by liberal values and attitudes.'[25] He argued that many socialist ideologists and historians of the movement believed that the liberal tradition of Britain has been incorporated into the movement.[26] While some positive reports of events in the USSR by members of the party during the 1930s suggested that the authors had dictatorial leanings, Gwyn rejected this, indicating that these authors were guilty only of 'wishful thinking and self deception.'[27] He identified two different strands of opinion within the socialist movement and the Labour Party concerning government bureaucracy and the freedom of the individual, which he informally described as liberal socialist and Fabian or Webbian opinion. He noted that the Gaitskellite new generation of right wingers within the party had adopted a more traditional Liberal stance to constitutional reform. Supporters of the traditionally Liberal view generally believed that the balance of power between Parliament and the cabinet needed changing. The primary aim of this loose grouping was to preserve the freedom and personal liberty of the individual from both private and public monopoly and control, particularly in regard to the nationalised industries and the power of the government.[28] This group believed that the cabinet effectively ran the House of Commons, and that there was a general lack of scrutiny and accountability within Parliament. Liberal socialists believed that this needed reforming and Parliament needed the power to scrutinise legislation more thoroughly.[29] This obviously had to be balanced with the ability of a government to pass legislation through Parliament which might not be popular with many of its members. Within this group Gwyn included Roy Jenkins, Tony Crosland and Richard Crossman who, during the late 1940s and early 1950s was generally assumed to be aligned with the left wing Bevanite group.[30] However, on this issue he did not fit in with the wider Bevanite group. Many left wing MPs were suspicious of private power and bureaucracy, preferring governmental bureaucracy as a way of implementing change. However, Gwyn did not develop this left wing position further. This may be due to a lack of consensus on the left of the party with some, such as Stafford Cripps in the 1930s, seeking a temporary dictatorship to implement socialist plans, while others were seeking more accountability to counteract government bureaucracy. Additionally a lack of left wing interest in the creation of an ombudsman, an issue liberal socialists were interested in and the main focus of Gwyn's writing, may be a key contributory factor.

The second group which Gwyn identified were the Fabian or Webbian strand of opinion. This group included individuals such as Herbert Morrison and later Labour ministers such as Patrick Gordon-Walker. Gwyn stated that the members of this group believed that Parliament in its existing form was effective and only very minimal reform was needed. It was simply necessary for a Labour government to use the existing mechanisms to its own advantage:

> Many socialists who value liberty highly have failed to see a threat in administrative activity because of their belief in the great merit of the British constitution. Governmental power is safe because it is kept responsible to the British people through their parliamentary representatives.[31]

These individuals concluded that the existing parliamentary system was a sufficient safeguard against excessive government bureaucracy. This lack of unity within the Labour Party on this issue would lead to difficulties for Crossman and the Wilson government in 1966 as the absence of unified aims led to a lack of consensus on what the result of reform should be or whether it was even necessary.

Kevin Theakston outlined four persistent themes which are observable when studying the Labour Party's views on Whitehall and governmental bureaucracy. He indicated that firstly there was a Fabian critique, 'accepting the political neutrality of the civil service, but suggesting that its *efficiency* needs improving.'[32] Secondly, the issue of bureaucratic power had been of concern to many within the Labour Party, including Crossman, often leading 'to a concern with finding ways of strengthening the political impulse in government through devices such as ministerial *cabinets*, political appointments to the civil service and so on.' Thirdly, Theakston identified a strand of opinion concerned with the class of the higher civil service and how the service recruited its members. This recruitment also raised questions as to whether a particular type of person with specific views were favoured, and if that inhibited the actions of a reforming government. The fourth theme which he identified was Whitehall's democratic accountability.[33] Crossman considered these four themes within his publications and diaries, not necessarily concluding that all were a problem but recognising the perceptions and attitudes which existed. As Theakston pointed out 'these approaches [except for the issue of recruitment and class] are not distinctly "socialist", finding advocates and supporters beyond the Labour Party. Neither are they necessarily distinct, for figures such as the Webbs, Laski and Benn can be found espousing reform packages drawing on elements of each.'[34] Theakston could have easily added Crossman to his list.

During the 1920s and particularly the 1930s, certain writers within the Labour Party, most notably Harold Laski and the Webbs, raised the issue of how a conservative Parliament could pass radical socialist policies without reform or even abolition of the existing system. The Webbs, writing in 1920 set out a radical plan of constitutional reform which they believed would make the parliamentary system fairer and more suitable for a Labour government intent on implementing social change.[35] *A Constitution for a Socialist Commonwealth of Great Britain* set out a wide-ranging and complex plan of reform, taking power away from civil servants and even individual ministers, and instead creating two different Parliaments with the Social Parliament being responsible for the control of departments.[36] This would ensure that the entire Labour Party, not simply the leaders, would take a role in government. The Webbs argued that ministers were too busy to run their departments effectively arguing that after fulfilling all his other engagements, 'he [the minister] had no time or energy left with which to supervise the day-to-day administration of the public service over which he presides.'[37] They concluded that in the current system, civil servants held more power than was acceptable and that while they were not inherently dishonest, the situation was compounded by the actions of ministers. 'The great mass of government today is the work of an able and honest but secretive bureaucracy, tempered by the ever-present apprehension of the revolt of powerful sectional interests and mitigated by the spasmodic interventions of imperfectly comprehending ministers.'[38] It should be noted though that as early as 1920 the Webbs were arguing that the real work of government was no longer carried out on the floor of the House of Commons, but was instead done 'in private conferences between ministers, with their principal officials...'[39] Their work on constitutional reform was extremely radical, and is more of an ideological book than a practical guide to constitutional reform. It is hard to comprehend any Labour government implementing the changes it advocated, as it would have destroyed the existing parliamentary system completely and there is no evidence to suggest that the party leadership took the recommendations seriously. Crossman borrowed the title *How Britain is Governed* from Ramsey Muir when writing his 1939 publication of the same name, so it requires consideration here.[40] Writing in 1930 Ramsey Muir, a Liberal supporter, was extremely critical of many facets of Parliament and the role of government. He concluded that the House of Commons did not properly control or hold government to account. He argued that while Whitehall was not blameless and tended to work for its own purposes, the cabinet controlled all governmental activity and therefore needed to be scrutinised by Parliament in a comprehensive and thorough manner. Crossman's guide to government is a much shorter, more superficial publication than Muir's critique of government. This may, in part be due to differing motives of publication. Crossman was writing a description of Parliament and government for the Labour Book Service, and adding his criticism and suggestions for improvement. He began by indicating that he was not writing a specialist text on government and Parliament, but was instead providing an overview of procedure in order to retain a more general readership, which was in contrast to Muir's more academic motives. Crossman decided that 'such specialist knowledge can safely be left to the experts.'[41] While there is no evidence to suggest that Crossman used Muir's book as a basis for his own work, the reader of Crossman's *How Britain is Governed* will be struck by the similarities it has to Muir's *How Britain is Governed*. Crossman described the 'temporary dictatorship' of the cabinet, echoing Muir's description of 'cabinet dictatorship'.[42] While his later writing on constitutional reform would place him 'at the heart of a key debate about power within British government in the 1960s and 1970s', this early work showed little of the insight required to achieve this.[43]

The left winger Harold Laski believed that Parliament as a whole was more suited to the actions of the Conservative Party, putting the Labour Party at a disadvantage in government.[44] The machinery of government had been built by the establishment and this, in his opinion, meant that the system was defending forces which the Labour Party did not support. He indicated that Parliament was essentially a rubber stamp for Conservative measures, while measures introduced by a Labour government received severe criticism, being either defeated, or heavily amended. He concluded, 'we cannot understand the parliamentary system in Great Britain unless we recognize that, beneath the appearance of democracy, this is the economic and social system it is intended to uphold.'[45] He was particularly critical of the House of Lords, which will be considered more fully later in this chapter. Without the ability to examine government bills, Laski concluded that the role of Parliament had been diminished with cabinet maintaining control of the parliamentary system.[46] He hoped to provide Parliament with the machinery to investigate governmental measures, balancing accountability with the required degree of power which every government needs, an aim which Crossman seems to have accepted. This overall theory was not one which Crossman supported, instead believing that Parliament required reform for a variety of other, non-partisan reasons.

Hanson, writing in 1957-8 indicated that while there had been a ground swell of support for parliamentary reform before World War II, contributed to by Muir, Laski, the Webbs and, to a much lesser extent, Crossman, after the war criticism of Parliament and government was greatly reduced. He attributed this to a loss of momentum during the war, when more pressing issues needed consideration, with disputes being 'swallowed up' by the war.[47] Not only had the British parliamentary system survived the rigours of two World Wars, it had adapted and provided a basis for victorious government in these circumstances. This success, coupled with

Parliament's role within the British establishment, meant that calls for reform, which implied criticism of the existing system, were far more muted than they had been before 1939. The reforming nature of the Attlee government, and the success of the party in the 1945 election also reduced calls for reform, the 'workability of the system has killed interest … in most of the radical schemes of reform that were so widely canvassed in the 1920s and 1930s'.[48] Once in power there was, in the eyes of many Labour MPs, particularly the leadership, far less need for reform, which might limit or even destroy their legislative programme and their new-found authority. As Hanson highlighted, echoing the views of many within the party such as Herbert Morrison, was fundamental reform necessary if all the measures which a socialist government introduced could be enacted using the normal channels?

> As it became evident that 'the job' could be done through the normal machinery of parliamentary government, there seemed little point in continuing to insist that this machinery was 'obsolete' or 'antiquated', or to demand that 'emergency' measures should be employed to get on to the Statute Book legislation which was actually being passed, without unusual difficulty, by the ordinary methods.[49]

The 1949 Parliament Act primarily changed only the delaying time of the House of Lords from two years to one. This reform did not affect the power of the House of Lords and was done for electoral reasons rather than as a response to obstruction.

Certain individuals, including Crossman, continued to press for parliamentary reform long after the end of the Attlee government. Crossman's pamphlet, *Socialism and the New Despotism*, written in 1956, did not consider House of Lords reform but did consider other areas of parliamentary reform.[50] His title was inspired by Lord Hewart's publication *New Despotism* published in 1929.[51] Gwyn indicated that this was significant as Crossman was expressing 'the same kind of exaggeration, oversimplification, and strong note of alarm as found in the words of the Tory Chief Justice.'[52] In his Fabian pamphlet, Crossman implied that various changes would be necessary to make the civil service work effectively for a future Labour government giving ministers eyes and ears, establishing a 'brains' trust, and a central fact-finding bureau.[53] He was also concerned that the government, regardless of its political complexion, was not accountable to Parliament, urging the increased use of parliamentary committees to rigorously vet the government's legislative programme in specific policy areas such as agriculture, defence and the colonies.[54] Here we see elements of Crossman's later goal of creating a much stronger, more robust parliamentary system which could provide backbenchers with an important role and allow more accountable government.[55] However, many were not in favour of the role which he anticipated for the Houses of Parliament. While there is some important writing on the issue of constitutional reform by socialists and Labour Party members, there is no singular clear aim which can be identified in the majority due to the various strands of opinion, although some themes do recur.

The Civil Service

Crossman never had a particularly high opinion of the civil service. It was not simply that he believed the civil service had more power than was desirable. He was fundamentally opposed to a number of facets of the service. Writing in 1939, he echoed Laski's concerns over recruitment to the service, arguing that 'its character and training are suited to keep the present machine in running order, not to reconstruct it.'[56] He was also apprehensive about the superiority of the Treasury as the home of the civil service, the internal grapevine of information and activities of civil servants, particularly high level officials in government, the role of the minister within departments and the lack of external specialists. These concerns led Crossman to question the value of the civil service in its current state. His concerns were shared by some, though not all, Labour ministers.

In *Doctrine and Ethos in the Labour Party*, Drucker indicated how the Labour Party as a whole reacted to the change between being in opposition and in government and how this affected ministers in varying ways.[57] He outlined a split between right and left wing ministers in their reaction to their positions in government. He indicated that more right wing ministers, using as examples Gordon-Walker and Morrison, were isolated from the outside political world by their civil servants. This isolation forced them to rely on their civil servants for information and guidance, encouraging them to follow the departmental view, at least in the short term. Drucker indicated that those individuals were so overwhelmed by their new positions of power that they felt they required guidance, not from their party, which did not really understand their work, but from the civil service who were accustomed to the departmental pressures. 'They become so drawn into the playing of the Whitehall game as, almost, to forget what it is for.'[58] However, there is no evidence to support his claim that Morrison fitted into this category. He was regarded by many of his peers as a very capable departmental minister, especially when dealing with domestic issues. While this theory requires consideration, Drucker's categorisation of individuals should be treated with caution.

Drucker argued that, in contrast, more left wing individuals, such as Crossman and Castle, were suspicious of their civil servants often failing to utilise the service properly and impeding their own progress. 'Castle and Crossman never trusted themselves or Whitehall sufficiently and so were unable to use the machine effectively. Both remained deeply suspicious of their role as ministers and both resisted its claims on them.'[59] As a consequence, the initial period in office of these ministers was often problematic and fraught with difficulties and personal disputes, something which can be seen in volume one of Crossman's *Cabinet Diaries*.[60] However, the categorisation of Crossman as a left winger in 1964 is very questionable, as he was, like Wilson, more of a centre-left figure by this time. It has already been noted that Gwyn did not categorise him as being left wing in relation to his views on constitutional reform. Instead he indicated that Crossman was a liberal socialist, rather at odds with Drucker's view. It seems likely that the behaviour of ministers to their civil servants was dependant on a variety of factors, their personality traits being perhaps one of the most important, while their political views were considerably less important. Crossman's experience as a Don and bullying behaviour undoubtedly contributed to his bullish attitude towards his civil servants, while a less confrontational minister would have undoubtedly had a different experience, such as Wilson who does not appear to have experienced these difficulties despite having similar political leanings to Crossman.

Barbara Castle's diaries contain almost no discussion of the civil service as a whole, instead concentrating on more specific incidents with her own civil servants. These incidents do not appear to have had a negative overtone, and she does not appear to have held any suspicion of the civil service from the date her diaries start in 1965. The only criticisms of the service which are listed are those dealing with their wage settlement in 1974.[61] However, writing in the *Sunday Times* in 1973 Castle described a very different civil service to that which is shown in her diaries.[62] She criticised many facets of the service but was particularly damning of its departmentalism, outlining how the department controlled a minister's life, describing it as 'the loneliness of the short-distance runner.' Her most fundamental criticism was regarding how the service reacted to radicalism. She noted that the civil service had impeded the government simply by saying 'we could not do some of the things our successors are now doing with considerable facility.' She concluded her damning article by stating that more political support was required in the departments to aid the minister, alluding perhaps to a type of *Chef de cabinet*. She argued that 'there are certain jobs you [the civil service] cannot do and should not attempt to do, in order to do the jobs you can do well: and that you need political men to help you.'[63] This article was completely at odds with Castle's day-to-day experiences and it should be noted that it was written while the Labour Party was in opposition. This period in opposition may have led her to re-evaluate her views on the civil service. However it is possible that this article was written to blame the inactivity and mistakes of the previous Wilson government on the civil service before the next general election.

Tony Benn's diaries contained far more criticism of the civil service than the Castle diaries, with Benn maintaining a suspicion of the service for much of his time in the Wilson government. He had troubled relations with his civil service Private Secretary, Tilling, whom he advised in 1964 not to go into his private filing cabinet.[64] He wrote in his diaries that 'the trouble with the civil service is that it wants a quiet life. The civil servants want to move slowly along the escalator towards their knighthoods and retirement and they have no interest whatsoever in trying to develop new lines of activity.'[65] He alluded to disquiet amongst some members of the party in 1965, indicating that Tommy Balogh, John Allen, Marcia Williams and himself had discussed 'how we could beat them.'[66] Patrick Gordon-Walker, a more right wing member of the government, expressed none of

Crossman or Benn's criticisms regarding the impartiality and abilities of the civil service. Writing in 1972 Gordon-Walker, like Morrison before him in *Government and Parliament*, provided an extremely positive outlook on the civil service.[67] He argued that the civil service made ministerial control much easier for new ministers as their 'whole instinct is to obey and carry out their ministers policy and, if necessary, to try and elicit one from him.'[68] Gordon-Walker's ministerial experience was very different to that of Crossman or Benn, but it is very questionable whether this was due to their differing political views or due to other factors, including personality and specific departments. Many Labour MPs, regardless of their political position, had at least some concerns regarding the civil service upon gaining office in 1964, and many of these concerns had taken root in opposition.

While Crossman was seeking to continue Bagehot's work with regards to describing the British constitution and the secretive nature of government in Britain, there was only one account of the civil service which he wanted to rewrite – Morrison's glowing review of the service. Morrison's *Government and Parliament* contains an overwhelmingly positive account of the work of the civil service, with almost no criticism included. This was Crossman's main criticism of the book, although he did not explain his reasons for taking such a dislike to this specific publication. Generally, he believed that Morrison's various publications created an inaccurate account of the civil service and departmental life generally. This was an opinion which he held before he entered the government in 1964 and he maintained his views until his death. In 1967 he wrote in his *Cabinet Diaries* that he had, for years been 'determined to write a book which would blow sky high Herbert Morrison's outrageous book *Government and Parliament*.'[69] He added to this in November of 1967, stating that he would write an analysis of political life showing how wrong Herbert Morrison's account was 'and how right I am.'[70] He alluded to the fact that he would have written this book in 1964 had he not gained a ministerial position.[71] However, it is difficult to see how he could have competently written such a book before 1964, as he had no comprehension of the system of government prior to this, and little knowledge of the workings of the civil service.

Crossman considered various methods of reforming the civil service including the spoils system. This system was prevalent in the USA where the minister appointed top level advisers, generally from the same party or political persuasion and they would leave their department when he left office. This system provided the minister with political allies within the department, advising on a political basis about the policy area in which they specialised. A spoils system provides a political element within the departments, creating an alternative political figure who could ensure that legislation was being written and planned with the appropriate political ideology at its heart, easing the load on the minister. Crossman did not advocate this system for Britain, describing it as 'harmful'.[72] He indicated that while it was an interesting idea, it would simply create another layer of officials within departments. Although the minister would have more control over the top levels of the service, the layers below these would remain unchanged and unreformed.[73] The political adviser may well be ignored or marginalised and viewed as a mere political appointment by the wider civil service, who, Crossman believed, would always attempt to ensure their departmental view was adopted. He indicated that 'were the minister to challenge and direct the ministry policy there would be no formal tension at first, only quiet resistance – but a great deal of it.'[74] It is likely that a similar situation would arise were departmental policy questioned by a political appointee. If the adviser had more specialised knowledge than the civil servants, which due to movement within the service would not be unexpected, this could lead to even greater problems. The civil servants might feel threatened by the advice of the adviser or the adviser could be unable to provide the political insight required for the position due to his lack of political experience. While indicating that it was vital for ministers to regain control of the state bureaucracy, Crossman did not expand on how the civil service should be reformed to achieve this.[75]

Harold Laski, writing in 1938, had discussed the French *Cabinet* tradition, whereby each department had a small group of advisers and specialists, something Crossman labelled a 'brains trust' in 1939.[76] Laski described it, not as another layer of administration but as

> a small and intimate group of men of his own policy or, at least, way of thought, in whose knowledge of his departmental problems he has confidence, and with whom he will feel able freely to discuss them in an atmosphere wholly apart from that of the official hierarchy.[77]

Laski concluded that the system was successful in France and that it might well be successful in Britain, providing the minister with a method of finding his 'way through the labyrinth he will encounter.'[78] His support for this system was undoubtedly encouraged by his personal criticism of the civil service. Crossman agreed that such a system of government had advantages. He used the *Cabinet* system as a model for this 'brains trust', which he attempted to implement to a limited degree while a minister by introducing a small number of external advisers into his departments. However, in 1967 Crossman stated that he believed 'the introduction of a "Cabinet" system in the French model would be a nonsense.'[79]

Laski argued that the civil service was important to the mechanisms of government, and provided a useful and vital service for ministers, but he was not uncritical of it.[80] One of his main criticisms was the way in which the service recruited. He argued that the service was not recruiting dynamic young people, but was instead engaging staid, conservative individuals who preferred the status quo to radical reform, a criticism very similar to that made by Crossman in 1956.[81] Laski argued that the civil service needed to provide a minister not only with the facts required to make a cohesive and beneficial decision, but they also needed to be aware of the obstacles. 'Its authority is that of influence, not of power. It indicates consequences; it does not impose commands.'[82] This role was compounded by the 'brake on innovation' which the civil service provided to a reforming government.[83] This slow and deliberate pace was adopted, Laski argued, to allow time for extensive investigation of the issues and to slow down the reforming process. Additionally the service 'tends to look at new ideas from the angle of how best they can be fitted into the existing scheme of things when the real need may be to depart from it.'[84] He concluded that while the civil service was not lacking in hard working, dedicated individuals, it did not contain enough innovators to provide adequate support for a reforming government.[85] This meant that reform was required, although he was not forthcoming on what that should be, hinting at reform of the recruitment process to encourage the necessary expert skills within the service.

Crossman first considered the role of the civil service in government in his publication *How Britain is Governed*, highlighting specific problems within the service which he believed would impede the progress of a socialist government. Crossman, who himself had graduated in Classics at Oxford and could read Latin and Greek, criticised those civil servants who were trained in the 'humane' tradition, taking Latin, Greek, languages, literature and technique. He indicated that this training did not provide them with the ability to 'understand a changing world and adapt our institutions to it'. He continued stating that the specific training which civil servants tended to receive at school made the civil service in Britain 'one of the most upright and one of the most inelastic institutions in the world.'[86] Many other writers, such as Laski, had made similar criticisms to Crossman, indicating that the service selection processes ensured that specific personality traits were encouraged, which might be detrimental to a reforming government. This lack of appropriate training was coupled, in Crossman's opinion, with the departmentalism of the civil service. The service suffered from 'excessive departmentalism and the growing domination of the Treasury.'[87] In his 1939 publication, he did not suggest any practical measures for dealing with his criticism. Others, including Edward Bridges (head of the civil service from 1945 to 1956), provided a more nuanced account of the views of the civil service, outlining that each department had accepted policy viewpoints which were based on internal departmental knowledge and experience, but Crossman avoided discussion of this.[88]

He did not consider the role of the civil service again in detail until the publication of *Socialism and the New Despotism* in 1956, when he not only outlined some of his criticisms of the civil service, but highlighted some proposals on how to remedy these. Crossman argued that it was impossible for ministers to make reasonable, appropriate policy decisions when they were so far removed from the rest of the political establishment or the wider electorate. He called for ministers to have more 'eyes and ears'.[89] While not recommending or supporting the American spoils system, he concluded that each department ought to have a board of experts. 'Some would be drawn from the civil service, some from the Universities, some from politics; and they would act as a team, reading the papers for him and enabling him to have a well-informed judgment *(sic)* when he faces the permanent officials.'[90] In actual fact, he was outlining the role which the civil service could fulfil, and in some cases did, but which he did not trust them to do. His suspicions were maintained until he became a minister in 1964, at which point they were gradually influenced by his experiences, though not necessarily contradicted. He recognised that many within the Labour movement did not agree with his views on the civil service, but he indicated that contrasting views were due to 'a difference of opinion about what is and what is not practicable for the next Labour government.' He was aiming for a radical Labour government, with democracy at its very heart, and while not suggesting it bluntly, he intimated that other Labour members were not looking for any of these traits in the next Labour government.[91]

When Crossman became a minister in 1964, it was his first experience of government and, despite being on the backbenches for nineteen years, he had almost no experience of parliamentary procedure or the Whitehall system. He admitted in his 1970 Godkin lectures that he 'had not even had the humble glimpses afforded to a Parliamentary Private Secretary' of the cabinet, its committees, the management of government departments and the politics of Whitehall.[92] This lack of experience meant he was almost completely ignorant of much of the parliamentary system and he quickly had to fill the gaps in his knowledge. The diary accounts of his time in his first ministry are littered with observations and criticisms of the civil service. The second and third volumes of his diaries do not contain the same level of detail or criticism as this first volume. This is undoubtedly due in large part to his growing exposure to this element of government. Additionally, as his experience and seniority increased, his ability to utilise the civil service may well have increased, leading him to have fewer difficulties with his civil servants.

Crossman was also concerned that due to his own lack of knowledge in 1964, his civil service were watering-down his proposals and ignoring his views. He believed that the main culprit for this was his Permanent Secretary, Dame Evelyn Sharp. The Dame, as Crossman labelled her, was unusual within the civil service.[93] She had, at one time, worked in the Treasury but had moved to the Ministry of Housing and remained there for a prolonged period of time. She had worked with Macmillan, Joseph and Sandys, and was familiar with the workings and constraints of the department, even taking personal control of the New Town's initiative, much to Crossman's consternation. As he pointed out 'she sees the New Towns as the great creations of her ministry and she loves them because they have been created autocratically from above.'[94] He believed that Dame Evelyn was thwarting his initiatives within the department by placing obstacles in front of his policy plans. Despite there being little evidence that his existing attitude to the civil service directly influenced his relations with them, it seems very likely that this was the case. Additionally, the mixture of Crossman and the Dame was explosive and bound to create tension which he did not experience with other civil servants to the same degree. He pointed out the difference Dame Evelyn's retirement made to his department and how his relations with her replacement were much better.[95]

Prior to gaining office in 1964, Crossman's shadow position had been Shadow Minister for Science and Higher Education. He had expected to become Minister of Education and it appears to have been a last minute decision which led Wilson to move him to the Ministry of Housing. This meant that Crossman was almost completely unprepared for his new job, and was completely unversed with the Labour Party's policy on this. This was compounded by a lack of detailed research of these issues.[96] This made work in the department initially slow, despite his ability to absorb information quickly. Despite his concerns, he indicated that the continuity of the civil service worked very well as it allowed ministers, such as himself, to gain knowledge and experience of the department without there being a break in the work of the department.[97]

Upon entering the Ministry of Housing in 1964, Crossman's fears regarding the civil service were almost entirely realised. He described his office as a padded cell, with his civil servants acting as nurses.[98] He believed that his staff kept him in almost complete isolation, making it difficult for him to see individuals from outside the ministry and making it equally difficult for people to make appointments to see him. Using this technique, Crossman believed the civil service was able to stop specialists and outside experts from contacting him. He described it using the hospital analogy, indicating that he was allowed visitors when he was good, with civil servants ensuring that he behaved himself.[99] The civil service, he believed, were suspicious of external specialists who might contradict the accepted departmental view, or recommend newer, more experimental courses of action. By excluding these individuals, the minister was, in Crossman's view, more likely to be unaware of external views or influences and more likely to adopt the departmental view on issues of importance.[100] In his case, however, while he bemoaned that fact that his civil servants kept experts away from him, his diaries are littered with incidents of dinners and meetings with specialists, something which Crossman indicated he needed to fight for. Writing in 1966, providing an overall impression of his experiences in the Ministry of Housing and Local Government, he maintained that the resistance of the civil service to external experts was immense. 'I found an intense dislike of bringing people in, whether they are politicians or experts.'[101]

While relations at the Ministry of Housing were never easy while Crossman was minister (Dame Evelyn describing him as 'really brilliant as a teacher – much better than as a journalist or a minister'[102]), a business routine was established. It is difficult to identify one factor which caused tensions to be slightly eased, and instead it seems to have been a combination of factors. Firstly, Crossman appears to have become more accustomed to the civil service machine, and they to him, with some compromises being made by both sides. Secondly, he was able to move some of his personnel around which allowed him to feel more comfortable. Thirdly, the legislation began to be written and he was able to see the valuable job which the civil service did and how they could aid him in his battles, both in cabinet and in the Commons. When Dame Evelyn retired, he was quite concerned as to who her replacement might be and whether she was really an asset to the department in comparison to other senior civil servants, although this view did not last for too long.[103]

Crossman gave evidence to the Fulton Committee in January 1967. The purpose of the committee was to consider the role of the civil service within government and suggest appropriate changes which could be made to improve the service. Many of the individuals who gave evidence to the committee had either served as ministers previously or were current members of the Wilson government. Of these Fry stated that 'Reginald Maudling and Enoch Powell were the most pro-civil service and Richard Crossman was the only really hostile witness among the politicians, possibly as a consequence of having to deal with Dame Evelyn Sharp when he had been Minister of Housing and Local Government.'[104] Crossman wrote in his diaries that he had 'fired off a considerable broadside which started with the declaration that before I became a minister I had found Tommy Balogh's chapter on the establishment the most important statement on the civil service. Now I had some experience, I was even more impressed by it.'[105]

In 1959, Thomas Balogh had written a damning critique of the civil service.[106] He argued that due to its historic tradition, experts were in very short supply. 'From the decision to elevate the general administrator, the mandarin, and grant to his corporation supreme influence, much of the present discomfort of the country has followed.'[107] Coupled with this amateurism was a lack of flexibility in the civil service structure. He indicated that key policy decisions lay with 'a handful of gentlemen', with experts managed by Permanent Secretaries.[108] Balogh criticised the governmental structure where civil servants enjoyed 'effective power without responsibility, the complete freedom from all criticism.'[109] His picture of an under-trained, unsuitably recruited, overly powerful civil service is completely at odds with the opinions of various other writers, some with considerably more experience than Balogh of the civil service, such as Edward Bridges. It is significant that Crossman should state his support for this publication during his Fulton Committee evidence in 1967. This particularly critical essay was not referred to again and his writing, both within his diaries and during the 1970 Godkin lectures, did not reflect these rather damning views.

Another criticism which Crossman recorded in his diaries, perhaps indicating his pleasure at being able to share it with the Fulton committee, was the issue of Treasury dominance over civil servants, an issue he had initially noted in 1939.[110] He wrote that he had told the committee

How the Treasury spies on ministers through ex-Treasury men in each department, how difficult civil servants find it not to feel a greater loyalty to the Treasury than to their ministers, and I then described the difficulty of the minister faced with the agreed solutions of official committees.[111]

His evidence to the Fulton Committee was fairly damning, arguing that the civil service simply took advantage of the existing departmental arrangements, meaning that reform was essential. He argued that Parliament needed to be strengthened, specialist committees should be introduced and external advice was also essential. For good measure, he mentioned that his officials had listened into his phone calls, forcing him to have a private line installed while at the Ministry of Housing and Local Government.[112] It is clear that he was absolutely delighted to be able to express his views to the Fulton committee and criticise the civil service viciously after his two years in government. It should also be noted that by 1967, he was Leader of the House of Commons, a political appointment which meant he was not in daily touch with the service. These opinions were carried from his earlier political career and he believed that his first two years in government had confirmed them completely. He concluded his diary entry by stating that 'to cheer them up I concluded with the description of the excellence of the Private Office system and how I'd been converted to the view that one shouldn't substitute a *chef de cabinet* system for the Private Office system.'[113] Crossman's views on the service appeared to have mellowed slightly since 1964, although he had obviously encountered many problems with the service which are described at length in his diaries. It could be that the opportunity to criticise the service encouraged him to exaggerate his problems and concerns. Perhaps his overly negative account led the committee to take more notice of his evidence, as was suggested by Michael Simons.[114]

When Crossman entered the department of Health and Social Security in 1968 he did not seem concerned about his civil servants. For all his evidence to the Fulton committee, his opinions had mellowed and he accepted that it was the job of a minister to give a lead to a department and ensure the civil service followed it. The references to the civil service within his diaries during his time in the Department of Health and Social Security are fairly limited but there is a perceivable change in his views from the period 1964-66. In May 1968 he argued that while the civil service were constantly attempting to gain control of any minister, this was encouraged by Wilson, who moved ministers from one department to another on a regular basis. He wrote 'too many job changes in three years means a tremendous decline in the power of the politician over the civil service machine and a tremendous growth in the power of the Whitehall departments, both to thwart central cabinet control and to thwart departmental ministers' individual control.'[115] He also commented on the completed report of the Fulton Committee, describing it as 'a second-rate report written in a very poor style.'[116] Between 1968 and 1970 his views on the civil service weakened, with Crossman beginning to look at the actions of the government to explain the activities of the civil service, an attitude which was expressed in his 1970 Godkin lectures. This was due to his experience within government, but it was encouraged by his increasing age and the realisation that his political career was moving fairly swiftly towards its conclusion. The reader of his diaries will note the different styles evident in the first and third volumes of his diaries, with Crossman initially being driven and enthusiastic towards his department and government. By 1968 this enthusiasm appears to have waned and his wider participation within cabinet reduced as other stronger members took a much larger role, such as Roy Jenkins.

In his 1970 Godkin lectures, Crossman again argued that the civil service would use any methods possible to ensure that their departmental view was accepted and implemented. He indicated that the civil service would brush off old ideas which had been rejected by one minister, and present them to their next minister. He used his successor at the Ministry of Health and Social Services, Keith Joseph, as his example, indicating that Joseph was being presented with ideas which he had previously rejected. In this way, the civil service, as the most constant feature in any government department, eventually had the policies which they preferred implemented.[117] He concluded that civil servants routinely implemented their preferred policies, taking numerous day-to-day decisions without referring them to the minister due to the time constraints. Once these decisions were taken, the minister was duty bound to accept them and support them publicly, although not necessary privately.[118] It is important to note that the Godkin lectures made clear that the failure of any government could be blamed on only one set of people – the politicians. The civil service, while being able to make life very difficult for ministers and coming in for heavy criticism, were not responsible for governmental failures. 'I would say that normally when a government fails it is not because the civil service blocks its plans, but because the government team has not had a clear enough sense of direction.'[119] It was the responsibility of any minister to ensure that their decisions were carried through, and he indicated that a strong minister could ensure that the civil service was working in accordance with his wishes.[120] This view was evident in his writing from 1968, but his criticisms of the service remained, noting an important change in emphasis.

Many writers, such as W. Ivor Jennings, have indicated an alternative viewpoint to that of Crossman regarding the departmental views of the civil service, which may be the cause of the confusion and hostility. While Jennings' writing is generally not held in as high regard as that of Sir Edward Bridges (Permanent Secretary to the Treasury and Head of the Civil Service 1945-1956), Crossman praised Jennings' work, commented that his 1934 publication *Parliamentary Reform* contained 'some excellent suggestions on this point [the efficiency of the House of Commons] which should be studied by socialists who wish a Labour government to carry through legislation.'[121] Jennings indicated in his later work that the civil service had a fundamental duty to point out the deficiencies of any scheme which a minister favoured, and may inadvertently recommend their own approach.[122]

Sir Edward Bridges made the same point in his 1950 Rede lecture, arguing that it was 'the duty of a civil servant to give his minister the fullest benefit of the storehouse of departmental experience; and to let the waves of the practical philosophy wash against ideas put forward by his ministerial master.'[123] He stated that the civil service tended to 'hedge or confine themselves to what has already been said' due to concern over radical policy, not due to their conservatism, as Crossman believed.[124] He indicated that this concern was caused by the position the civil service occupied within government, being answerable to their minister, who will in turn 'get the praise and blame for what they do.'[125] He argued that, while the civil service should advise a minister on any cause of action, 'on all important questions it is necessary to make sure that the minister approves what is being done,' a view somewhat at odds with those of Crossman.[126]

Crossman believed that if a minister were strong-willed and determined, he would force the civil service to adopt his policies, regardless of their personal reluctance. 'We have to fight very hard to get a chance of this kind because every possible difficulty is discovered; and though each is duly surmounted it all takes time if the department doesn't like the direction in which we are moving.'[127] While he never stated that civil servants shouldn't have their own opinions, he did believe that they should always follow the lead of a minister, as Bridges had stated. However, he believed that strong leadership was required to do this. He concluded that after taking office his civil servants believed he was 'far too rough with them, scare them stiff, make hasty judgements and very often scrawl rude things on paper which upsets them.'[128] This was a deliberate attitude which he adopted in his departments, bringing him into conflict with many of his civil servants. His overall conclusion was that while the civil service would and perhaps should maintain its own opinions, the wishes of the minister had to be paramount. This required a strong minister who could push through this work instead of being weak and following a purely departmental line.

The civil service came in for a great deal of criticism, particularly from left wing individuals, such as Laski. However, it appears that there was no overall consensus of opinion on this issue. As Theakston pointed out there was 'no single, coherent "Labour Party view" about the nature and problems of the civil service or its reforms.'[129] Laski and Crossman agreed that while the civil service was a flawed institution, it was not responsible for the failures of government. Crossman stated this very explicitly in his 1970 Godkin lectures, 'where we failed, it was because we failed. We just have not done our job when we had the chance to.'[130] His views on the civil service did not improve over time, but his time in office does seem to have adapted his view slightly. The idea which Crossman had in 1956 of having a brains trust was never instituted and he did not mention such a plan while a minister. However, he did attempt to introduce experts and outside advisers into his departments to provide the same kind of information which such a group would have collected. The experience of office seems to have made him more practical and orthodox in his views of the civil service. While recognising the service as an imperfect organisation, he did not pin the failures of government on it, instead blaming this on all cabinet ministers including himself. His lack of knowledge of the Ministry of Housing and Local Government was a considerable problem for Crossman initially, and put even greater strain on his relations with his civil servants. Laski indicated that it was the responsibility of the Prime Minister to ensure that any minister was not at an automatic disadvantage by lacking in knowledge on the policies of his ministry, as Crossman was in 1964. This would then mean that business could be carried out smoothly and efficiently. 'It means, in the first place, that a cabinet must take office knowing what it wants to do and that its Prime Minister must so distribute the posts at his disposal as to constitute the team most likely to effect its purpose.'[131]

This leads us to consider whether it is better for a minister to be a specialist or a generalist, a question which Crossman frequently asked of the civil service. Morrison, writing in 1954, concluded that a politician should be a generalist about specific policy areas but a specialist on the public:

> He [the Permanent Secretary] is not and should not be a politician, but he should know enough about politics and politicians to be on his guard against blunders and indiscretions, although it is the minister rather than the Permanent Secretary who is paid for his political expertise and understanding of the public.[132]

Crossman worked in one department during his career which he was fairly well versed in, the department of Health and Social Security between 1968 and 1970. He knew almost nothing about Housing or Local Government before 1964, and while having written on constitutional reform before 1966, he was almost completely ignorant of the workings of the House of Commons, something he was in control of from 1966 to 1968. He indicated that he felt his lack of knowledge had been a difficulty. 'We would have done better if I had had more political experience. It took me fifteen months before I realized what was wrong.'[133] While he did not directly consider the generalist vs. specialist argument, his statement here indicated that a politician with some specialist knowledge of their ministry was preferable to a politician with no knowledge of their ministry. While it seems unlikely that his relations with his civil servants would have been good had he entered a ministry about which he had detailed knowledge in 1964, it seems to have been a contributory factor to his poor relations with the service.

Prime Ministerial Government

The different styles which a cabinet and a Prime Minister could adopt were an issue which was focused upon particularly during the 1950s and 1960s. John Mackintosh published *The British Cabinet* in 1962, identifying the characteristics of different styles of cabinets using the examples of various Prime Minister from Lloyd George through to Macmillan.[134] While not specifically naming these different styles, two prominent styles were identified throughout his book, which have been subsequently labelled as prime ministerial and cabinet government. He argued that the modern cabinet was not a place for discussion or policy decision making. The cabinet in a prime ministerial government was overworked and tended to make decisions based on the inaction of its members. Decisions, while not generally made at cabinet, were reported to it, and any major issues which had not been resolved at departmental or committee stage could be considered here. The power of the Prime Minister in this style of government was important, but he was not an isolated figure. In order to retain his power at the head of a cone of influence which Mackintosh described, he needed to retain the confidence and support of other high ranking cabinet ministers. Without this loyalty, the Prime Minister would be lost and the government would collapse until another individual who could command this loyalty was found.

Generally the style which a Prime Minister adopts is influenced by his preferred style of conducting cabinet and any previous experience he may have as a cabinet minister. Mackintosh used examples of various Prime Ministers, both Conservative and Labour, to show how different individuals had influenced their party. The style which has been labelled prime ministerial government appears to have been adopted by the vast majority of modern Prime Ministers. In a cabinet government the Prime Minister was first amongst equals, with more decisions being made in cabinet with a guiding hand from the Prime Minister. This was a collective style of government, where the cabinet as a whole, generally dominated by the Prime Minister and the more senior members, make policy decisions. However, he concluded that this has not existed since the latter half of the nineteenth century.[135] His accounts of different governing styles meant that traditional views of how the government worked were now called into question. Crossman concluded that the cabinet style of government, which Bagehot had commented on in 1867, no longer existed.

Mackintosh argued that in Britain, the prime ministerial system had become predominant, but his earlier examples generally from pre-1940 showed that virtually all Prime Ministers had preferred the cabinet style of government. He argued that the role of the modern cabinet in a prime ministerial government was to co-ordinate administration, ensure that legislation proposals were acceptable and to keep senior ministers in touch with the activities of the government. This was very different from the traditionalists' view of the role of cabinet.[136] Ministers generally spent their time dealing with decisions within their departments using the policy frameworks which had been worked out previously. These policies were often decided upon while in opposition by the larger party, although of course some policies had to be thrashed out while the party was in government. Departmental decisions could be made at a variety of levels within government depending on what the issue was. These could be decided by civil servants, departmental committees, the departmental minister or even, in a limited number of cases, the cabinet. Decisions would often be taken with very little discussion and many may never have come to the attention of the cabinet, or even the departmental minister. When issues were referred to the cabinet, this was often due to conflict at the committee stage. In these instances, the cabinet acted as an appeal court, not deciding policy but instead deciding what specific measures should be adopted to institute a policy which had already been decided. Alternatively, decisions could be made based on the specific circumstances, with issues of practicality taking precedence. However, in the battle between departments, and with the input of the Treasury, ever eager to cut costs, the support of the Prime Minister was vital for these policy decisions to pass through cabinet without rejection or considerable rewriting. The Prime Minister gained further influence and power by being at the middle of the political system and knowing the majority of the policy decisions being made.

When Mackintosh's book was published in 1962, Crossman had no experience of the workings of government or the cabinet. He had not given the issue of governing style any real consideration until reading Mackintosh's book in 1962 which he then commented on in his weekly column for *The Guardian* written in June 1962. He outlined the three main themes of the book as being that '(1) cabinet government had been replaced by prime ministerial government, that (2) the Commons had become only one of many interests which a Prime Minister had to consider when making decisions, and that (3) prime ministerial government was a retreat from democracy.'[137] He believed that Mackintosh's book was extremely good, describing it as 'a monumental new book' which contained 'the first serious academic analysis of where power lies and how decisions are made in our present system of government.'[138] His column was fairly short and so his critique of Mackintosh's book is brief but there are some striking observations which he made that it is important to note. Firstly, he supported Mackintosh's assertion that the Prime Minister can make all the big decisions of government. Indeed, he went further stating that 'it is entirely at his discretion whether he consults members of the cabinet, civil servants, outside advisers, or representatives of big interests.'[139] He continued with Mackintosh's conclusions, stating that this hand-over of power from cabinet to the Prime Minister meant that the Commons was now little more than one interest among many, with the Prime Minister more able to rely on other communication methods to reach out to the public at election time.[140] He indicated that the Prime Minister did not have any other reason to communicate with the public other than during elections. This meant that democracy as it had been traditionally accepted, no longer existed as discussion no longer influenced decision making. 'The only kind of discussions a modern Premier need hold before a decision are secret consultations with civil servants, or outside interests, and secret meetings with a party caucus.'[141] The picture which Crossman painted of government, using Mackintosh's book as his starting point, was one which he re-evaluated when he entered government in 1964, when he had gained the knowledge and experience which allowed him to make more credible conclusions.

Between 1964 and 1970, Crossman's views were not stationary, changing and adapting when new experiences or decisions contradicted his earlier assumptions. Initially, he concluded that while there was more scope for decision making in cabinet than he had initially thought, there was also more scope for interference by the Prime Minister in decision making. He was surprised by the level of discussion which was available in cabinet, and appears to have been surprised at the freedom which both the cabinet and the Prime Minister had.[142] One month after recording his initial views in his diaries, he returned to this theory and considered the cabinet and Wilson's role within it again, coming to very similar conclusions. While noting the power of other senior ministers within the cabinet, particularly George Brown, Crossman indicated that Wilson was allowing his departmental ministers to get on with their work 'without running to him for assistance.'[143] The main criticism which he had of the cabinet was that it was too departmental and that almost no-one has an overall impression of all the activities of the government except Wilson, with Brown being well-versed on domestic issues but lacking in foreign affairs knowledge at this point. Crossman failed to consider whether this knowledge helped Wilson fulfil a prime ministerial role, placing him in a far more powerful position than his closest senior ministers, but it should be assumed that it increased his relative position with the cabinet.

By December 1964, Crossman had more clearly identified a theme which was to recur within his diaries for much of his ministerial career. He argued that individual ministers did not have wide-ranging discussions within cabinet on policy. Instead, 'the twenty-three of us come, each with his particular pressures and problems, trying to get what we want. And we do avoid any collective discussion of general policy except perhaps on defence and foreign affairs.'[144] This departmentalism was an issue which he continued to be aware of, repeatedly urging Wilson to create a small inner cabinet which could help him to co-ordinate policy and consider the wider political picture. Wilson did not act upon this advice despite Crossman's belief that he would.

From 1965 until 1970, Crossman's views on the style of the Wilson government remained relatively static, only fluctuating when he felt Wilson had acted in a distinctly different style on specific issues. From the middle of 1965 he began to indicate in his diaries that while Wilson was very careful to create the impression of cabinet government, he was instead acting in a more prime ministerial way, fixing decisions with individual ministers, making more decisions and being at the very centre of his government.[145] While being critical of this style of government, Crossman utilised it, relying on Wilson at certain key points to ensure decisions were made and agreed by cabinet. In 1966 he began to note a change in Wilson's style. 'The PM has run the govt completely prime ministerially, he has decided to allow decisions to be taken by George Brown and Callaghan sparring with each other, and in every other way he has retained decision taking in his personal domain.'[146] In June 1967 when he again commented on Wilson's handling of cabinet regarding the issue of D-Notices, indicating that Wilson dominated the handling of the affair by carefully preparing the timing of the cabinet meeting, ensuring that the discussion took no longer than half an hour, limiting criticism and ensuring that the white paper on the issue was published after the cabinet meeting. Crossman described this as the 'first occasion when I can remember him taking the strictly presidential line.'[147] He maintained in his diaries that from this occasion on, Wilson became more prime ministerial in his style with the cabinet. He concluded that the 1967 cabinet reshuffle allowed Wilson to take more control of his government, 'now that phase is over and he is taking the lead himself, laying down the policy in SEP (steering committee on economic policy) and then telling the full cabinet of the decisions.'[148] It seems likely that this gradually changing style was due to Wilson's increasing confidence in his role as Prime Minister and his reshuffle of cabinet. After this point, Crossman did not comment upon the style of government, instead becoming more involved in his reform programme and later his departmental business. It can be assumed that he did not fundamentally alter his view that Wilson acted increasingly in a prime ministerial way, with his cabinet relegated to the role of rubber-stamp on legislation, a situation which had developed since 1964 when his presentation style had been very different.

During the Godkin lectures in 1970, Crossman again returned to the issue of governmental style. He argued that he and Mackintosh had come in for acute criticism for their theory of government style, though one suspects that Mackintosh, as the original author, came in for more criticism than his supporter.[149] He indicated that the power of the Prime Minister had been increased due to the expansion of government and the unique role which he occupied within the party, within Parliament and with the civil service.[150] Crossman stated that his view in 1963, that cabinet government had been replaced by prime ministerial government, had been confirmed by his time in government. He suggested that one of the other most fundamental changes to the style of government was due to collective responsibility. Instead of decisions being made at cabinet level, decisions were made by a much smaller number of ministers, indicating it was often two, three or four. These decisions were then minuted and became covered by collective responsibility, meaning that they were 'binding on a hundred-odd members of the government.'[151]

He concluded that this change contributed to the creation and prevalence of prime ministerial government. He indicated in his lecture that

> It does not mean that he [the Prime Minister] is a dictator; it does not mean he can tell his ministers what to do in their departments. But it does mean that in the battle of Whitehall this man in the centre, this chairman, this man without a department, without apparent power, can exert, when he is successful, a dominating personal control.[152]

He concluded that prime ministerial government had become prevalent, and while having some practical benefits, removed more democracy from Parliament and cabinet creating a temporary dictatorship, something he had first referred to in 1939.

The Role of the Party

In *Socialism and the New Despotism* Crossman considered how democratic government could best be achieved by the next Labour government. He pointed out that 'a government is no longer fully responsible to Parliament', indicating that 'this transfer of responsibility from Parliament and the individual Member to the cabinet (and to the shadow cabinet) has…gone perilously far.'[153] He concluded that it was essential to create a situation where governments, regardless of which political party they represented, were accountable to Parliament:

> Certainly a socialist will want to be sure that the next Labour government will have sufficient power to carry through its programme speedily, and that requires a strong political leadership and a disciplined party at Westminster and in the country to back it up. But the next Labour government … will [need] to democratise the vast institutions, already theoretically responsible to it.[154]

In order to do this he outlined, for the first time in print, his idea of parliamentary standing committees. These committees, which will be discussed later in this chapter, would be set up for each nationalised industry, removing administrative chores for ministers, allowing them to focus on policy making and providing backbench MPs with more involvement in government activities.[155] Some writers would take issue with Crossman's definition of the role of a minister, creating far-reaching policies within cabinet as opposed to within the party prior to election. However, his continued support for more parliamentary scrutiny of government business was, by 1956, taking him in new directions. He was not simply considering the position of the Prime Minister and cabinet, he was also considering how individual MPs could be utilised and their skills developed, giving them more to do than being just one vote for the Whips.[156] This would help to create the accountability which he felt was essential, as well as providing an informal training ground for backbench MPs. It might also help with issues of discipline, providing MPs with more responsibility, an issue which would occupy his mind considerably between 1966 and 1968.

By 1956, Crossman believed that the government and the cabinet were no longer answerable to Parliament, and therefore it was essential to allow MPs to question their leaders within the House of Commons. His views on discipline were linked to his views on the accountability of government. While he considered the government to lack rigorous parliamentary scrutiny, he believed it was important for backbench MPs, such as himself, to be able to hold the government to account within the House of Commons both in terms of questioning and voting. He concluded that it was vital for backbench MPs to be included in the work of government, not simply instructed how to vote:

> No sensible politician denies the need for unity and discipline at Westminster, in Council Groups and, to a lesser extent, in the party organisation outside. But are unity and loyal support of the leadership best

achieved by elaborately drafting Standing Orders, which enforce acceptance of majority decisions on threat of expulsion?'[157]

In this statement the impact of Bevan's numerous battles with the party leadership can be felt, with Crossman calling for more involvement of backbenchers in government, creating less of a separation between the leadership and the rank and file members of the parliamentary party. However, when he became a member of the government, and was able to implement this, his views appear to have begun to change. This was not particularly evident between 1964 and 1966, before he became Leader of the House of Commons. It seems to have been this role which adapted his views and turned them on their head. After 1968, he was no longer in favour of allowing backbench MPs to follow their own agenda when voting on specific issues, as the voting public was not interested in their personal views, but the policies of the party. As well as being keen to increase accountability, he was now concerned with the authority and the power of the government and its ability to pass legislation without too much difficulty. The battering ram of change, the party, had to be maintained, while the individual whims of an MP could be ignored, a view which is almost completely irreconcilable with his views before 1966.[158]

While Crossman had maintained his belief that MPs needed a way of questioning ministers on their policies, by 1970 he was outlining a slightly different position. Before 1968, he had been in favour of holding departments to account by select committees, but he was no longer in favour of this kind of scrutiny. In a memo to Wilson he wrote, 'is it really politically prudent and is there an administrative advantage to be gained from encouraging backbench Members of the House to think up proposals for extracting more information from Whitehall?'[159] This gradual change in his views was evident when he considered the issue of party discipline in his Godkin lectures. Rather at odds with his previously held views, he concluded that individual MPs tended only very rarely to be elected on individual attributes or local issues. Instead, they were usually elected as the representative of the wider party, and as such owed their loyalty to the party, on all issues other than those of conscience. While questioning of ministers was still acceptable to him in certain circumstances, voting against the party was not. He referred to the 'battering-ram' of change, where the individual MPs came together to form a group which would force change through the House of Commons.[160] This was a contradiction of his earlier, more liberal views, and was undoubtedly influenced by his own experiences of trying to impose discipline on the party. His main concern now was that the party be maintained as the 'battering-ram' of change, as opposed to allowing the individual member freedom to express themselves, as he had previously believed was important, except when the survival of the party was at stake, as it was between 1964 and 1966. He concluded that in order to institute change, discipline was needed, more so in the Labour Party than in any other.[161]

House of Lords Reform 1966-68

Reform of the House of Lords was widely debated within the Labour Party almost from its conception. The party questioned how a socialist programme of reform could be adopted when there was such a large Conservative majority in the upper House. This majority ensured that even when the Conservatives were not in government, they still held the reins of power. The Labour Party at the beginning of the twentieth century had, in some quarters, favoured the abolition of the Lords. While this view was not predominant after 1945 there were contrasting views on how the House of Lords should be reformed to best serve a Labour government and whether this was even necessary. Many on the right of the party concluded that the existing constitutional arrangements could be used to implement the party's programme with only minimal alteration, such as a reduction in the delaying power of the House of Lords as was implemented by the Attlee government in 1949. Some on the left of the party, such as Michael Foot, concluded that the powers of the Lords needed reducing and extensively reforming. Crossman appears to have been in a minority, believing that the composition of the Lords needed considering in conjunction with the powers it held to create a useful second chamber, not necessarily a weakened one. He recorded in his diaries a conversation he held with Wilson in 1968, where he told him 'we *have* to deal with composition and powers together... Composition *is* their power and if you try to pass a bill destroying their powers, while you are passing it they will do everything possible to sabotage our programme.'[162]

The first occasion when Crossman considered the House of Lords was in 1939 when, like Laski, he used Norway's second chamber as a model, indicating that what was needed in Britain was a 'small expert body which would carefully examine legislation passed by the Commons and tidy it up.'[163] While he wrote about various aspects of constitutional reform, the House of Lords was not an issue which he considered in any depth, and his 1939 writing did not fully examine the issues raised by the reform of the Lords or the impact of reform on the wider constitution. While he wrote on constitutional reform several times during his political career, he was not a key individual within this debate, failing to produce a work comparable with Crosland's pivotal work on social democracy on the subject of constitutional reform.[164] However, in comparison to his cabinet colleagues he had more knowledge of the reform debate than many of them, a fact which may have influenced his appointment as Leader of the House of Commons. Of those on the right of the cabinet, Roy Jenkins and Anthony Crosland had similar views to Crossman. However, Crosland had shown little inclination to the reform debate, while Jenkins was such a key member of the cabinet, he was filling the powerful positions of Home Secretary from 1965 to 1967 and Chancellor from 1967 to 1970.

On the left of the cabinet, Barbara Castle was really the only other high-ranking member at this time. However, again she had shown little interest in the Lords reform debate. Additionally, she was not, in 1966, a powerful enough minister to warrant being Leader of the House of Commons and Lord President of the Council. Wilson, in his book *The Labour Government 1964-70* gave little indication as to why Crossman was moved to his new position in 1966. Crossman stated in his diaries that Wilson had told him he was being moved so he could work with him more closely and also to organise the party and 'ensure the rank and file feel themselves linked with the leadership.'[165] Additionally, he claimed that Wilson wished him to push through constitutional reform, though he did not indicate exactly what this would include. Wilson may well have assigned him his position as Leader of the House of Commons due to his interest in constitutional reform, but his hand may well have been forced due to a lack of any other candidates for such a job. Also the lack of high ranking cabinet positions which Crossman could occupy may have also been a factor. Bernard Crick indicated that his appointment to the role 'was a shrewd political move. His [Crossman's] known leanings in favour of parliamentary reform, but his realism about the carrying on of government; his restless and impulsive intellectuality, but his personal toughness and truculence...' made him suited to the job.[166]

When Crossman became Leader of the House of Commons and Lord President of the Council in 1966, he did not simply focus on House of Lords reform. His overall aim was to increase scrutiny of legislation and provide constructive ways of improving policy documents. In order to rigorously vet legislation the second chamber would need to be strengthened, but would need a governmental majority within the House for the life of the government. When Labour was in power, there would be a Labour majority in the House of Lords and a Conservative government would have a Conservative majority. This was a policy which was designed as a sensible solution to the two main problems which he saw with the House of Lords. Firstly it would resolve issues over the composition, and secondly it would provide a scrutiny of the government which had been lacking. He concluded, presumably with support from Wilson, though this is not explicitly stated in his diaries, that the most sensible way to implement these changes was to have cross-party talks on the issue of House of Lords reform and see if a common view could be found. [167] This approach would have a better chance of success within the Houses of Parliament as, with agreement from the other political parties resistance would be minimal.

These talks were fairly successful, with agreement being reached until 18th June 1968, the second evening of debate on Rhodesian sanctions in the House of Lords. Janet Morgan indicated that Lord Shackleton, who was not in favour of reform 'had been hinting for some time that by rejecting the Southern Rhodesia (United Nations Sanctions) Order the Tory Peers might thereby sabotage the inter-party talks and the opportunity to secure an agreed reform scheme.'[168] The government was defeated by nine votes, but Crossman's hopes of cross-bench co-operation collapsed and Wilson 'according to some sources, attacked the dream world of the inter-party conferences and confidences.' Morgan indicated that this was due to the increasingly bitter political climate.[169] This statement highlights Wilson's frustrations over the scheme, but as there is no suggestion that Crossman was acting independently of the Prime Minister, it seems likely that he had changed his views over cross-party talks due to the defeat of the government in the Lords. The talks were abandoned and the reform bill was introduced into the House of Commons. Individuals such as Enoch Powell and Michael Foot became unusual bedfellows, each of them opposing the bill for different reasons. Those on the right, such as Powell, believed that the House of Lords worked well enough as it was and did not require reform of this magnitude, if at all. Those on the left, such as Foot, believed that the bill did not go far enough and that more radical reform was needed.

The approach which Crossman adopted and the general success of the cross-party talks was jeopardised by the Conservative front bench, the transient support of the cabinet and an unusual coalition of backbenchers from both parties. Crossman, believing that he had an undertaking from Heath to support the bill, began the difficult process of passing the bill in the House of Commons. While some members of the Conservative front bench were sympathetic to the reforms, the powerful opposition groups made progress very difficult. The cross-party talks which were meant to provide a workable solution created more difficulties than they solved. The Lords were, on the whole, very much in favour of the reforms. Many believed they were a positive move forward, while others concluded that while reform may not be a move forward, the bill at least would stop calls for more reform and would be acceptable if not desirable. If this bill were rejected, the next call for reform may propose more radical action which might strip the Lords of any power or influence. This support from the Lords made many within the Commons very suspicious. How radical could this bill be if the House of Lords was supporting it? There was also a belief amongst some, particularly those on the left, that the Labour Party should not have discussed its plans with the opposition and should instead have implemented their own plans regardless of opposition. It should be noted here that in matters of constitutional reform both parties tend to be involved in some form of discussion, even if these are only minimal, due to the nature of the change.

When the bill came to the House of Commons, the grouping of those on the left and right came together to make progress very slow. Each clause was debated at length and many divisions went on late into the night, delaying government business and angering many members of the Commons. These difficulties were compounded, in Morgan's view, by the lack of enthusiasm which Callaghan as Home Secretary showed for the bill, despite him introducing it into the Commons. Additionally, Crossman had been moved to be overlord of the huge department of Health and Social Security, meaning that while he remained committed to the reform bill, his attention was diverted elsewhere, and the new Leader of the House of Commons and Lord President of the Council, Fred Peart, did not have the will to push the bill through.[170] The government was faced with a dilemma. Should the reform bill be pushed through, regardless of how long it took, or should it be ended quickly, and other government business used to replace it, such as the

Industrial Relations bill which Wilson was personally committed to? Constitutional reform was not seen as a vote winner and with a general election less than two years away, this might have been a factor in Wilson's thinking. The decision was taken to withdraw the bill, and replace it with the Industrial Relations bill, which Wilson was considerably more enthusiastic about.

While Crossman took this further than many might have preferred, he did so with the support of the Prime Minister and he believed that a workable and useful solution had been negotiated. He was bitterly disappointed when his reform bill fell, and continued to argue that it had been a real opportunity for change which would not be revisited for some time to come, suggesting a lack of enthusiasm from Wilson and senior cabinet members.

Parliamentary Reform

When Crossman became Leader of the House in 1966, the only concrete proposals which he had inherited from the previous Leader, Bert Bowden, was a commitment to trial morning sittings in the House of Commons and a scheme to trial the televising of proceedings in the House of Lords. He was not personally committed to either of these schemes but he did attempt to implement them in spite of resistance from both cabinet and Parliament. This section will focus primarily on the issues which caused most resentment, those of morning sittings and select committees as well as the televising of the Houses of Parliament. While the trial of televising the House of Lords was fairly quickly and quietly forgotten, morning sittings aroused some very strong feelings from the House of Commons. These feelings were compounded by Crossman's attempt to reform the House of Lords and also by his insistence that select committees be introduced, in selected departments initially.

The Labour government was committed to the televising of the House of Lords as part of the reform packages. Prior to 1966, Crossman did not discuss or even consider the idea of televising the Houses of Parliament. The trial scheme had been considered by a select committee which had concluded that for the length of the trial, the floors of both Houses should be recorded and then the tape released to television companies to do with as they wished. He believed that this was 'expensive and impracticable. My own personal belief is that if we have the House televised it should be done much more simply by having the facilities there and using them occasionally for live broadcasts of debates, as a number of European countries do.'[171] His diaries do not really consider the televising trial very thoroughly, with it only being mentioned on occasion, such as when he ensured the funding for the experiment at cabinet despite the reservations of the Chancellor, Roy Jenkins.[172] The televising of the Lords appears to have raised objections from the majority of Peers, although Crossman concluded that this was due to the House of Lords being a 'very introverted place. It's made up its mind about television and it doesn't want to change its mind.'[173] The scheme was dropped fairly quickly and Crossman was not particularly perturbed by this.

The experiment to extend the number of select committees was something which he had been calling for for some time. In *Socialism and the New Despotism*, he had called for a standing committee to be set up for each nationalised industry, one each for the National Assistance Board and the Agricultural Marketing Board, one for defence issues and another for colonial issues.[174] He outlined a number of advantages to the scheme. Firstly it would raise the status of backbench MPs, it would reduce the need in the House of Commons for 'shadow boxing or for idle gossip'. Its main objective would be to 'remove from the cabinet and from individual ministers some part at least of the detailed administrative chores which prevent them from concentrating on their main task of formulating national policies and preparing plans which require legislation.'[175]

His opinions on what was practical and advantageous were clouded by his perception of the work of a minister, something he had no experience or knowledge of in 1956. It is questionable how much any individual minister formulates national policy or prepares plans which require legislation, but for Crossman it was essential to set up these committees to allow for such policy making, and to ensure that backbench MPs were included in a more rigorous, more accountable parliamentary system. In his evidence to the Fulton Committee he had argued that these committees would put pressure on civil servants and provoke dissension. 'They would examine both ministers and officials, and he hoped that many of the hearings would be public, although it would be necessary for some of the work to be done in private.'[176] Upon becoming Leader of the House and being in a position to implement some of his ideas, he began to set in motion his plans for select committees. He only managed to establish two while he was Leader of the House, an agriculture committee and one on science and technology. His scheme ran into difficulties, not from backbench MPs, but from the Chief Whip and other cabinet ministers. He recorded incidences in his diaries when backbench MPs complained to him that select committees were being packed with individuals who would not hold the government to account and showed no independence. He responded by saying 'I am beginning to realize that the complete control which the Chief Whip keeps on the selection of members and the assumption which he and each minister has that they will in future be able to control the business and forbid the committee to do anything of which they disapprove is really unconstitutional.'[177]

It can be concluded from this incident that other cabinet ministers and the Chief Whip had different aims to Crossman. They were simply looking to stop the committees from interfering in departmental business while he was looking for more accountability. Anthony Howard indicated that there was also a lack of unity between Wilson and Crossman on the issue of parliamentary reform, indicating that 'whereas Dick believed passionately in the cause, the Prime Minister – as conservative in his attitude to the Commons as in much else – was never really prepared to pay it much more than lip service.'[178] Crossman recognised that Wilson advocated two different views on constitutional reform, believing this was due to pressure from Whitehall. 'When he's alone with me he's always in favour of specialist committees but in cabinet he's always accepting ministerial objections.'[179] The trial of select committees that he established eventually blossomed into an accepted fact of parliamentary life after 1979, but his own experiences were not particularly successful, despite his commitment to the scheme.

Another reform which Crossman was not personally committed to, but which took up much of his time, was morning sittings in the House of Commons. It had been recommended by a single vote by the select committee on Commons' procedure and therefore he began to implement this reform upon becoming Leader of the House. In his diary he insisted that 'it's a half measure which I would never have dreamt of introducing if I hadn't inherited it.'[180] Morning sittings were introduced in an attempt to keep business within reasonable hours ending the all night sittings of the House. By starting in the morning it was hoped that the House could finish at an earlier hour. While this all seemed very sensible, it was bound to interfere with the routine and life of those MPs who held a second job while on the backbenches.[181] As a backbench MP, Crossman had held an additional job and did not spend as much time in the House of Commons as he could or perhaps should have done prior to 1964 so he understood the concerns of many. In an attempt to convince the dissenters in both parties that this experiment was worthwhile, it was decided that non-controversial business would be pushed through in the new morning sittings, so if MPs were unable to attend, it would not necessarily be too damaging to democracy. However, the Conservative Party, which was not in favour of the experiment, attempted to disable the scheme by ensuring that debates did not end until the early hours of the morning. This ensured that the Labour MPs were too exhausted to attend the House the next morning.[182] Despite the continuation of the scheme for eight months, until November 1967, it was eventually dropped and was not considered a success. Crossman concluded early in March 1967 that it could never succeed without the support of the whole House, and he does not appear to have been particularly unhappy with the abandonment of the scheme.[183]

His programme of reforms for the House of Commons was not particularly successful. While select committees have been maintained and extended to include other policy areas, they were not a success during his political career, and morning sittings were completely unsuccessful. The main problem which these reforms faced was opposition to the aims of the reform, although this was not always from the same source. Select committees raised serious issues of increasing accountability, which some senior members of the cabinet disagreed with, such as Jim Callaghan. Morning sittings were objected to primarily by the Conservatives, although they raised questions for many Labour MPs who had external employment, a protest which Crossman sympathised with completely. It is important to indicate that of these reforms, the introduction of select committees was the only one he was personally committed to and which he had initiated. Morning sittings and the televising of Parliament were initiatives which he inherited, and he was not convinced of their merits. As Crick concluded on the Crossman reform package, 'the changes were great. But in terms of any new "opening up" of British government, of radically increasing the flow of knowledge of how we are governed, the reforms are less impressive – the end of the a beginning, certainly, but not the beginning of the end.'[184]

The Monarchy

Crossman was particularly proud that he vocally complained about the pomp and circumstance of the British establishment. His dislike of ceremonial dinners and morning suits was an important part of his character.[185] While never portrayed as a 'man of the people' due to his background, the more ceremonial elements of government did not sit well with his socialist views. Pimlott described him as 'a Wykhamist rebel – an Establishment-reared opponent of his contemporaries with a sophisticated understanding, both social and intellectual, of the system he attacked.'[186] This extended to the role of the Monarchy. Bagehot had described the Monarchy as a dignified part of the constitution and Crossman subscribed to this view. While never being a supporter of republicanism, he objected to the ceremony which was attached to the Monarchy. His views might never have been particularly important, but his position as Lord President of the Council from 1966 to 1968 forced him to deal with the Queen and reconsider his opinions in light of his new experiences.

He only considered the role of Monarchy in Britain twice in his writing. In his 1939 publication, *How Britain is Governed*, he argued that the Monarchy was a useful symbol of national unity and that 'Royalty, which is genuinely non-party, is one of the best safeguards against a revolutionary dictatorship, since it enables the Left when it reaches power to show itself as the real national government, His Majesty's Ministers of State.'[187] In this writing, he was primarily concerned with the protection of the non-partisan role of the Monarchy. He indicated that it served a constitutional purpose, but he did not go beyond that, simply accepting it as part of the constitution. It was not until 1963 that he considered the role of the Monarchy again. Again he indicated that it was an important symbol of national unity but he also argued that cabinet government was protected by the secrecy of Monarchy, which was far better than any republic could manage.[188] While he was aware of the flaws of Monarchy, and concerned about the role it could play in government, particularly a left wing government, he also saw the benefits of the Monarchy.

His first practical experience of Monarchy came in 1964 when he became a minister. As a new member of the Privy Council, he was required to take part in the 'kissing hands' ceremony. This was the kind of event which Crossman hated, where he was required to learn a specific protocol and follow it rigorously and, in his opinion, pointlessly. 'I don't suppose anything more dull, pretentious, or plain silly has ever been invented.'[189] Pimlott argued that 'where lower-middle-class and sentimental Harold Wilson loved the ceremonial aspects of Monarchy, Crossman was impatient with them. At any rate, this was the theory.'[190] While he objected to the ceremony of this occasion, when new ministers were eager to get on with their new jobs, he drew an important distinction between the Monarchy as an element of the constitution and the Queen as an individual. Despite having only very limited contact with her at this first meeting, he did seem to like the Queen. 'I found it was perfectly simple and straightforward to get on with her. Indeed she puts one at ease immediately and we were able to chat about other things fairly happily.'[191] He concluded that she did not really like the ceremonial fuss either, something on which he was in total agreement.

It was during the period 1966 to 1968 that Crossman came into much greater contact with the Queen. His role meant he was a point of contact between the Queen and the government, explaining the purpose of legislation and the actions of government to her. He again seems to have liked the Queen as an individual. However, he again objected to the system which surrounded her. An example of this was the Privy Council meeting held in September 1966:

> It's interesting to reflect that four ministers, busy men, all had to take a night and a day off and go up there [to Balmoral] with Godfrey Agnew to stand for two and a half minutes while the list of Titles was read out. It would be far simpler for the Queen to come back to Buckingham Palace, but it's *lese-majeste* to suggest it.[192]

The outdated procedure which prevailed between the government and the Monarchy was an irritation to Crossman. It did not fit in well with his position in a 'socialist' government committed to modernising Britain.

Crossman did not favour a republic and he did seem to like and respect the Queen. However, he did not approve of the elaborate ceremony which surrounded her. As an atheist, the Monarch's position as head of the Church of England was not particularly important to him, and he never gave it any consideration. He seems to have favoured a more modernised, slimmed down Monarchy, cutting out all of the unnecessary and excessive ceremony. 'Surely there must be a limit to which busy ministers are compelled to sacrifice their time to suit royal private engagements. This I think is unchivalrous.'[193] While not seeking to actively reform the Monarchy, something he would have been incapable of doing, he did not approve of its existing form, as a dignified part of the constitution with limited use.

Conclusion

While Crossman believed that he was a devoted advocate of constitutional reform, this was not an accurate depiction of his political career. As with many issues, while he had maintained an interest over many years and written some small-scale pamphlets and articles, he had not written anything particularly influential. His publications tended to be a continuation of the work of others, this being reflected in his desire to write a follow-up to Bagehot's *The English Constitution*, and his use of John Mackintosh to write the first drafts of his 1970 Godkin lectures, which he eventually discarded, writing an alternative script himself. This lack of innovation seems to have been due to his perception of an MP's life. It was not uncommon for MPs to have other jobs, often utilising their position in Parliament. However, this does not seem to have prevented others from dedicating themselves primarily to the House of Commons, becoming involved in the disputes and intrigues of the House, a balance that Crossman did not attain. Firstly, his position as a journalist, coupled with his tendency to speak his mind, led him into conflict with other MPs which was counter-productive and harmful to his political career, separating him from aspects of parliamentary life which he needed to experience to write a book on constitutional reform. He stated in 1974 that he knew 'no academic could write this book. It could only be done by someone who knew party politics from inside, and that must include council politics, parliamentary politics and, if possible, the politics of Whitehall and No. 10.'[194] Secondly, his journalism allowed him to become diverted from key debates and prevented him from effectively being at the heart of political life.

Some of his views developed and changed during his political career, but others were held as strongly in 1974 as they had been in 1939. He had initially believed that individual MPs needed to follow their own beliefs, even if this meant criticising their own party as he frequently did, particularly while a member of the Keep Left group from 1947 until approximately 1950. However, perhaps influenced by his time as Leader of the House of Commons, he considered in his 1970 Godkin lectures the idea of the 'battering-ram' of change:

> It is a humbling thought, for it reduces the sense of self-importance of any MP. It makes me realise that I am sent to Parliament because they want the party, the battering-ram, the mandate, not me. That's what left-wing politics are about; and that's why left-wing politics are rather more disciplined than right-wing politics.[195]

In addition, he was also forced during his career to consider elements of constitutional reform which he had never focused on before. The policy of morning sittings was not one which he supported, but he was required to implement it and consider how best to make it work. House of Lords reform was another issue which he was forced to consider in considerable detail, where he had previously limited himself to only the briefest of discussions on the issue in 1939 and 1956.

Some of his opinions, while not being significantly altered by either his time on the backbenches or his ministerial career, were mellowed as he grew older. While he heavily criticised his civil servants both in his cabinet diaries and in his evidence to the Fulton Committee, by 1970 he was moving the blame for inactivity and failure from the civil service to the cabinet and the governing party, indicating that it showed a lack of direction.[196] Crossman's aim for an accountable government remained strong, as did his commitment to select committees and the reform of the House of Lords. In 1970, four years before his death, he was still arguing that 'there are great difficulties in maintaining the morale of Parliament if you turn it into a forum with a sham battle between political oligarchies of this kind.'[197] On issues such as parliamentary accountability, Crossman's views changed very little, with the broad outlines being retained for much of his life.

The advantage which Crossman maintained over many other writers on constitutional reform was his position as a minister. This meant that unlike Mackintosh, Bagehot, Laski or Muir, he might actually get chance to institute change instead of simply writing about it. When he became Leader of the House of Commons in 1966, he was given a golden opportunity to implement change and secure his position within the constitutional reform debate, not as a thinker but as a doer.[198] However, his golden opportunity was not perhaps all that it initially seemed. He was fundamentally inexperienced in the House of Commons, leading him to make mistakes and accept information which a more experienced man would not have accepted so easily. His naivety could perhaps have been overcome were it not for the lack of enthusiasm displayed by the cabinet primarily. His plans, while interesting and perhaps shrewd, were never implemented despite his best efforts, and he moved to the Department of Health and Social Security, a department about which he knew quite a bit more. Had Crossman's reforms being instituted with more government backing, it is quite possible that they would have been considerably more successful and perhaps become a permanent feature of Parliament, as some of them have since. Had he managed to reform the House of Lords in 1968, his place in the constitutional reform debate would have been guaranteed. However, due to a combination of his own inexperience and his party's lack of unity on the issue, many of the reforms were lost at least in the short term, and he was relegated to a minor position within the constitutional reform debate.

6

Conclusion

Richard Crossman was an unusual individual within the Labour Party. He occupied several different roles within the party, and it was the combination of these that make him worthy of study. Not only was he an intellectual within politics, he was also a left wing MP in his early career, gradually becoming more of a centre-left figure, a supporter of Bevan and later Wilson, having difficult relationships with Attlee and later Gaitskell. He was a 'part-time' MP, often focusing his considerable attention on his journalistic writing, but he failed to produce in his lifetime a really important or influential book.[1] While his newspaper articles provided him with a platform from which he could argue and publicise his personal or party views, this often caused him considerable problems with other party members. While he tended to focus his personal attention on a limited number of issues, often maintaining an interest in them for much of his life, his journalism gained him a reputation as fickle and unfocused, flitting from one issue to another, a reputation which I have argued was not accurate.[2]

Socialism and Social Democracy

As was considered in chapter 3, the future of socialism was an area of conflict within the Labour Party before the Second World War, with differences being noted between the left and right wings of party. However, the debate seems to have become more entrenched and bitter when the Labour Party formed a government in 1945, a situation which continued after the party left power. Those on the left of the party, such as Bevan and Mikardo sought more nationalisation than the Attlee government had instituted, continuing the process that had been started. Those on the right of the party were hoping after 1950 to consolidate the nationalisation which had been introduced, allowing these industries to adapt to their new circumstances. The publication in 1956 of Anthony Crosland's *The Future of Socialism* offered another alternative, arguing that nationalisation was becoming less relevant in the developing industrial sector of Britain, due to the changing hierarchies within industry. Crosland argued that a Labour government needed to focus more on management to make effective changes:

For practical purposes, therefore, economic decisions in the basic sector have passed out of the hands of the capitalist class into the hands of a new and largely autonomous class of public managers ... of course, this leaves open the question of whether nationalisation is always the only, or the best, method of achieving this result.[3]

While Crossman was one of the most formidable intellectuals on the left of the party, he was not a great thinker about socialism, certainly not in the same way as Crosland or Durbin.[4] He supported nationalisation in principle in the late 1940s and early 1950s, but he only advocated it in a limited number of small-scale industries coming to believe that it was really a secondary issue.[5] Often, he focused on more peripheral issues relating to socialism, including the economic development of the Soviet Union immediately after the Second World War and the related issue of liberty and personal freedom, both of which were being sacrificed in the USSR in pursuit of economic development. While he periodically wrote on the future of socialism and the economic situation in the USSR, this issue could not really be considered a constant priority for Crossman. Instead, he considered the issue more fleetingly, failing to be regarded an expert on the issue or produce a definitive account of his, or the Bevanite group's, approach to socialism and nationalisation.

However, Crossman did produce four pamphlet length works on socialism, focusing particularly on the USSR and individual freedom which was very much closer to his heart. He believed that the five-year economic plans of the USSR were an important tool for improving the economic situation of the country, perhaps something which could be adapted and introduced in Britain – an outcome he alleged would be very beneficial.[6] He believed that the government needed to be involved in the planning of the industrial sector, but he did not outline any specific policies or actions which could achieve this, or even which particular aspects of economic planning would be advantageous.[7] His views on nationalisation were already in flux by the time his Fabian pamphlet, *Labour and the Affluent Society* was published in 1960. These had never been particularly deep-rooted, with him focusing on other issues, such as Israel, to a far greater extent.

The reasons for this change seem to have been his personal circumstances and his move away from the Bevanites to becoming a Wilsonite in the mid-1950s. News of humanitarian atrocities was beginning to emerge from the USSR, but while Crossman noted in his writing that the preservation of individual liberty was of paramount importance, he did not reject the achievements of the USSR, merely criticising the abuses of power and noting that all socialists detested the denial of freedom in the communist State.[8] This seems very strange for an individual who was so deeply committed to personal freedom as Crossman. He appears to have been swept along by the 'economic miracle' which the USSR was experiencing, unwilling to extensively criticise them when they were being so successful economically. It seems likely that he was not particularly interested in the issue, having some knowledge of the totalitarian regime's practices, but failing to speak out.

While never a strong supporter of nationalisation as a practical policy, Crossman nonetheless remained relatively positive about its use in certain circumstances for much of the 1950s. In 1959/60, Crossman along with Wilson questioned the merits of challenging Clause IV, as Gaitskell was. However, it seems that Crossman had begun to view nationalisation as a fairly redundant policy. His 1960 Fabian pamphlet, *Labour in the Affluent Society*, argued that the five year plan and nationalisation might be usefully adapted to suit Britain but this pamphlet is very different in tone and content to any of his other writing and it seems likely that it was a reaction to the Clause IV debate and his break with Gaitskell.[9] The opinions which he expressed in this pamphlet were very short lived and he told David Isaacs that 'I never felt deeply about nationalisation. But I knew that the sentiments of the Left had this irrational attachment to it.'[10] Isaacs did not report when Crossman made these comments, but they were a reaction to Gaitskell's attempt to re-write Clause IV of the Labour Party's constitution in 1959. They illustrate how far Crossman had moved away from the left wing and calls for nationalisation during his political career which, as was noted earlier, he had supported in 1951 in selected industries.

Crossman's views on liberty and the preservation of individual freedom were an important element in his writing on socialism and social democracy. He believed that it was vital that the public be taught how to defend their individual liberties against government, regardless of its political complexion, protecting the individual against the excesses of the state. William Gwyn stated that some members of the Labour Party were worried about 'the stigma of illiberalism and bureaucracy which their political opponents have attributed to them.' He argued that the illiberal or statist image which the party had gained was electorally damaging and therefore individuals within the party, such as Crossman, needed to promote libertarian policies.[11] While Crossman never expressed a great concern for the electoral implications of his views, he did believe that by teaching and educating the public on how to resist governmental forces, violent revolution could be avoided.

Gwyn noted that the Labour Party was made up on two main strands of opinion in regard to freedom and liberty. The first group, which Gwyn labelled liberal socialists, adopted the traditions of liberalism in regard to liberty. Within this group he included Crossman, Crosland and Jenkins along with the majority of the Gaitskellites, though he also noted that Bevan and Foot were passionate defenders of personal liberty. Unlike the more conservative Fabian group within the party, the liberal socialists believed that individual liberty was an important part of socialism which required protection and even reform. The existing constitutional arrangements were not enough to protect people from government.[12] Gwyn concluded that Crossman was a 'persistent and influential [reformer]' based on his long-term interest in the defence of liberty and personal freedom.[13] Secondly he identified a group within the party based around the Fabian or Webbian argument that the existing parliamentary arrangements were enough to protect individuals and prevent abuses of the system. This group also tended to believe that the civil service in Britain was 'the most capable and trustworthy in the world' so maladministration was not a genuine concern.[14]

Crossman's views on socialism and social democracy, like many of his political views, became less radical during his lifetime with an accelerated conservatism becoming evident during his time as a minister. His views on socialism became of only marginal importance to him after 1964, with his diaries instead filled with departmental details and personal comment. While reluctant to admit it, Crossman gradually realised his more establishment attitudes, attributing this to his time in government and the impact of his lifestyle at his manor house. Interestingly, he asked himself if the basis of his socialist views made him more immune to an affluent lifestyle. He noted in early 1967 that 'my radical passions have never been based on a moral or egalitarian philosophy. It's been really an expression of my bump of irreverence, based on my conviction that governments and establishments are fools and that participation by the people will probably improve government in this country.'[15] As part of that government and establishment, he failed to consider if that made him and his colleagues fools.

One issue which he noted within his diaries as having a big influence on his life was Prescote, his 360-acre farm near Banbury. Crossman's continual self-analysis forced him to consider whether his surroundings and increasingly affluent lifestyle had had any impact on his political views, both in terms of his radicalism and in terms of the issues which he was interested in. Additionally, he was concerned that perhaps Prescote was reducing his interest in his political life, providing him with an alternative focus to the House of Commons. Writing in 1965, he addressed these issues head-on:

> What a difference it makes to be able to come back here to the sheer comfort of Prescote, and its beauty and rootedness, which is more and more influencing me. Is it making me more conservative? Well, in one sense being rooted is being conservative. But I don't think it is making me less adventurous in my ideas, less prepared to take risks. On the contrary I am more self-confident as the result of my married life, more ready to try radical measures even if they risk my being thrown out of my job. The radical measures which excite me are not anti-property measures in the sense that they would require us to accept the confiscation of Prescote. On the other hand I am sure Prescote has taught me a lot more about economic growth, about capital investment, about business, about tax law, than I knew before.[16]

While he may have concluded that Prescote had not particularly affected his radicalism, this was a piece of self-deception. Prescote, coupled with his ministerial position after 1964 compounded Crossman's increasingly conservative attitude to certain issues, reflected in his attitude to the student demonstrations in Europe in

1968. He commented on 'how depressing is the student movement all over the Western world, these curious student revolutionaries in America, France and West Germany and, of course, to a lesser extent in Britain.' He described those who took part in the demonstrations and riots as the 'spearhead of anarchist, Maoist, Che Guevarist revolutions, all infantile.'[17] While he might never have supported the political views of those involved in the movement, he would have, in the 1940s and 50s, defended their right to be heard in a peaceful way. Here we see how Crossman's attitude to popular movements during his political career had changed.

While Crossman favoured, early in his career, the ability of the public to resist governmental action, by 1967 he noted that his earlier views have been abandoned. 'Ever since I was a young Don I've believed in the WEA [Workers' Educational Association], in training the mass of the people for responsibility for self-government and I've been convinced that if we used education for that purpose we would be able to substitute genuine social democracy for oligarchy.'[18] His earlier desire for a true representative democracy had been abandoned by 1967, probably due to his experience as a minister and his attempts at reforming the constitutional arrangements in Britain. He explained his disillusionment in early 1968, in a fit of depression on the future of British democracy:

> I can't help wondering if the whole of my life has been lived in vain and if that is not the reason why I'm so glad to have given up adult education and journalism and taken on a spell as a professional politician – a member of the ruling establishment … I've abandoned the aims in which I believed in the WEA and I now accept that the settled and just management of society by a progressive oligarchy is possibly the best we can hope for.[19]

These periods of disillusionment became more frequent in the last two years of his ministerial career. While Crossman argued that his changing views were not influenced by his life at Prescote, there are numerous occasions in his diaries where he links his changing views with Prescote and the change he perceived in his own social standing. In 1968, he experienced a moment of rare clarity and understanding on the impact his affluence had made on his views. 'Does this wealth blunt our socialism? The answer, I'm afraid, is that of course it does. It means that we look at things from the top and this stratospheric approach is accentuated in my case by the little attention I have to pay to my constituency.'[20] He believed that his new status as a landowner, of which he was so proud, affected how others responded to him, even the Prime Minister. He noted in 1965 that 'Harold's strength is that he has no kind of inferiority complex but lives his own real, natural life. He doesn't respect the upper classes for having superior cultural tastes which he would like to share. He won't hold it against me that I live in a lovely manor house in the country and he doesn't.'[21]

While Crossman may have shrunk back from the label, he became part of the establishment he so fiercely criticised but so desperately wanted to join when he moved to Prescote. While he still maintained his juvenile opposition to wearing dinner jackets and attending formal functions, this was really the last remnant of his radical nature. He described his response to the 'idiotic flummery' of the Privy Council meetings and how he felt 'morally superior to his colleagues in despising it.'[22] While Prescote may well have widened Crossman's horizons in terms of the policies he was interested in, it should be noted that he did not utilise this knowledge in cabinet, where he sometimes fell asleep, or ignored discussion until his own departmental business was raised. Writing in 1967, he commented that he could not really record in his diary the content of Roy Jenkins' Race Relations Bill 'because I was sound asleep.' Either as a reassurance to himself or his readers he continued 'I do sometimes sleep in cabinet but I've never failed to wake up before we reach my item on the agenda.'[23] Additionally, it must be remembered that he spent the bulk of every week living in Vincent Square in London rather than in Banbury, and that he and his wife, Anne had a manager for the farm, Pritchett, who dealt with much of the day-to-day business.

Crossman's basis for socialism, his 'bump or irreverence' was not only rather narrow, it was also incredibly flimsy and rootless. Essentially, his brand of socialism was whatever he considered radical or unpopular with the ruling classes, regardless of the policy details. Healey noted an argument he had with him where Crossman argued that as a socialist it was his duty to 'automatically … oppose anything which was being proposed', a situation Healey thought was intolerable.[24] While Crossman remained convinced that his bump of irreverence remained intact during his time as a minister, the conventional way in which he admitted he dealt with problems and his acceptance of privilege indicates that this was not the case, with him becoming an accepted part of the establishment.[25] His developing views on socialism and his gradual withdrawal from the issue reinforced the view that he became more conservative, and less socialist, throughout his lifetime.

Foreign Policy

As chapter 4 outlined, Crossman's thinking on foreign policy was somewhat more coherent than his thinking on social democracy. In his early political career, he tended to confine himself to writing on foreign affairs, as he believed that his wartime experience qualified him to offer an opinion on certain foreign policy issues.[26] Radhika Desai argued that the Bevanites tended to focus on foreign policy issues due to a 'lack of concrete proposals for domestic reform.'[27] While Crossman spent much of his time before 1955 focusing on Israel, he also spent time writing and speaking on several other foreign policy issues, including the gradual rehabilitation of Germany after the Second World War, the position which Britain should occupy within Europe, and Britain's role in the Cold War. While his views changed and developed, after 1955 his preoccupation with foreign affairs began to diminish and he lost interest in many of these issues. Even those of particular interest to him, such as the future of Israel, became much less important after 1955.

From 1945 until 1950/1 Crossman favoured some form of united Europe. While he did not envisage an organisation like the EEC, he did favour some form of loose European grouping where discussion could lead to greater understanding across the continent. While not an idealistic thinker, his views on the future of Europe were optimistic, calling for a third force with Europe being a 'superpower' along with the USA and the USSR. 'The security of each and all of us depends on preventing the division of Europe into exclusive spheres of influence.'[28] This force would provide Britain with an alternative power base, rather than being a pawn of one of the two larger superpowers. Crossman's thinking on this issue was in line with many of those on the left wing of the Labour Party at this time, highlighted by his role in the 1947 publication of *Keep Left*, a pamphlet which was supported by the members of the group of the same name.[29] This publication called for Britain to implement a socialist foreign policy, preserving Britain's role within the world, supported by Europe and the USSR if necessary. The USA was viewed with suspicion and distrust with a distinctly eastern focused policy being advocated. Calls for a socialist foreign policy were almost immediately dropped after the publication of *Keep Left* and Crossman did not call for such a policy again. The reason for this seems to have been the changing international situation, with the USSR gradually retreating behind the iron curtain and the USA participating in the rebuilding of Europe.[30]

His views on Europe began to change during the early 1950s as the ECSC (and later the EEC) began to develop, becoming more federalist in nature than he would have hoped for or accepted. By 1962 he was having reservations about Britain's role within such an organisation, which turned into hostility for the community by 1967, stating that he was in favour of Britain becoming an 'off-shore island'.[31] As early as 1969, Crossman was describing himself as a 'little Englander'.[32] In 1972 he wrote a letter to the Duchess of Bedford, outlining his objections to Britain joining the EEC:

> I am afraid I regard January 1 next year as a black day in our history; more particularly since we are being dragged into the Market against the will of the majority of the voters and in a state of complete economic disarray which will render us quite incapable of standing up to the rigours to which we shall be submitted.[33]

As Crossman's views on a socialist foreign policy and Britain's role in Europe were moulded by external events, he began to reassess his views on Britain's relationship with the USA. While he had been hostile to the USA and critical of her influence over Britain, there seems to have been a fairly rapid change in his views in 1947-8. This was caused by the activities of the USSR and her eventual disengagement from the western world, and by the willingness of the USA to become involved in the rebuilding of Britain and other European countries, primarily through Marshall Aid. Henry Pelling noted that the left wing of the party viewed the USA as 'the greatest stronghold of private enterprise, on which the reform of the New Deal had made little impression.'[34] It can be seen that Crossman, Mikardo and Foot all concurred with this view of the USA in *Keep Left*. Pelling argued that the offer of Marshall aid encouraged those on the left to view America with less suspicion. However, by 1950 when the Korean War began, the left wing of the Labour Party had changed their views on the USA again, external forces heavily influencing their opinions:

> Just as, in the period of the Marshall Plan, the Labour Left had found ideological reasons for its friendship with America by emphasizing the significance of the Fair Deal and Truman's Fourth Point, and exaggerating the political importance of the American labour movement, so now the Bevanites justified their alienation by stressing the instability of American capitalism, the likelihood of an early economic depression in the United States, the influence of 'big business' in the counsels of the Republican Party ... and finally, the irresponsible character of the anti-communist "witch-hunt" which reached its climax under Senator McCarthy's leadership in 1953-4.[35]

While Pelling noted the general trends of left wing thinking, Crossman did not fit easily into this mould from 1948 onwards. His views on the USA began to change in late 1947 or early 1948, due to the announcement of Marshall aid, and the actions of the USA in Palestine. From 1946 onwards, Crossman was in favour of the partitioning of Palestine and the creation of a Jewish homeland, opinions which were in step with those held by many of the American administration. This convergence of views coupled with the investment in European reconstruction seems to have led him to alter his views on the USA, though he remained opposed to Britain become an American satellite. In 1951 he said 'I believe that, as socialists, we have to accept the fact that we have far more in common with the United States than we ever had, or could have had, with the USSR.'[36] While he was never enthusiastically pro-American, being far more interested in maintaining Britain's international position by working with various other informal groupings and individual nations, events had overtaken his earlier views, encouraging him to view America with less suspicion. Crossman's views on America were not particularly popular among the left wing of the party, and his gradual acceptance of the US seems to shadow his ideological move within the party, moving from being on the left wing to being more of a centre left figure by 1955-6.

Israel was the foreign policy issue closest to Crossman's heart, and an issue in which he maintained an interest for much of his life. While he had been ignorant of the situation in the Middle East before joining the Anglo-American Commission in 1945, once he was educated on the subject, he wholeheartedly supported the creation of a Jewish homeland. His main period of activity on the issue of Israel was between 1945 and 1949, writing pro-Israeli articles and encouraging the

Labour Party, along with several other high-profile individuals, to support Israel and recognise it once it had declared its independence in 1948. However, once it had been established and its survival seemed more assured, he began to disengage gradually from the issue. After 1955, he maintained his interest in Israel while losing interest in other foreign policy issues, though his writing was considerably decreased. He remained good friends with Chaim Weizmann until his death in 1952 and gave three lectures in Israel in 1960, published as *A Nation Reborn* focusing on Israel's past and future.[37] Israel was very important to Crossman and while he remained interested in its survival and prosperity, once its survival was assured, he began to step back from the issue. This shift was highlighted by Crossman in 1967 when he referred to the two totally committed Zionists in the cabinet being Ray Gunter and Bert Bowden, failing to include himself in this description.[38]

Constitutional Reform

As was considered in chapter 5, Crossman's interest in constitutional reform was long-term but intermittent. He had first written on the constitutional arrangements of Britain in 1939, but he failed in *How Britain is Governed* to offer recommendations for reform.[39] He did not write on the issue again until he published *Socialism and the New Despotism* in 1956, offering in this Fabian pamphlet some detail on his preferred reforms for the future, linking his views on liberty and personal freedom with constitutional reform.[40] His most famous publication on the constitution was the introduction he wrote for the 1963 reprint of Walter Bagehot's *The English Constitution* where he considered various styles of cabinet, building on John Mackintosh's 1962 publication *The British Cabinet*.[41] Crossman was eager to produce another work like Bagehot's book on the constitution, going beyond describing the constitution and including proposals for reform. His ambition was to write a comparable study on the modern working of Parliament, using his experience as a backbencher to support his views. 'By 1961 I had collected enough firm information to write a book on the working of the two-party system inside and outside Westminster, but my knowledge of government was all gathered from academic textbooks and the gossip of the smoking room.'[42] It is difficult to conceive how he could have written this book without the experience and knowledge he gained as a minister.

Crossman's interest in constitutional reform might have remained sporadic were it not for his appointment in 1966 as Leader of the House of Commons and Lord President of the Council. His position meant that he could be involved in the reform of both House of Commons procedures and the composition and power of the Lords, utilising his theorising to put in place practical reforms. Unfortunately, his plans were never instituted and while he continued to write about constitutional reform from time to time, most notably in his 1970 Godkin lectures, his interest in even this issue began to wane.[43] When he left government in 1970, he failed to write his book on constitutional reform because of other commitments, such as his biography of Chaim Weizmann which was itself left unfinished, due to his declining health. Crossman focused his attention instead on the editing of his political diaries.

One issue which was of particular interest to Crossman, showing his developing thinking on various elements of constitutional reform, was the importance of the individual MP. While he had been, in his early career, a rebellious MP, acting on his own instincts and defending the left wing views of his constituency first and foremost, he gradually began to accept over time that the required role of the MP might be very different to that which he had occupied. His nineteen years as a backbencher gave Crossman plenty of time to reflect on this issue, though he admitted that he had not learnt much about House of Commons procedure from his time on the backbenches, something his civil servants were well aware of.[44] Influenced by his time as Leader of the House of Commons, where it was part of his job to maintain some form of discipline and unity within the party, he considered in his 1970 Godkin lectures the idea of the 'battering-ram' of change.[45]

This theory placed emphasis on the role of the party rather than the individual MP, noting that the electorate tended to vote for a party representative rather than for an individual MP or candidate:

> It is a humbling thought, for it reduces the sense of self-importance of any MP. It makes me realise that I am sent to Parliament because they want the party, the battering-ram, the mandate, not me. That's what left-wing politics are about; and that's why left-wing politics are rather more disciplined than right-wing politics.[46]

Crossman argued that left wing politics tended to be focused on the movement, not on any one individual MP. This is a complete contradiction of his earlier opinions or the role in which he cast himself when he first became an MP. He was a rebel, aligning himself with the left wing of the party, becoming extremely unpopular with some of the most powerful figures in the Labour Party. His gradual move to a more central position in the party made him equally unpopular with those on the left of the party. Mikardo described Crossman and Wilson as 'operators, wire-pullers, bargainers, persuaders, dealers, manoeuvrers, fixers.'[47] Had Crossman believed he was part of a 'battering-ram' at this point, his actions would undoubtedly have been different, causing him to have less fractious relationships with other individuals within the party.

While Crossman's time as Leader of the House forced him to consider discipline and the importance of individual MPs, the Silkin-Crossman disciplinary code was not particularly restrictive, suggesting that he was not convinced of the case while Leader of the House of Commons. It seems likely that his views did not fully change until he had become Secretary of State for Health and Social Security. While he would not have discouraged conviction politicians, as in his early career he could have been considered one of these himself, over issues such as Israel or the rearmament of Germany, he began to appreciate the difficulties of maintaining a united party line, and the problems which this posed in the Commons. The reason for this change seems to have been his increasing age and his time as Leader of the House of Commons. His views on individual freedom changed over time, so that by 1970, on the majority of issues, MPs could be viewed as only one small part of a collective.

Some of Crossman's opinions while not being significantly altered by either his time on the backbenches or his ministerial career, were mellowed as he became older. While he had heavily criticised the civil service in his cabinet diaries and in his evidence to the Fulton Committee, his 1970 Godkin lectures failed to blame the service for inactivity and failure, arguing that they had not deliberately blocked government plans. Instead, he blamed the cabinet and the governing party for a lack of direction in policy which had led to a lack of cohesive or radical action.[48] His desire for an accountable government, which was at the root of much of his thinking on constitutional reform and the basis for the proposed House of Lords reform, remained strong, as did his commitment to select committees and the reform of the composition and power of the Lords. In 1970, four years before his death, Crossman was still arguing that 'there are great difficulties in maintaining the morale of Parliament if you turn it into a forum with a sham battle between political oligarchies of this kind.'[49]

Crossman had a rather negative view of civil servants when he entered government. As a backbencher, he had become convinced, probably wrongly, that certain ministers, such as Gaitskell and Bevin, were being hoodwinked by their civil servants into accepting policies which were not suited to a Labour government, one of these being an abandonment of Labour's pre-1945 election pledge to support a Jewish homeland in Palestine.[50] In 1946, he and Michael Foot argued that 'these officials [within the Colonial and Foreign Offices] are the advisers and the executants of the policies of a Labour Foreign Secretary and a Labour Colonial Secretary, and we can be sure that they have not been backward in presenting Mr Bevin and Mr George Hall the case for a political ceiling on Jewish immigration, and against the full development of the National Home.'[51] Writing in 1939, he had voiced his concerns over recruitment to the service arguing that 'its character and training are suited to keep the present machine in running order, not to reconstruct it.'[52] Harold Laski had already raised this issue the previous year. He had argued that 'a civil service ... needs not only the able routineer; it needs also the ardent inventor who can disturb the routine; and my own doubt is whether the system either breeds that type or is able adequately to assimilate it when it rarely discovers one.'[53] As can be seen here, Crossman relied very heavily on the work of others, often simply reaffirming or building on their original ideas. It is rare, both in terms of his views on constitutional reform and on other issues, for the original idea to have been his. Instead he utilised the work of others, often failing to give them credit, as in the case of Laski above.

Henry Drucker argued that the political leanings of ministers and MPs affected how they viewed the activities and motives of their civil servants. He argued that those on the left wing of the party were distrustful of their civil servants, failing to utilise them properly at least in the short term. Speaking about Crossman and Castle, he argued that 'both remained deeply suspicious of their role as ministers and both resisted its claims on them.'[54] He categorised Crossman's views on the civil service as being left wing, but by 1964 he was certainly not on the left wing of the party.

While Crossman can be identified as a left wing MP from 1945 until the early 1950s, by 1955/6 when Gaitskell became leader of the party, he was not a Bevanite, and was instead much more of a Wilsonite. His views on many issues were incredibly simplistic for such a gifted individual, and there does not seem to have been, at this time, any consistent set of ideological principles supporting them. He seems to have considered many issues on an individual basis rather than within any ideological framework, meaning that some of his views remained fairly left wing in character, such as his desire for a more accountable and reformed House of Lords, while his views on other issues were far more right wing, such as his developing views on taxation. Additionally, there are numerous examples of left wing ministers who enjoyed good working relationships with their civil servants. Barbara Castle, who Drucker argued was initially suspicious of her civil servants, had very good relationships with them, and Michael Foot noted that Bevan also had good relations with his civil servants in the Ministry of Health. 'Any fears of a boorish intruder vanished. He was positively gentle. The one place where he schooled his temper most successfully was with his ministerial department.'[55] Bearing this in mind, the categorisation that Drucker made is very difficult to defend and does not accurately represent Crossman's developing views or indeed the actions and attitudes of many left wing ministers. His argument, while interesting, needs to be treated with caution due to the lack of subtlety in his categorisation.[56]

When Crossman became a minister in 1964, he was intent on making his presence felt in his new department, which is exactly what he did. His relationship with Dame Evelyn Sharp, his Permanent Secretary and a formidable civil servant, was notoriously difficult and his attitude was often disliked by civil servants, who felt he was a bully and very difficult to work for.[57] His evidence to the Fulton Committee in 1967 showed the civil service in a very negative light, a view which was not universally shared or accepted. As has been previously mentioned, many ministers on both wings of the party, had very good relationships with their civil servants, including Patrick Gordon-Walker, Barbara Castle, Ernest Bevin, Aneurin Bevan and Harold Wilson. The majority of the views expressed to the Fulton Committee by Labour MPs and ministers were very positive in terms of the attitude and capabilities of the civil service.[58] However, Crossman's views on the civil service began to change during his ministerial career, influenced by his experience. While he accepted in 1964 that civil servants would bury legislation they disliked and could bring bills to a standstill while they were being researched and written in the department, he began to see them in a different light, musing in 1966 that perhaps their lack of activity was more understandable than he had initially thought.[59] In his 1970 Godkin lectures, he accepted that the civil service was not responsible for the failures of the Wilson government, indicating that they had been handicapped, as many ministers had, by the lack of any concrete plans both before entering government and during their tenure. Crossman argued that where the Labour government failed 'it was because *we* failed. We just have not done our job when we had the chance to do it.'[60]

While Crossman had started his career as a rebellious backbencher, his actions gradually became less factious and, while he was still able to cause chaos and difficulties for the party leader and his colleagues, this was often unintentional. His opinions also mellowed over time, undoubtedly reflecting his increasing age as well as other external factors. In 1967 Crossman wrote that,

> In my old age I find that the moral motives for radical change (which in my case were never very strong) tend to weaken and I see the case for change more and more either in strictly functional terms – the adaption of institutions to changing circumstances in accordance with most strictly utilitarian and technical considerations – or alternatively in terms of my ever-growing conviction that –at least in our British public life – whatever is is *(sic)* likely to turn out on investigation to be an entrenched defence of selfish and usually rather stupid vested self-interest.[61]

Here, not only can the effect of his age be seen, but also the flimsy nature of his earlier views which, like those he held on socialism and social democracy, were based on a very weak basis – that of radicalism for the sake of it.

While Crossman did maintain his interest in certain issues, he considered issues he was less interested in only briefly, often lacking any real understanding of the fundamentals of the debate or detailed proposals for change. These include devolution for Scotland and Wales and electoral reform, which Crossman seems to have almost completely overlooked, tending to focus on them only when forced by external circumstances, or by the persistence of his Parliamentary Private Secretary (PPS), Tam Dalyell. Duncan Tanner argued that 'although Crossman edited out some of his growing enthusiasm for regional assemblies all round the published versions of his diary, the uncut version of the diary and letters in other collections show that he too was enthusiastic about regional parliaments.'[62] While the unpublished diaries do show the amount of time which Crossman spent on this issue while Leader of the House of Commons was more than the published diaries suggest, the reasons for this are not clear. Tanner indicated that he had deliberately edited his published diaries to omit details of devolution, as he was no longer in favour of the scheme he had been working on briefly.[63]

However, it has been previously noted in chapter 1 that Janet Morgan took on much of the editing of the *Cabinet Diaries*, especially volumes 2 and 3 covering his time as Leader of the House and Secretary of State for Health and Social Security, with the specific remit of preventing Crossman from rewriting his career. Other policy areas were expunged or minimised by Morgan, seemingly on the basis that while they occupied Crossman for a short time, they were not issues he had maintained any interest in beyond the first flash of inspiration, and they were not particularly important within the larger context of his career such as the economic development of China, and it seems likely that regional assemblies fell into this category.

Intellectuals in Politics

The Labour Party during the 1950s and 60s contained numerous individuals who could easily be labelled as intellectuals in politics. Radhika Desai has argued that the Labour Party had initially been hostile to the 'theorization of its programme and strategy,' but by the early 1960s, the party had consolidated its position as the 'thinking man's party'. 'There was a remarkable increase of intellectuals in the Labour Party and, in a reflection of the importance accorded to them in British state and society generally during wartime and post-war reconstruction, there seemed to be a greater welcome and far less suspicion of them in the Labour Party too.'[64] Desai identified certain intellectuals in politics, including Hugh Gaitskell, Douglas Jay, Anthony Crosland and Richard Crossman amongst many. While Harold Wilson and Barbara Castle were both university-educated and very capable MPs, Desai did not categorise them as intellectuals in politics.

An intellectual in politics is distinguished from an intellectual politician in this biography by their desire to theorise party policy, something which Wilson and Castle rarely did. Both Ben Pimlott and Philip Ziegler noted in their biographies of Wilson that he was not particularly interested or concerned with theorising or ideologies, instead focusing on practical policy issues. Ziegler described Wilson as the 'Gritty Yorkshireman', an observation which Crossman had also made, noting that these kind of men 'are also expected to be pragmatic and to distrust, if not invariably avoid, flights of fancy or reflective theorising. Henry Kissinger marvelled as Wilson's indifference to abstract ideas.'[65] Pimlott noted that *The Observer* 'counted it an advantage, as far as the approval of rank-and-file trade-unionist MPs were concerned, that – though brainy – he [Wilson] was not an intellectual in the normal sense…'[66] Geoffrey Goodman noted that

Denis Healey is wrong in his assessment of Wilson as a man who had 'neither political principle' nor 'sense of direction'. Wilson did have both – embedded not in ideology but in his intuitive sense of decency and his powerful drive to try and spread that decency among his fellow citizens. Not classical socialist doctrine, but a profound belief that the Labour Party was the instrument in his hands for the establishment of social decency.[67]

Wilson's more practical approach seems to have been popular with the electorate, but his lack of theorising while an MP excludes him from the category of intellectuals in politics.

Intellectuals in politics could be seen to fulfil specific roles within political parties. In her book *Intellectuals and Socialism*, Desai struggled to find a suitable definition for this category of politicians. Instead she worked on Gramsci's definition of an 'organic intellectual'. 'The intellectual function in socialist politics hitherto has actually tended to be performed by those Gramsci called 'traditional' intellectuals (not linked to either capital or labour) who were capable of elaborating larger visions of social order which could form the basis of its hegemonic ambitions.'[68] For the purpose of this study, the definition which will be used has a fairly wide scope. An intellectual in politics will be defined as an intellectual who occupied a political role within a party and utilised their intellectual ability to theorise on specific policies and ideologies. Crossman noted that 'the intellectual in politics is always "unbalanced" in the estimation of his colleagues. He peers round the next corner while they keep their eyes on the road; and he risks his faith on unrealized ideas, instead of confining it prudently to humdrum loyalties. He is "in advance" and in this sense, an "extremist."'[69] This definition is interesting for two reasons. Firstly, it is a useful definition of what an intellectual in politics is and how they differ from other MPs. Secondly, and perhaps more importantly, it is the definition which Crossman gave to these kind of MPs, and it seems to have been a category which he wanted to be included in.

As thinkers and 'deconstructers' of complex ideas, it seems plausible that intellectuals would bring these skills with them to the political arena as well as any relevant specialist knowledge they might have, such as Crosland's economic training. For certain individuals, such as Crossman, their academic speciality was not relevant to their political career (he studied and taught classics which had rather limited direct use in the political arena) but their general academic approach could certainly be utilised. Intellectuals could often highlight the pitfalls of policies or ideologies and be charged with the task of remoulding these. This tendency could make intellectuals particularly unpopular within their own parties, encouraging the perception that they lacked loyalty to the party, focusing instead on policy initiatives.

While intellectuals in politics may have different methods to other types of MPs, their motivations remained very similar. However, the personality differences between intellectuals would affect their behaviour, making some more popular or more problematic than others. As with the other types of politicians, such as trade union MPs or MPs with a business background, some intellectuals in politics seemed to have revelled in their unpopularity while others avoided it whenever possible. Crossman did not seem to mind being unpopular, perhaps even enjoying his notoriety. Obviously, the differing positions these individuals occupied within the party affected their views, with leadership candidates needing to maintain their popularity. It is important to consider the varying roles that intellectuals within political parties fulfil, particularly individuals who occupy differing sectors of the political world. By studying these traits and varying roles, we can add another dimension to our study of Crossman, and discover whether personal traits and opinions motivated his actions, or whether they were stimulated by his intellectual training, therefore being more widespread among intellectuals in politics. It can also be determined whether he was representative of all intellectuals within politics or a specific set of intellectuals, perhaps limited to his political party.

In order to analyse these issues, this section will consider the different attitudes and activities of four intellectuals, both MPs and influential figures within the parties. These will be Harold Laski, Anthony Crosland, Richard Crossman and Keith Joseph. These four intellectuals have been specifically chosen as they share some obvious similarities but have differing traits and experiences, ensuring that the conclusions reached are not skewed due to party preference or time period. Laski, Crosland and Crossman were all Labour Party members, while Joseph was a Conservative MP. Crosland and Crossman were commonly seen as occupying opposite wings of the Labour Party, but were both active in the same time period as Joseph, though Joseph's career lasted longer, continued on into the 1980s, while Laski was a left wing member of the Labour Party earlier than the other intellectuals, though not an MP. He was, however, an influential member of the NEC, being chairman from 1945 to 1946 like Crossman, who was chairman from 1960 to 1961. It can then be concluded whether Crossman was an intellectual in politics.

It is necessary here to give some details of our chosen intellectuals. Harold Laski was not an MP, and he is therefore slightly different to the other intellectuals who are considered here. Laski was a Professor at the London School of Economics and Political Science, but this was coupled with his position within the Labour Party. He was a member of the NEC, published numerous books and articles on his own political views and on aspects of political science. Anthony Crosland is often regarded as being a typical intellectual in politics, combining his role as an MP with a prolific and influential publishing career and he is generally considered a great thinker within the party. Crossman noted in 1969 that Crosland had 'not proved himself a good minister, he is too dilettante, too much of an intellectual.'[70] Another typical example is Keith Joseph, a Conservative MP who many believe was Margaret Thatcher's Svengali, being, at the very least, an influence upon her economic ideology. Hugo Young described the Thatcher-Joseph relationship as 'one of the most formative political relationships of modern times.'[71] He was credited as being the driving force behind the formation of the Centre for Policy Studies (CPS) within the Conservative Party.

It is important firstly to consider whether intellectuals in politics have similar motivations to MPs with other backgrounds or interests. Intellectuals are often considered to be unrealistic, being more committed to abstract ideas and ideologies than to practical policies and actions. This suggests a lack of dedication or loyalty to the party or its ideological framework. However, Richard English and Michael

Kenny have suggested that as an intellectual becomes more integrated into their political party, they become more loyal to the organisation rather than the ideology that underpins the policies. 'A popular explanation is that in the British case intellectuals were particularly prone to integration within the political and cultural establishments and that there was a consequent diminishing of space for public intellectuals to operate in an autonomous or independent fashion.'[72] Their article focuses primarily on public intellectuals, though no definitive definition of a public intellectual is provided. It seems likely that public intellectuals are individuals who are accepted as intellectuals by the academic community and engage with the public, focusing on world issues. This group therefore does not seem to include intellectuals in politics, who are working within the political arena. However, Miliband categorised Laski as a public intellectual.[73] Without a definition it can be difficult to accurately categorise an individual, due to their varied activities. However, for the purposes of this study, for the reasons outlined above, Laski will be categorised as an intellectual in politics. Intellectuals in politics are already integrated into the political party or establishment when they become party members or MPs and therefore while the impression of disloyalty may linger in the minds of their colleagues, there seems to be little truth in this.

The careers of Crossman and Crosland seem to reflect this gradually increasing loyalty to the party. Both started their careers with a specific ideological approach, though Crosland's seems to have been more coherent and therefore more firmly held, but these developed and changed over time. In Crosland's case, he was able, due to his intellectual capacity, to write some very influential material which had a considerable effect on the views of others. Crossman was undoubtedly gifted, being referred to by Desai as a man whose 'intellectual vitality often outshone that of the revisionists...'[74] However, he very rarely disciplined himself, leading his arguments to be simplistic, lacking in detail and unable to survive close scrutiny. For Crossman, it seems that he excelled in verbal argument and persuasion rather than in detailed written explanation. In his 1960 introduction to *The God That Failed*, he explained that even this project 'was conceived in the heat of argument.'[75] This was coupled with his tendency to use the work of others as the basis of his writing, rarely developing a completely original idea or theory. Greg Rosen accurately described him as 'an intellectual magpie.'[76] Crosland was able to find a circle of friends and associates within the party who shared his views, providing him with a support group as well as an unofficial working group or 'think tank' – the Gaitskellites. Crossman failed to find this working group, instead finding friends and associates within the Bevanites.

Laski and Joseph appear to have remained committed in the first instance to their ideological views. In order to reconcile this with their parties, they attempted to change the views of party members to reflect their own, creating groups and organisations or using publications to achieve this. Crosland's writing also affected the views of others, but he and Joseph achieved differing levels of success and Crosland was already a member of a political grouping. Joseph's views were only adopted initially by a small group within the Conservative Party, but that group included Margaret Thatcher. Anthony Crosland's views and particularly his 1956 publication *The Future of Socialism* have remained important within the Labour Party, informing subsequent generations of the changing nature of social democracy in Britain, an ideology which is often very different to that seen on the continent.[77] In the longer term, his writings have remained prominent while Crossman's publications have faded into the background. Considering the future of social democracy and whether it has outlived traditional socialism within the Labour Party, Tudor Jones argued that 'as a political ideology it [social democracy] has prospered in the past through its flexibility and pragmatism. Yet the task of revitalising social democracy, or, in the preferred phrase of probably most Labour politicians, democratic socialism, remains an uncertain prospect.'[78] While social democracy may face an uncertain future, socialism has gradually become less important within the party. It is clear that Crosland's influence on the debate within the party on the future of socialism and the development of social democracy was far greater than that of Crossman, who in terms of this debate was, at best, a secondary figure.

However, Crosland's position within the Gaitskellites, as their leading thinker, was not replicated by Crossman's position within the Bevanites. While playing a large part in various campaigns such as *Keep Left* in 1947, Crossman failed to be considered the great thinker of the group (though no one else seems to have adopted this role either) and his views by the early 1950s were beginning to create conflict within this group. Rather unfairly, considering his own reputation, Ian Mikardo argued that 'Dick entered into … machinations [within the party] because he was amused by them and enjoyed them as a challenge, particularly as he was very good at this kind of operation and knew it: political power-broking was for him the breath of life.'[79] Desai argued that 'the intellectuals of the Bevanite/Tribunite left were generally exceptions who proved the rule that intellectuals in the party were generally revisionist.' She attributed the left wing allegiances of certain intellectuals to frustrated ambition, naming Bevan and Wilson as examples of this.[80] Crossman should also be placed in this category. While his views in the late 1940s were left wing in origin, his political position changed during the 1950s, influenced by circumstance, suggesting that some of his views were not particularly deeply rooted to begin with. He seems to have become less ideologically driven as his career progressed, so while he maintained his deeply held views on individual freedom and liberty and the rights of the individual over the excesses of government, the way in which he pursued these aims became less radical and more conventional, though he was still capable of being rash and impulsive.

Practicality is not always a consideration for intellectuals, but it is essential for politicians and would therefore indicate how integrated into the political arena an intellectual was. Crossman, Crosland and Joseph were forced to become practical politicians in their ministerial posts. As these individuals became integrated into their political parties and hoped for and achieved high ministerial office, they became involved in detailed policy planning. Joseph was, according to one close aide, 'addicted to work, paying obsessive attention to minor matters' while Secretary of State for Health and Social Security.[81] Crossman, particularly while Minister of Housing and Local Government, wanted to be involved in all aspects of his department, objecting when plans were drawn up without his prior agreement.[82] While he tended not to get involved in the detailed planning of his departmental documents, like most ministers, he liked to be involved in the decision-making process behind this planning. Joseph and Crossman had not been particularly detailed planners before they became ministers, but their position obviously forced them to consider legislation in great detail.

Crosland's writing, on the other hand, had often been very detailed and his time as a minister encouraged him to continue with this style of working. Jefferys noted that Dick Leonard argued that Crosland 'in the 1970s was able to speak not as a theoretician but as an experienced minister, one whose reputation in Whitehall had been built through a combination of administrative skill and innovative thought.'[83] This practical approach to ideological issues is what marks out a true intellectual in politics as opposed to an intellectual or a purely pragmatic politician. Of the intellectuals considered here, only Laski tended to lack practicality or detailed planning for the majority of his career. Due to his lack of high office in the Parliamentary Labour Party, he was able to support certain policies without having to work out the practical details for implementation. It seems that while many intellectuals in politics begin their careers in a rather idealistic way, as they gradually develop, they tend to become more practical and more detailed in their planning. Very few individuals are able to hold important governmental posts without this practical attitude.

The development of practical policies using a specific ideology is often facilitated by 'think tanks'. The term 'think tank' has several different definitions. Denham and Garnett defined three different types of think tanks. The first type are 'large institutions with considerable staff, mostly academic researchers, working mainly on book-length projects'. The second category of think tank 'serve government agencies and private sponsors on a contractual basis by executing research solicited in a number of fields.' The third type are entitled 'advocacy tanks … [which] have a strong policy partisanship and campaign aggressively on current policy issues.'[84] For the purposes of this study the term 'think tank' will be used in its cognitive sense, a variation of the third category which Denham and Garnett described; a group of individuals who work together with specific ideologies, on either individual issues or on general policies, with the purpose of influencing the political establishment, both ideologically and into actioning practical measures.

The Fabian Society has traditionally run alongside the PLP, linked to it while lacking official affiliation status. The society provides a forum for ideas to be discussed and debated in the form of published pamphlets, tending to be an umbrella organisation for individual members. While being a member of the

Fabian Society is not compulsory for Labour Party members, dual membership is common and individuals within the party, often write pamphlets on a wide-range of policy areas and issues, including Laski, Crosland and Crossman. While the Fabian Society can certainly be labelled as a think-tank, it does not have a rigid mission statement and is often reliant upon the individual work of its members rather than a more collective research group. The pamphlets which are produced for and published by the Fabian Society include the disclaimer:

> This pamphlet, like all publication of the FABIAN SOCIETY, represents not the collective view of the Society, but only the view of the individual who prepared it. The responsibility of the Society is limited to approving the publications which it issues as worthy of consideration within the Labour movement.[85]

The opinions which the society publicises are not officially endorsed by the society though inevitably many support party policies. Additionally, the society tends not to undertake active group research, generally encouraging the production of small pamphlets, often authored by only one or two individuals, outlining a specific policy issue or debate.

The fact that the Fabian Society is closely linked to the Labour Party while remaining an independent body suggests that it is a slightly different type of think tank to more general, research based think tanks, which often produce research either for general use or for specific commissioning groups. Laski, Crosland and Crossman were all linked to the society, and it seems that it was important to them to be part of an intellectual forum in which they could publicise their views and opinions, as they all did on numerous occasions. However, none of these intellectuals undertook any kind of collective work, instead producing individual works or working with just one other author. This suggests that in this regard these intellectuals were operating in a more individualistic political sense rather than in a collective intellectual sense.

While the Fabian Society is linked to the Labour Party, the Conservative Party has a think tank which is very similar in its work. The Centre for Policy Studies (CPS) was established by Keith Joseph and Margaret Thatcher primarily to provide intellectual bedrock for their ideological beliefs. The CPS is bound to the Conservative Party and is a more traditional think tank than the Fabian Society in that it has supporters and staff but no subscribing members. It seems to have been important to Joseph to be involved in the intellectual development of policies and ideologies, a trend which has been noted in our other intellectuals. Joseph also worked with the Institute of Economic Affairs (IEA) and this allowed him to develop his views:

> Prior to 1964, Joseph's arguments for economic liberalism had been relatively unsophisticated; they had arisen chiefly from instincts which, while not

exactly untutored, lacked the support which years of specialised study would have lent them. Contact with the IEA provided him with 'an intellectual back-up system and a sounding board.'[86]

Denham and Garnett argued that this development changed Joseph's reputation, leading his 'technocratic' image 'to be surpassed by an image of one who was at home with ideas as well as with practical problems.'[87] However, unlike our other intellectuals, Joseph was heavily involved in the CPS, working as part of a much larger group to research certain policy areas. In this respect, Joseph seems to have a different approach to other intellectuals. This might be due to personal preference, but it may well reflect Joseph's continued commitment to research, which Crosland, Crossman and Laski gradually lost.

It is also vital to consider whether intellectuals in politics all exhibit a certain type of attitude and temperament. It might be expected that, due to their adherence to ideas and perhaps a lack of practical planning skills, they would be unpopular, both within their own parties and within government departments, where their lack of practicality and detailed planning would make them difficult to work for. Susan Crosland noted that Tony Crosland had 'the non-academic's desire to translate ideas into action', highlighting the perception that intellectuals are unable or unwilling to institute practical action.[88] David Isaacs felt that on certain issues (he focused on the debate over Clause IV), Crossman was more of a realist than a theorist, certainly being more realistic than certain members of the Gaitskellite group, including Gaitskell himself.[89] Of our four intellectuals, Laski was the only one not to gain ministerial office. He was viewed with suspicion and dislike by many of the leading members of the Labour Party, including Attlee and Bevin. This could have been due to his left wing politics, or even perhaps anti-Semitism, something which Bevin was perhaps unfairly accused of. However, it seems to have been Laski's attitude and lack of political judgement or common sense that enraged his colleagues. 'For what is truly remarkable about Laski was the courage, often bordering on recklessness, which he displayed in expressing views which he knew to be unacceptable to people whose friendship he valued, and in openly criticizing men of power whom he might have been expected ... to flatter rather than excoriate.'[90] He demonstrated this tendency by writing to Attlee in 1944, informing him that 'your resignation of the leadership would be a great service to the party.'[91] He seems to have been a demanding individual, often overstepping the boundaries of his position, a trait which we can see in another of our intellectuals. Crossman was widely mistrusted by many within his own party, and his difficult relationships with his civil servants while a minister were legendary. Dame Evelyn Sharp described him as a 'bull in a china shop' and a bully.[92] While Laski and Crossman used their intellect as a weapon, this was due to their personality traits, not their positions as intellectuals in politics.

However, Crosland and Joseph seem to have had very different attitudes towards their civil servants. Crosland was widely liked and praised by those civil servants who worked for him in his various departments despite his arrogance, though there does seem to have been some resentment over his willingness to utilise the skills of outside advisers, a resistance which Crossman also encountered within the Ministry of Housing and Local Government.[93] Joseph was also widely respected by his civil servants and by some very influential members of the Conservative Party. By coincidence, Joseph worked at the Ministry of Housing and Local Government and the Department of Health and Social Security as Crossman did, but his relationships with the civil servants were considerably more amiable:

> For the first time [at the Ministry of Housing and Local Government] he could rely on a team of diligent civil servants to unearth reassuring information about rubbish tips etc. – and unlike Crossman, he was always glad of their assistance, which relieved him of the burden of making personal decisions on the myriad of routine issues which cropped up.[94]

Dame Evelyn Sharp seems to have enjoyed working for Joseph far more than for Crossman, something Crossman attributed to Joseph being more easily influenced by his civil servants.[95] While, in the run-up to the 1970 election, Joseph 'had hinted darkly that senior civil servants were a potential obstacle to change ... this seemed to be forgotten as soon as he was back on office.'[96] This suggests that these views were not deeply held by Joseph, perhaps being used tactically. Here it can be seen that while intellect might influence the relationships which they had with their departmental staff, their personality traits were the determining factor. The hostility which these intellectuals generated were not due to their intellect, but due to their personalities. Different intellectuals had different ways of working and thinking through policy, some of which were more popular than others.

    A career in journalism tends to have a rather negative impact on the reputation of intellectuals in politics. It can often be seen that their journalistic career has impacted on their political activities, making them into a 'jack of all trades and master of none'. Instead of focusing on a handful of issues, journalistic MPs are forced to consider a multitude of policies and issues, all in a fairly superficial manner, rarely getting a chance to look deeper into the issues. As Kramnick and Sheerman pointed out when writing about Laski, in a statement which could easily have been directed at Crossman, 'He wrote too much in general and far too much journalism in particular.'[97] Both Laski and Crossman wrote newspaper columns for much of their careers, and this popular journalism, while giving them a voice outside the party and Parliament, diverted their attention from other issues, and seems to have been very unpopular. While their colleagues may have been unimpressed by their writing, it undoubtedly raised their public profile and gave them a platform from which to publicise their personal views. Laski argued that 'intellectuals needed to have the courage to shun wealth and respectability and to speak the truth as they saw it.'[98] Crossman wanted to educate the public about political issues and his journalism could be seen as a way of doing this. Laski's teaching background may have inspired him to do the same. While their activities might have been viewed as self-publication, it may have had more altruistic origins than this. This did not prevent it from adversely impacting on their careers or generating hostility from within their own party.

Crosland and Joseph did not have journalistic careers, avoiding weekly columns and instead confining themselves to occasional articles in academic journals or pamphlets and books. In the 1950s, Crosland was able to maintain his academic reputation while writing occasional articles for national newspapers on an ad hoc basis. 'He was frequently called upon to provide accessible but informed commentary upon the Conservative government's economic policy.'[99] These activities did not prevent Crosland from referring to Crossman as a 'vulgar journalist', showing the impact that journalism could have on the reputation of an intellectual in politics.[100] This may reflect their own wish to educate, but in a more restricted way, instead of the mass-education which Laski and Crossman seem to have been pursuing. While having similar motives, the differing styles of these individuals led to them being treated differently by their colleagues within their parties. Crosland and Joseph were regarded as true intellectuals in politics who were not seeking notoriety or fame, while Laski and Crossman were treated with suspicion and hostility. This seems to have been linked in some ways to their prolific journalistic writing, which some viewed as being problematic to the wider party.

While being an intellectual in politics does not seem to have substantially affected the political convictions of these individuals, there do seem to be some links and similarities in the way in which these individuals worked and interacted with their colleagues. Laski, Crosland, Joseph and Crossman were all very capable, intelligent individuals who had the ability to drive themselves extremely hard and work excessively. It should be noted at this point that all four died at relatively young ages. Indeed, Laski, Joseph and Crossman all suffered from serious illness sporadically, and it is possible that this was due to the extreme stress these individuals worked under and the single-minded approach they took. While being dedicated to the exploration of ideas, the integration of these individuals into their parties seems to have encouraged them to be loyal to their party or at least a certain section of it, tending to move away from ideological arguments to more practical measures which would implement these. While often being viewed with suspicion by those within their party, this does not seem to have impeded the careers of these intellectuals in politics, though it does seem to have caused them sporadic problems with other groups of MPs. As with all MPs, where there were delays or failures in their careers, it tended to be for other reasons, with their intellectual background being of secondary importance.

While the motives of these intellectuals in politics may have been similar, their methods and attitudes were very different, reflecting their personalities. While Laski and Crossman tended to be very direct and even bullying, causing them to be disliked by many, Crosland and Joseph adopted a more flexible approach, leading to a higher level of respect being achieved within their departments. While Crosland was generally respected, he was not particularly popular within his departments, having a reputation as being rather arrogant. Joseph, on the other hand, seems to have been quite a popular minister, leading to accusations that he was a lamb in government but a lion in opposition.[101] Both of these approaches seem to have had some value, with policy decisions being made in different ways. The activities of our intellectuals also seem to have been different, with some venturing into journalism while others restricted themselves to more academic publications. This seems to have affected the reputations of our intellectuals, but it is possible that the motivations of these intellectuals was the same – the desire to educate, something which the majority of our intellectuals had done professionally at some point in their early career, Joseph being the exception. While intellectuals in politics are not a uniform group with identical traits and behaviour patterns, there does seem to be some common behaviour which is likely to be linked to their intellectual background.

Crossman's Traits

Crossman gained a reputation during his political career for losing interest in policies and ideas fairly quickly, becoming something of a gadfly, as David Marquand labelled him.[102] In addition to his perceived lack of sustained interest in many policy areas, he was considered by some within his own party, such as Ian Mikardo and Denis Healey, as well as the Conservative Party, as being fickle, changing his views time and again. Healey wrote about one particular example of this in his 1989 autobiography:

> He [Crossman] and I once ruined dinner with a friend by a fierce four-hour wrangle about what Dick considered to be a socialist's duty, automatically to oppose anything which was being proposed. The next night my friend heard Dick lecturing a Fabian meeting with equal ferocity that whether or not a socialist should oppose a proposal depended on whether the proposal made sense – the obvious point I had been making the night before.[103]

Ian Mikardo described how Crossman 'enjoyed the game for its own sake, and revelled in his ability to dribble round opponents.'[104] His surname made him an easy target for the nickname 'Double Crossman'. However, these impressions of Crossman do not seem to be wholly accurate. While he did not have a great deal of interest in numerous policy areas, he was committed to several key issues for much of his career. This situation does not seem to be unique within political circles, where many MPs focus on a select number of issues for much of their careers, while considering other issues more fleetingly when circumstances dictate. David Judge specifically considered the specialisms of backbench MPs in his 1981 study.[105] The book outlines several different hypothesises on whether backbench MPs actually specialise in certain issues or if they merely accept the wishes of the government or their party leaders. Judge argued that it can be very difficult to state with any certainty that the majority of MPs specialise on only a few select issues, although some of his results suggest that many members confine themselves to a fairly narrow range of issues.[106] Judge suggested that this trend may change over time, though he could not conclude with any certainty whether MPs are more or less likely to specialise as their career progressed.[107]

However, while noting that Crossman was committed to a handful of important issues, there does seem to have been a change in his attitude in 1955/6. At about this time he seems to have lost interest in several foreign policy issues that had previously occupied much of his time. There were several reasons for this change, the primary one being Gaitskell's succession to the leadership of the Labour Party. While Attlee and Crossman had had a cool and distant relationship which had prevented Crossman from holding any official post within government, it seems likely that Gaitskell's succession as leader produced some changes in his attitude, at least temporarily. There seems to have been a division of interests with Gaitskell's growing interest in foreign affairs leading Crossman to change his areas of interest away from these issues.[108] The appointment of Crossman to the working group on Pensions seems to have been a successful way of cultivating his interest in domestic issues. While his reputation may have made a position of responsibility unlikely, Gaitskell noted that 'if you take people like Dick Crossman into your confidence, discard their foolish ideas, retain their sensible ideas, then, on the whole, you can really make some headway.'[109] While their relationship was not particularly good, Gaitskell's succession as leader made Crossman hopeful of advancement and therefore initially less rebellious. His appointment as spokesman on pensions in 1956 seems to have additionally encouraged him to focus his attention on domestic issues.

There seems to have been several additional factors within his private life that contributed to him losing interest in foreign affairs. It was a combination of both personal and professional factors which have previously been considered which encouraged Crossman to focus predominantly on domestic issues and selected policy areas he had been interested in for much of his life, including Israel and constitutional reform. His journalistic career also allowed Crossman to escape from his role as MP, forcing him to consider a huge number of issues briefly before passing on to other pressing concerns. He gradually became involved in issues which he adopted at the instructions of the party leader, firstly pensions, then science and higher education and later, housing, constitutional reform and health and social security. While a minister, he complained that he tended to focus on his departmental work, ignoring all other issues. In this, he reflected a departmentalism which he observed within other cabinet ministers.[110]

This perception of Crossman's changing views was an issue of concern to some within his own party. He believed that good ideas tended to come out in the course of a discussion or argument and this meant different viewpoints needed to be explored, a very Socratic attitude. In order to facilitate this, he tended to adopt differing viewpoints, acting as he had during his career as a Don. For many, including Dame Evelyn Sharp and Denis Healey, this was not an academic exercise but an example of his changing views and fickle nature. Dame Evelyn Sharp, speaking in 1975, noted that she had heard Crossman referred to as a 'flying saucer', noting that they 'have their uses, but not as ministers.[111] He refuted this claim and, while in conversation he does seem to have altered his opinions based on his company, there is little evidence in his written work to suggest that he actually changed his views or was inconsistent in his political opinions. On the key issues in his life, such as Israel and constitutional reform, this biography has shown that his views remained fairly constant with very little substantive change. While his argumentative style may have concerned and antagonised some of his colleagues, and given the Conservative Party and the press an easy target, there seems to be very little foundation in the claims that Crossman changed his opinions routinely. His time as a government minister would have been considerably more difficult if his views were constantly in flux.

There seems to have been two general trends which can be noted in Crossman's political career. Firstly, there is some validity in the claim that he began to lose interest in foreign affairs after 1955. While this had been his primary interest pre-1955 and his area of expertise up to this point, after 1955 he began to focus on domestic issues, often those requiring detailed research, such as the payment system of pensions. As his knowledge increased on these issues, he seems to have become more comfortable within these debates. The reasons for this seem to have been both professional and personal. The change in leadership of the Labour Party encouraged him to be, initially at least, less rebellious and his position as spokesman on pensions gave him an issue to focus his attention on. While good relations between Crossman and Gaitskell were not permanent, they did last long enough for his attention to be diverted from his traditional areas of interest.

The second general accusation, that Crossman changed his views depending on his audience, seems to be misleading. While he did take a number of different positions in discussions and arguments, this seems to have been a tool for learning which he employed to gain greater understanding, as he had during his career in university education. This argumentative attitude does not seem to represent any real change in his personal views, as the written evidence suggests that his views remained fairly constant. While his style may have been disagreeable and often misunderstood, this does not justify the nickname 'Double Crossman'. Politicians often develop their opinions over time and rarely focus on more than a handful of policies or issues for much of their career and Crossman followed the same pattern. While his time as a minister forced him to focus his attention on certain departmental issues, his backbench career saw him concentrate on a limited number of issues, with occasionally fleeting glances given to current affairs, as all politicians and journalists are forced to do.

Crossman's Legacy

Crossman spent much of his twenty-nine year House of Commons career on the backbenches. His membership of the Keep Left group and the Bevanites allowed him to be involved in some of the most explosive battles in Labour Party history before he finally moved onto the front bench in 1964. However, in terms of legislation, there was very little of his vision actually enacted. His main piece of legislation, his 1968 Parliament (No.2) Bill was withdrawn from the House of Commons, much to Crossman's annoyance. While he introduced other important legislation and tackled some important issues, such as his 1965 Rent Act and his publication of the report by Geoffrey Howe on abuse within Ely Mental Health hospital, these tended to be useful but unimpressive in the larger picture of the Wilson government's reforms and particularly when compared to the legacy of the Attlee government. It is more likely that if he had a legacy, it is to be found in his writing and activities while on the backbenches. He played a small role in two larger policy development groups, though he was not a central figure in these groups. In 1957 Crossman worked as part of the Labour National Superannuation Scheme, considering the development of Labour's pension policy. The real driving force behind the scheme, in terms of the initiatives, were Richard Titmuss, Brian Abel-Smith and Peter Townsend from the LSE. However, Crossman was not redundant in this group and the policy initiatives which the group formulated were the basis on which the Labour Party built its superannuation plans. His superannuation plan, which fell when the 1970 general election was called, was based on the research done within this group.

Another important group which he played a substantially smaller role in was the Radcliffe-Maude Royal Commission on Local Government reform. This investigative group was established by Crossman while he was Minister of Housing and Local Government, but this was the extent of his input in this area. While he had an influence on these policy areas by taking part or setting up committees to investigate specific issues, there does not seem to have been a great deal of individual initiative here which might lead to a personal legacy. Had his Superannuation bill not fallen in 1970 and instead been enacted, this would have established an important legacy, but that did not happen.

As has been previously discussed, Crossman was not a key or systematic thinker on the development of socialism. The majority of his views were held by other members of the party and the wider Labour movement. These opinions on the practical implications of socialism were not particularly radical and were often only marginally different from the accepted views of the wider party. Additionally, his writing tended to lack detail and he often failed to fully think through his policies, focusing on the more superficial policy outlines. Before 1955, the main divergence between his views on socialism and nationalisation and those of the wider labour movement was a matter of style over content. While Crossman and the Bevanite group criticised individuals such as Morrison for wanting to consolidate the achievements of the Attlee government from 1950 onwards, Crossman's own plans for further nationalisation were hazy and undefined. He was a centre-left member of the Bevanite group and gradually became more of a supporter of Wilson than he was of Bevan, no doubt influenced by Bevan's reconciliation in 1955/6 with Gaitskell and Wilson's gradual move to the centre-left of the party in the early to mid-1950s. As his views were not contentious or radically different to those of many of his colleagues, Crossman's work on nationalisation and the practical implications of socialism did not leave a legacy behind. His views are very rarely even mentioned in studies on socialism or social democracy. The two tables below consider how significant Crossman's actions and publications are in studies of socialism (table 6.1) and histories of the Labour Party (table 6.2). A selection of publications have been studied and the number of pages in which Crossman and other notable figures have been listed is included in these two tables.

As can be seen from the table below, while the individual publications on socialism and social democracy concentrate on different individuals, with some failing to mention Laski or Cripps, all of these publications consider Crossman to a very similar extent. Crosland and Tawney, probably the two most influential thinkers in our table, are considered to a much greater extent that Crossman or other thinkers such as Dalton.

Table 6.1: Showing the number of pages on which these notable figures are mentioned in specific publications on Socialism and Social Democracy

	The Labour Party's Political Thought [112]	British Socialism[113]	Remaking the Labour Party[114]
Richard Crossman	9	11	10
Anthony Crosland	21	11	55
Evan Durbin	10	1	2
Harold Laski	13	3	0
Stafford Cripps	7	0	0
Hugh Dalton	5	0	4
R.H. Tawney	6 (+ repeatedly in chapter 4)	27	15
S. & B. Webb	11	10	7

However, the way in which these individuals are dealt with by each author is very different. In Tudor Jones' *Remaking the Labour Party*, Crossman is only mentioned ten times, all of these discussing him as part of a larger group, either the Bevanites or as a supporter of Wilson. The only exception to this is Jones' consideration of the *New Fabian Essays*, of which Crossman was the editor.[115] However, the focus of Jones' writing on this issue is Crosland and his chapter within the book.[116] This is to be expected as Crossman wasn't a particularly well-respected thinker on socialism and certainly didn't have the same level of respect within this debate as Anthony Crosland, Evan Durbin or Hugh Gaitskell.

Table 6.2 below shows how the histories of the period deal with these individuals.

Table 6.2: Showing the number of pages on which these notable figures are mentioned in specific publications on the History of the Labour Party

	A History of the British Labour Party[117]	A Short History of the Labour Party[118]	The Labour Party Since 1945[119]	The Labour Party: A Centenary History[120]
Richard Crossman	5	2	7	15
Anthony Crosland	15	4	12	19
Evan Durbin	3	0	0	1
Harold Laski	6	4	0	3
Stafford Cripps	17	9	11	9
Hugh Dalton	18	15	16	15
R.H. Tawney	3	0	0	6
S. & B. Webb	14	6	0	24

As can be seen from the table above, in the general histories of the Labour Party, Crossman is still considered far less than many other individuals. It might be expected that Crosland would be discussed to a greater extent, as has been seen in table 6.1, due to his position as the leading revisionist thinker. It is interesting to note that Crossman is considered in wider histories to a far less extent that other government ministers, such as Cripps or Dalton. This suggests that not only is he overlooked by texts on the development of socialism, he is also marginalised in accounts of the Labour Party, an omission which this book has gone some way to remedying. It is also interesting to note that the contribution of Evan Durbin is widely overlooked.

Tony Benn noted in his diary that Crossman had failed to write a book on socialism 'because if he did he thought he would discover he wasn't a socialist.'[121] It is clear that Crossman was not completely comfortable with his socialist views, and we have already noted the shaky foundations on which they were built. Any large-scale explanation of these might have made him aware of this. While he may not have been a particularly influential writer on the practical implications of socialism and nationalisation, he was considerably more interested in the associated issues of liberty and individual freedom. In all of his writing on socialism, he considered this issue. He may have been inspired by the claims which were often made by opponents of socialism, who raised concerns over the lack of individuality within totalitarian states such as the USSR and Nazi Germany and the lack of personal freedom within 'socialist' Russia, though his lack of discussion of these issues might more accurately suggest a lack of interest in this issue (see Chapter 3). In his 1960 publication, *Labour and the Affluent Society*, Crossman referred to the 'inefficiencies and brutalities perpetuated by their [the communist States] totalitarian rulers...'[122] However, his criticism seems very weak, undoubtedly influenced by his admiration for the economic activities of the USSR. He was keen to note that socialism did not, and should not, mean a compromise in individual freedom. This would require the revival of 'Parliament's traditional function of controlling and checking the executive.'[123] While this was a policy area where Crossman was particularly prominent, his views were not particularly contentious. His writing on this issue was not particularly well known and, due to the wide acceptance of his views, he does not appear to have directly affected the opinions of others on this issue. This can be noted by the absence of writing on Crossman generally in contrast to that on other leading Labour figures, including Cripps and Crosland, and the overlooking of his writing on this issue in academic studies on social democracy. In the debate on socialism, nationalisation and individual liberty, Crossman was a secondary character and he seems to have left very little legacy.

Crossman seems to have left a larger legacy behind in terms of Britain's foreign policy, particularly due to his pro-Zionist stance. In the wider debate on Israel, he was certainly not the most high-profile Labour MP calling for British support of the Jewish population of Palestine and, later, for British support of the Israeli state. Herbert Morrison, Aneurin Bevan, Hugh Dalton, Stafford Cripps and Hugh Gaitskell were all far more high-profile supporters of Israel in the late 1940s and 1950s with many of them able to take part in cabinet discussions over the future of the Middle East between 1945 and 1951.[124] While these individuals were all in favour of the establishment of some sort of home within Palestine for the Jewish displaced persons within Europe and the protection of Jews already within Palestine, there were a number of different solutions offered by these individuals. The most striking difference was between those who were calling for the partition of Palestine into two separate countries and those who were seeking to make Palestine into a bi-national country.

Crossman's time on the Anglo-America Commission gave him first-hand experience of the issues and a central position in the debate prior to Britain handing back the UN protectorate mandate for Palestine in 1948. While his support was gladly received by Israeli leaders, and his role on the Commission was important and affected its recommendations, it seems likely that he was unable to single-handedly influence the opinions of others on this issue.[125] Despite this, William Roger Louis noted that he 'played such an important part as conciliator in the clash between the British and the American points of view...'[126] While Crossman was still a devoted supporter of the Israeli state in the 1960s and early 1970s, he gradually began to withdraw from debates over Israel from 1955 onwards, as with all foreign policy issues, though he remained interested in the future of Israel. He did not leave a large legacy in regard to this policy area, though his actions on the Anglo-American Commission did influence the activities of interested groups and therefore the shape which Israel took.

Crossman was only able to adopt an unofficial leadership role on foreign policy issues while he was a member of the Keep Left group in 1947. He was closely associated with calls for a more 'socialist', eastern focused foreign policy, as Bevin noted at the 1947 Labour Party conference.[127] However, the calls for this sort of policy quickly became redundant, being overtaken by events almost as soon as *Keep Left* had been published in 1947. Pelling identified the reasons for this as being 'the formation of conservative governments in France and Italy and …the generous offer of economic help for all European countries which was made by General Marshall…'[128] While there have occasionally been calls for the Labour Party and government to adopt a more socialist foreign policy in the intervening period, this does not have the same meaning as it did in the late 1940s. It is no longer possible for Britain to look to Russia or a loose grouping within Europe to secure its world role. Instead, British foreign policy has become linked to that of the USA and Europe has become a far more cohesive grouping in the form of the EU. Crossman's influence on later generations in regard to this policy has been small, though the work of the Keep Left group has been considered several times in publications on foreign policy.[129]

One area in which Crossman was able to make a tangible individual difference and leave an important legacy behind was his work on the Anglo-American Commission in 1946 on the future of Palestine and calls for a Jewish homeland. At this time, rather unexpectedly, he was able to take a key role in the international effort to decide the future complexion of the Middle East. Any further influence which he had over specific foreign policies seems to have been exercised before 1955, and his influence beyond the commission cannot be separated from that of the wider groups which he was perhaps unintentionally a member of due to his views. Joseph Gorny included him in a small group of influential figures within the Labour Party on this issue. The group also included Attlee, Bevin, Morrison, Dalton, Brailsford and Laski. He also, rather interestingly, noted that those on the left wing of the group, in which Crossman was included in the late 1940s, 'preserved the socialist humanistic traditions of the labour movement in their attitude to Zionism, while the opponents, particularly Attlee and Bevin, deviated from these traditions.'[130] He was, despite his battles with Bevin, returning to the more traditional position of the Labour Party on this issue.

Crossman's views on the regeneration of Germany following the Second World War, were not unique and in some respects, his views were not particularly influential. On the issue of the rearmament of Germany, in 1954 he worked with a much larger group of MPs, consisting of Bevan, Castle, Driberg, Mikardo and Wilson. The pamphlet, *It Need Not Happen: The Alternative to German Rearmament*, argued that Germany should not be rearmed, as this would contribute to the continued separation of Germany, encouraging an armed stand off.[131] The main concern of the group was that 'any German forces, whether in the West or the East would only fight for German national interests and not to suit the convenience of either the USA or the USSR.'[132] This would encourage nationalism within Germany, which was obviously viewed with suspicion. This is an example of Crossman working with his Bevanite colleagues, expressing a left wing foreign policy view, but not taking a leading or isolated role in the debate. He was one amongst many, and he rarely took a leading role in the debates on these issues.

His influence on the constitutional reform debate is more tangible than in other policy areas. The constitutional reform debate was one within which he had a fairly unique position. Not only did he write about constitutional reform intermittently during his career, but he was additionally able to try and enact some of his proposals while Leader of the House of Commons from 1966 to 1968. This was coupled with his dissatisfaction about the existing arrangements for ministers and concern over the role and influence of civil servants, worries that other Leaders of the House had either not shared, as was the case with Herbert Morrison, or had not acted upon in the same enthusiastic way, such as Fred Peart, Crossman's successor.

However, the potential of Crossman's situation was never fully realised. The all-important legislation which he attempted to introduce in order to reform the House of Lords was lost, due to his own inexperience within Parliament and a combination of hostility from both the cabinet and the members of the House of Commons as well as a series of unfortunate and perhaps unavoidable events. His other reforms in both the Commons and the Lords were, with hindsight, seen as useful, with the televising of the Commons and specialist committees both being successfully introduced at a later date. However, during Crossman's lifetime, the vast majority of his reforms were met with disquiet amongst MPs and ministers. While Miles Taylor described him, along with Morrison, as probably doing 'more to overhaul the ordinary procedure of the Commons than any politician since Gladstone', in practical terms Crossman's reform package seems to have been written-off by many of his colleagues and he seems to have received very little recognition for some of his useful and practical reforms. [133]

Crossman's writing on constitutional reform, while sporadic, was an important part of his thinking and his legacy. The four longer publications which he produced in which he discussed constitutional issues were important in the on-going debates over constitutional reform and the role of Whitehall since the Second World War. In particular, his introduction to the 1963 edition of Bagehot's *The English Constitution* is a landmark publication in its own right, building on and developing the work of others.[134] While Humphrey Berkeley noted that Crossman was 'the only leading politician in the last half century to have expressed any genuine concern about the future of Parliament before becoming Leader of the House', he argued that Crossman's 1963 introduction was out of date almost as soon as it was published. 'Paradoxically, just as at the time when Bagehot was writing the House of Commons was already being transformed into one of the dignified parts of the constitution, so is Crossman's analysis ceasing to be valid. For the House of Commons is no longer the main battleground between the great political parties.'[135] However, Crossman was well aware that many decisions were made outside the Commons ,or even the cabinet, adding weight to his views on the emergence of prime ministerial government:

> When I wrote the introduction to Bagehot, I gave a description of prime ministerial govt, which fits what has happened in the last twenty months with absolute precision. The PM has run the govt. completely, prime ministerially. He has decided to allow decisions to be taken by George Brown and Callaghan sparring with each other, and in every other way he has retained decision taking in his personal domain.[136]

It was not until 1970 that Crossman again wrote about constitutional reform and the experience he had gained as Leader of the House of Commons, delivering the Godkin lectures on the subject of the constitution (published in 1972's *Inside View*).[137] In these three lectures, he used his own experiences, as well as the work of others, to recommend reforms to the constitutional arrangements in Britain. While his views were not revolutionary, they do seem to have survived, while those who supported either the retention of the existing arrangements with very few alterations, or the abolition of the House of Lords completely, with only minimal reform of the House of Commons have not. The reforms which he tried to institute and his overall aims were continued by the Study of Parliament Group. This group had been established in 1964 and 'pressed for reforms, including investigative specialized select committees.'[138] Crossman was not a member of this group, but the reforms he attempted to introduce were in line with many of its aims. The group continued to call for reform after he left his position as Leader of the House of Commons in 1968.

While the reform programme which Crossman attempted to implement was not successfully or popular during his lifetime, certain elements have been successfully applied since his death. Specialist committees in particular have been widely accepted and are now an important part of Britain's parliamentary arrangements. The combination of his position as Leader of the House of Commons and his writing on constitutional reform allowed Crossman a rather unique and important role within the debate over the future of Parliament, and his reforms allowed a 'trial run' of several types of constitutional reform. While the Study of Parliament group's aims were in line with much of his thinking on making Parliament more accountable, the views of the Labour Party were far more diverse. As Theakston pointed out 'there is and has been, in fact, no single coherent "Labour Party view" about the nature and problems of the civil service', and this is equally true of constitutional reform as a whole.[139] There seems very little evidence to suggest that Crossman's views directly influenced constitutional reformers who followed him. It seems more likely that his views fitted into the overall aims of the Study of Parliament group, who continued to push for reform after Crossman left government. However, it seems that the majority of his views were at least based on the work of others, including John Mackintosh, Thomas Balogh and, from an earlier era, Harold Laski.

While Crossman was influential in the constitutional reform debate, he does not seem to have directly influenced other MPs who followed him, and there is no evidence to suggest this. It was in another area where he influenced his contemporaries and those politicians who followed him. The publication of his diaries in 1975, 1976, 1977 and 1981 seem to have been his finest and most enduring legacy, one which outlasted virtually all of his other activities and publications. By 'disclosing the secret operations of government which are concealed by the thick foliage which we call the myth of democracy'[140] in a detailed diary, Crossman opened the door through which numerous other politicians have followed, including Tony Benn, Barbara Castle and Alan Clark.[141] As Castle noted 'I was initially shocked by Dick's breach of collective responsibility, of which I was a rather prim supporter, but then I discovered that his belief in open government was justified. The heavens did not fall.'[142] The battle which Crossman's executors fought on his behalf, and the publicity which it generated, sparked the interest of many, allowing the public and politicians alike to read very detailed accounts of cabinet meetings and his personal opinions of his cabinet colleagues.[143]

Crossman was only occasionally given credit for his groundbreaking diaries by other diarists, and his diaries are often criticised by academics for their gossipy style and one-sided commentary. However, they are still the most detailed account of governmental life from 1964 to 1970 which is available. Wilson argued that the diaries which were published might have been quite different had Crossman been alive at the time of their publication. 'Some of the facts he recorded are almost masochistic in frankness, and few politicians are masochistic.'[144] Tony Benn noted that Crossman's diary entries were 'most unattractive – personal, gossipy, unrooted in political principle and disconnected from the labour movement. It showed Crossman and politics in a bad light, and correctly so. The awful thing is that my diary for 1968, which is now being typed, is equally unattractive.'[145] While the Castle diaries are extremely detailed on the work of the government and her departments, they do not provide the reader with the same sort of information which the Crossman's diaries provide. The Crossman's diaries are particularly honest and telling, providing detailed information on the personality of their author and of the other personalities in government.

The legacy which Crossman has left behind is rather unevenly balanced, with his influence on certain issues being far greater than on others. The most long-lasting legacy of Crossman was his work on the Anglo-American commission on the future of Palestine, his writing on and attempted reform of the constitution and, obviously, the publication of his diaries, for which he is often solely remembered. It is interesting to note that much of the influence which he had was after his death when, perhaps, his personality and the preconceptions others had about him were forgotten. It seems that Crossman's personality was both a blessing and a curse for him, meaning he was rarely forgotten and that many never forgave him.

Conclusion

Crossman was a very important individual, for a number of reasons. His very detailed account of his time in Parliament and government gave the academic community an overwhelming amount of information and detail on the daily life of an MP and a minister. He seems to have had very similar interests to other MPs and ministers, though he had a reputation for changing his mind frequently. David Judge's study on the level of backbench specialisation in the House of Commons draws a very distinct line between those MPs who consider themselves, or are considered by their colleagues, to be specialists and those who have taken part in relevant debates, committees or research groups. He argued that 'a majority of respondents [to Judge's questionnaire] indeed consider themselves and the bulk of their colleagues, to be fairly highly specialised in their parliamentary work.'[146] This is an impression which could easily be applied to Crossman, when taking into account his work and devotion to Israel or the British Constitution. The impression which he provided, of being fickle in his views, seems to have been an inaccurate perception, and not a true representation of his opinions. He believed that it was important to argue issues out in order to reach a useful conclusion, and this often meant him taking a position he did not actually support, in order to generate the argument. This approach does not seem to have been adopted by other ministers and it did cause considerable consternation among Crossman's colleagues. Manny Shinwell described him as suffering from 'intellectual indigestion'.[147] While he did consider a huge number of issues fairly briefly, as was the nature of his political and journalistic career, he maintained his commitment to and interest in a few key issues – the importance of individual freedom, the creation and existence of Israel and constitutional reform. However, there does seem to have been a change in his interest within foreign policy issues in 1955/6, caused by a number of personal and professional changes.

His work within his government departments also seems to have been personally driven. His 'bump of irreverence', which he spoke so proudly of seems to have been a hindrance to him as well as a help.[148] As has been previously discussed, this was an extremely slim basis on which to build an ideology and a parliamentary career spanning twenty-nine years, but this was the basis which Crossman accepted for his views. It allowed (or forced) his views to be flexible or temporary, depending on your viewpoint. Nonetheless he was a hard-working minister, unafraid to make unpopular decisions if he believed they were correct and he bullied his civil servants, viewing them with suspicion from his first day in government to his last. Anthony Crosland noted that '...the officials hate it [ministers who believe they can get their own way by shouting], and so they should. You don't shout at people like this in other forms of life, and you've absolutely no need to in order to get your way.'[149] Additionally, Crossman was unable when he entered office to fully utilise his civil service, due to a lack of knowledge and experience. While he admitted in 1970 that he did not hold the civil service responsible for the actions of the Wilson government, he did treat them badly while a minister, causing them to complain about him.[150] Drucker has attributed this attitude to his left wing complexion, but it would be very difficult to label him as left wing by 1964. His attitude to the civil servants was certainly not caused by his role as an intellectual within politics, and it seems likely that it was a product of Crossman's own personality, as well as his perceptions of the activities of civil servants and their effect on other ministers, such as Bevin at the Foreign Office in 1945 to 1951.[151]

Crossman was not a great thinker within the Labour Party. Despite his intellectual capabilities and hard-working nature, he failed to fulfil his potential. His publications, while interesting and enlightening about the views of those on the left of the party generally, failed to be particularly influential or widely read outside the party. Additionally, he managed to irritate some leading members of the party, including Attlee, Bevin and later Gaitskell. This meant that his hopes of high office were frustrated for nearly twenty years. When he finally did become a minister in 1964, he was hard-working and dedicated to his departments. Sometime his dedication almost became an obsession, with Crossman noting that he was becoming departmentalised, failing to notice what was happening in other departments or on wider policy areas.[152] His time at the Ministry of Housing and Local Government was a baptism of fire for Crossman, working with the formidable Dame Evelyn Sharp. During his time in government, he became much better at working with his civil servants as opposed to working against them, and the responsibility of office seems to have made him less rebellious and difficult. However, his time in office did not stop him from making terrible gaffes, such as before the 1969 local elections. 'Crossman was genuinely surprised when his announcement of an increase in charges on teeth and spectacles three days before the local elections in 1969 produced an explosion of anger in the party. A Machiavelli without judgement is a dangerous colleague.'[153]

Crossman was a unique individual, with a fairly difficult temperament. However, his life and career highlight many influences and issues, allowing wider conclusions and observations to be made. While he was not the great thinker or writer that he believed that he was, his role as an MP, a journalist, a member of the Keep Left group and the Bevanites early in his career, his friendship and working relationship with Wilson and his time as a minister make him an important individual within the Labour Party and an individual certainly worthy of research and investigation.

Notes

Chapter One

1 Wilson, Harold, "A Desire to Educate", *The Listener,* 5th January 1978 p.4.

2 Theakston, Kevin (ed.), *Bureaucrats and Leadership,* Basingstoke, Macmillan, 1999, p.4.

3 Hamilton, Nigel, "Wanted: Cult of Personality" *The Times Higher Education Supplement,* 10th March 2000 p.19.

4 Derry, John, "Political Biography: A Defence (2)" *Contemporary British History* 10/4, Winter 1996 p.76.

5 Wilson, Harold, "A Desire to Educate", p.6.

6 Shepherd, Robert, "The Challenge of Political Biography" *British Journalism Review* 8/1, 1997 p.28.

7 Hamilton, Nigel, "In Defence of the Practice of Biography" *Contemporary History* 10/4, Winter 1996 p.81.

8 Pimlott, Ben, "The Future of Political Biography" *The Political Quarterly* 61, 1990 p.222.

9 Edel, Leon, *Literary Biography*, London, R. Hart-Davis, 1957, p.11.

10 Croft, Pauline, "Political Biography: A Defence (1)" *Contemporary History* 10/4, Winter 1996 p.72.

11 Derry, John, "Political Biography: A Defence (2)", p.79.

12 Theakston, Kevin (ed.), *Bureaucrats and Leadership*, pp. 1-11.

13 Theakston, Kevin (ed.), *Bureaucrats and Leadership*, p.3.

14 Nicholson, Harold, *The Development of English Biography,* London, The Hogarth Press, 1927, p.60.

15 Harris, Jose, *William Beveridge: A Biography*, Oxford, Clarendon Press, 1977.

16 Marwick, Arthur, *The Nature of History*, 3rd Edition, Basingstoke, Macmillan Education, 1989, p.165.

17 Theakston, Kevin (ed.), *Bureaucrats and Leadership*, p.4.

18 Theakston, Kevin (ed.), *Bureaucrats and Leadership*, p.3.

19 Beattie, Alan, "Biographies of 1992 and the Limits of Biography" *Parliamentary Affairs* 46/1, January 1993, p.430.

20 O'Brien, Patrick, "Is Political Biography a Good Thing?" *Contemporary History* 10/4, Winter 1996, p.61.

21 O'Brien, Patrick, "Is Political Biography a Good Thing?" *Contemporary History* 10/4, Winter 1996, p.64.

22 Croft, Pauline, "Political Biography: A Defence (1)" p.71.

23 Croft, Pauline, "Political Biography: A Defence (1)" p.70.

24 Harris, Jose, "William Beveridge in Whitehall: Maverick or Mandarin" in MacLeod, R (ed.), *Government and Expertise: Specialists, Administrators and Professionals 1860-1919*, Cambridge, Cambridge University Press, 1988, p.244.

25 Catterall, Peter, "Autobiographies and Memoirs" in Catterall, Peter, and Jones, Harriet, *Understanding Documents and Sources*, Oxford, Heinemann, 1994, p.33.

26 Crossman, Richard, *The Diaries of a Cabinet Minister*, Vol. I, London, Hamish Hamilton and Jonathan Cape, 1975, p.84. Entry for Friday 4th December 1964.

27 National Archive BA 1/6, *Civil Service Department: Committee on the Civil Service (Fulton Committee). Minutes, Papers and Report 1966-69*. Report of Crossman's oral evidence to the Fulton Committee.

28 Crossman, Richard, *Cabinet Diaries*, Vol. I, p.13.

29 'Since ex-cabinet ministers are entitled to access to secret documents when they publish their memoirs, and rely for their accounts of cabinet proceedings mainly on memory, how much to publish is not a matter of government ruling, far less the Official Secrets Act, but a concern of personal taste and personal conscience.' Crossman, Richard, *Cabinet Diaries*, Vol. I, p.13.

30 Details of the court case can be found in Young, Hugo, *The Crossman Affair*, London, Hamilton and Cape for the Sunday Times, 1976.

31 Jones, George W., "The Value of Recent Biographies, Autobiographies and Diaries" *Parliamentary Affairs* 34/2, Spring 1981, p.336.

32 Castle, Barbara, *The Castle Diaries 1964-76*, Paperback edition, London, Papermac, 1990, pp. vii/viii.

33 Benn, Tony, *Out of the Wilderness; Diaries 1963-67*, London, Arrow, 1989.

34 Crossman, Richard, *Cabinet Diaries*, Vol. I, p.12.

35 Crossman, Richard, *Cabinet Diaries*, Vol. I, p.15.

36 Castle, Barbara, *The Castle Diaries, 1974-76*, London, Weidenfeld and Nicolson, 1980. Castle, Barbara, *The Castle Diaries 1964-70*, London, Weidenfeld and Nicolson, 1984. Benn, Tony, *Out of the Wilderness; Diaries 1963-67*, London, Arrow, 1989.

37 Benn, Tony, *Out of the Wilderness; Diaries 1963-67*, London, Arrow, 1989, p.462. Entry for Thursday 28th July 1966.

38 Castle, Barbara, *The Castle Diaries 1964-76*, p.80. Entry for Thursday 28th July 1966.

39 Castle, Barbara, *The Castle Diaries 1964-76*, p.80. Entry for Thursday 28th July 1966.

40 Crossman, Richard, *Cabinet Diaries*, Vol. I, p.591. Entry for Thursday 28th July 1966.

41 Crossman, Richard, *Cabinet Diaries*, Vol. I, p.591. Entry for Thursday 28th July 1966.

42 Nicholson, Harold, *The Development of English Biography*, London, The Hogarth Press, 1927, p.131.

43 Tosh, John, *The Pursuit of History,* 2nd Edition, London, Longman, 1991, pp.78/9.

Chapter Two

1 Crossman, Richard, "My Father" *The Sunday Telegraph* 16th December 1962.

2 Howard, Anthony, *Crossman: The Pursuit of Power*, London, Jonathan Cape, 1990, p.16.

3 Morgan, Janet (ed.), *The Backbench Diaries of Richard Crossman*, London, Hamish Hamilton and Jonathan Cape, 1981, p.604. Entry for Tuesday 17th September 1957.

4 Howard, Anthony, *Crossman,* p.19.

5 Howard, Anthony, *Crossman,* p.13.

6 Crossman, Richard, "My Father".

7 Crossman, Richard, "My Father".

8 Crossman, Richard, "My Father".

9 Howard, Anthony, *Crossman,* p.24.

10 Crossman Papers, Modern Records Centre, University of Warwick Library, MSS.154/3/BR/2/4-18. Transcript of "A Chance to Meet" with Cliff Michelmore, BBC programme, no date but appears to be 4th April 1970.

11 Howard, Anthony, *Crossman,* p.24.

12 Howard, Anthony, *Crossman,* pp. 24/5.

[13] Crossman, Richard, "My Father".

[14] Crossman, Richard, *Palestine Mission: A Personal Record*, London, Hamish Hamilton 1947, p.15.

[15] Howard, Anthony, *Crossman*, p.36.

[16] Howard, Anthony, *Crossman*, p.40.

[17] Howard, Anthony, *Crossman*, pp.54/5.

[18] Howard, Anthony, *Crossman*, p.67.

[19] Crossman, Richard, *The Charm of Politics and Other Essays in Political Criticism*, London, Hamish Hamilton, 1956, p.7.

[20] Crossman, Richard, *Plato Today*, London, George Allen and Unwin, 1937.

[21] Howard, Anthony, *Crossman*, p.69.

[22] Crossman, Richard, *The Diaries of a Cabinet Minister*, Vol. I, London, Hamish Hamilton and Jonathan Cape, 1975, p.11.

[23] Crossman, Richard, *How Britain is Governed*, London, Labour Book Service, 1939.

[24] National Archives FO 1110/220, *Psychological Warfare: Paper by R.H. Crossman*, 1949.

[25] For a more detailed account of Crossman's activities during the Second World War, see Howard, Anthony, *Crossman*, Chapter 8, pp. 88-107.

[26] 'The luck of my being chosen in 1937 [in Coventry] has kept me in Parliament with a huge cast-iron majority and with a particular kind of party behind me which has deeply influenced my thinking, keeping me much more on the Left than I would be nature have been.' Crossman, Richard, *Cabinet Diaries*, Vol. I, p.416. Entry for Saturday 18th December 1965.

[27] Crossman concluded that it was not his earlier relations with Attlee which had adversely affected his career, but his opposition to Bevin's Palestine policy. Crossman, Richard, *Cabinet Diaries*, Vol. I, p.11.

[28] Crossman, Richard, *Palestine Mission*, p.12.

[29] Wilson, Harold, "A Desire to Educate", *The Listener* 5th January 1978, p.4.

[30] Morgan, Janet (ed.), *Backbench Diaries*, p.219. Entry for Wednesday 22nd April 1953.

[31] Crossman, Richard, *Palestine Mission*, p.12.

[32] Crossman, Richard, *Palestine Mission*, p.11.

[33] Crossman, Richard, *Palestine Mission*, p.66.

[34] Crossman, Richard, *Palestine Mission*, p.23.

[35] Crossman, Richard, *Palestine Mission*, p.66.

[36] Crossman, Richard, *Palestine Mission*, p.192.

[37] Crossman, Richard, *Palestine Mission*, p.198.

[38] Crossman, Richard, *Palestine Mission*, p.198.

[39] Crossman, Richard, *Palestine Mission*, p.201.

[40] Crossman, Richard, *Palestine Mission*, p.204.

[41] Crossman, Richard, *Palestine Mission*.

[42] Labour Party Conference Annual Report 1947, p.179.

[43] Crossman, Richard, Foot, Michael and Mikardo, Ian, *Keep Left*, London, New Statesman and Nation, 1947. Fifteen individuals officially authored the pamphlet.

[44] Crossman, Richard, *Keeping Left*, London, New Statesman and Nation, 1950. 12 individuals officially authored the pamphlet.

[45] Mikardo, Ian, *Back-bencher*, London, Weidenfeld and Nicolson, 1988, p.109.

[46] Crossman, Richard, *Cabinet Diaries*, Vol. I, p.12.

[47] Crossman Papers, MSS.154/3/BE/8-10. Letter from Crossman to Bevan dated 31st March 1955.

[48] Shaw, George Bernard (ed.), *Fabian Essays in Socialism*, London, Fabian Society, 1889.

[49] Crossman, Richard (ed.), *New Fabian Essays*, London, Turnstile Press, 1952.

[50] Howard, Anthony, *Crossman*, p.164.

51 After his election to the National Executive, Crossman was due to give a speech. On reaching the rostrum, he said 'I will tell conference quite frankly that for the very lively and fiery things I decided to say yesterday, I felt – and I think conference will know the reason why – it was wiser to substitute less controversial things.' Labour Party Conference Annual Report 1952, p.107.

52 Morgan, Janet (ed.), *Backbench Diaries*, p.125. Entry for Wednesday 23rd July 1952.

53 Morgan, Janet (ed.), *Backbench Diaries*, p.313. Entry for Wednesday 21st May 1954.

54 Morgan, Janet (ed.), *Backbench Diaries*, p.315. Entry for Wednesday 21st May 1954.

55 Morgan, Janet (ed.), *Backbench Diaries*, p.341. Entry for Friday 13th August 1954.

56 Morgan, Janet (ed.), *Backbench Diaries*, p.341. Entry for Friday 13th August 1954.

57 Thorpe, Andrew, *A History of the British Labour Party*, 2nd Edition, Basingstoke, Palgrave, 2001, p.130.

58 Crossman, Richard, *Cabinet Diaries,* Vol. I, p.11.

59 Morgan, Janet (ed.), *Backbench Diaries,* p.466. Entry for Thursday 19th January 1956.

60 Crossman referred to them set as the 'Hampstead poodles'. Morgan, Janet (ed.), *Backbench Diaries,* p.796. Entry for Friday 23rd October 1959.

61 Thorpe, Andrew, *A History of the British Labour Party*, p.137.

62 Morgan, Janet (ed.), *Backbench Diaries,* p.797. Entry for Tuesday 27th October 1959.

63 Crossman, Richard, *Cabinet Diaries*, Vol. I, p.11.

64 In 1957 Crossman and Brown came to blows in the House of Commons after Brown took offence to one of Crossman's articles. Howard indicated that Crossman, who had played rugby at school and was fairly well built, knocked Brown to the floor and sat on him. Howard, Anthony, *Crossman,* p.211.

65 He stated that 'about this job I knew virtually nothing.' Crossman, Richard, *Cabinet Diaries*, Vol. I, p.12.

66 Crossman, Richard, *Cabinet Diaries*, Vol. I, p.69. Entry for Sunday 22nd November 1964.

67 Jenkins, Simon, "Dame Evelyn Hits Back", *The Sunday Times* 5th October 1975, pp.16/17.

68 Crossman, Richard, *Cabinet Diaries,* Vol. I, p.631. Entry for Wednesday 24th August 1966.

69 Morgan, Janet, *The House of Lords and the Labour Government 1964-70*, Oxford, Clarendon Press, 1975, p.196.

70 Morgan, Janet, *The House of Lords*, p.188.

71 Crossman, Richard, *The Diaries of a Cabinet Minister,* Vol. III, London, Hamish Hamilton and Jonathan Cape, 1977, p.408. Entry for Tuesday 11th March 1969.

72 Crossman, Richard, *Cabinet Diaries*, Vol. I, p.11.

73 Crossman, Richard, *Cabinet Diaries*, Vol. I, p.12.

74 In his introduction to the first volume of his Cabinet Diaries, Crossman outlined his reasons for publishing his diaries so close to events. Crossman, Richard, *Cabinet Diaries*, Vol. I, pp.13/14.

75 Morgan, Janet, *The House of Lords and the Labour Government 1964-70.*

76 Crossman, Richard, *The Diaries of a Cabinet Minister*, Vol. I, *The Diaries of a Cabinet Minister*, Vol. II, London, Hamish Hamilton and Jonathan Cape, 1976, *The Diaries of a Cabinet Minister*, Vol. III. Morgan, Janet (ed.), *The Backbench Diaries of Richard Crossman.*

77 Howard, Anthony, *Crossman,* p.6.

78 'He's [Wilson] absolutely loyal to me, but he is removing himself inevitably into a professional stratosphere.' Morgan, Janet (ed.), *Backbench Diaries*, p.1023. Entry for Friday 26th July 1963.

79 Crossman, Richard, *Cabinet Diaries*, Vol. I, pp.217/8. Entry for Thursday 13th May 1965.

Chapter Three

1 Thorpe, Andrew, *A History of the British Labour Party*, 2nd Edition, Basingstoke, Palgrave, 2001, p.106.

[2] Jefferys, Kevin, "The Attlee Years, 1935-55" in Brivati, Brian and Heffernan, Richard (eds.), *The Labour Party: A Centenary History*, Basingstoke, Macmillan, 2000, pp. 81/2.

[3] Jefferys, Kevin, "The Attlee Years, 1935-55" in Brivati, Brian and Heffernan, Richard (eds.), *The Labour Party: A Centenary History*, p.82.

[4] Morgan, Janet (ed.), *The Backbench Diaries of Richard Crossman*, London, Hamish Hamilton and Jonathan Cape, 1981, p.905. Entry for Tuesday 8th December 1960. Account of Tawney's Birthday celebrations.

[5] Thorpe, Andrew, *A History of the British Labour Party*, p.122.

[6] Freeden, Michael, *Ideologies and Political Thought: A Conceptual Approach*, Oxford, Clarendon Press, 1996.

[7] Freeden, Michael, *Ideologies and Political Thought: A Conceptual Approach*, p.4.

[8] Writing about the period 1956-59, Pimlott argued that 'Wilson by this stage had become hard to pigeon-hole: he might best be described as a tribal Bevanite, a tactical Centrist, and an ideological revisionist. Inherent in his revisionism was a belief in the need to avoid electorally unpopular policies, of which nationalization was one.' Pimlott, Ben, *Harold Wilson*, London, HarperCollins, 1992, p.218.

[9] Freeden, Michael, *Ideologies and Political Thought: A Conceptual Approach*, p.418.

[10] Mikardo, Ian, *Back-Bencher*, London, Weidenfeld and Nicolson, 1988, p.152.

[11] Mikardo, Ian, *Back-Bencher*, p.152.

[12] Crossman, Richard, *Keeping Left*, London, New Statesman and Nation, 1950, p.3.

[13] Thorpe, Andrew, *A History of the British Labour Party*, p.38.

[14] Jefferys, Kevin, "The Attlee Years, 1935-55" in Brivati, Brian and Heffernan, Richard (eds.), *The Labour Party: A Centenary History*, p.70.

[15] Jefferys, Kevin, "The Attlee Years, 1935-55" in Brivati, Brian and Heffernan, Richard (eds.), *The Labour Party: A Centenary History*, p.75.

[16] Jefferys, Kevin, "The Attlee Years, 1935-55" in Brivati, Brian and Heffernan, Richard (eds.), *The Labour Party: A Centenary History*, p.74.

[17] Mikardo, Ian, *Back-Bencher*, p.66.

[18] Crossman, Richard, Foot, Michael and Mikardo, Ian, *Keep Left*, London, New Statesman and Nation, 1947. The details of how the pamphlet was planned are to be found on the inside cover of the pamphlet.

[19] Crossman, Richard, Foot, Michael and Mikardo, Ian, *Keep Left*, p.11.

[20] Crossman, Richard, Foot, Michael and Mikardo, Ian, *Keep Left*, p.15.

[21] Crossman, Richard, Foot, Michael and Mikardo, Ian, *Keep Left*, pp.24/5. These committees were established to increase worker co-operation with management.

[22] Crossman, Richard (ed.), *New Fabian Essays*, London, Turnstile Press, 1952.

[23] Shaw, George Bernard (ed.), *Fabian Essays in Socialism*, London, Fabian Society, 1889.

[24] Crossman, Richard, "Towards a Philosophy of Socialism" in Crossman, Richard, *New Fabian Essays*, p.2.

[25] Crossman, Richard, *New Fabian Essays*, p.27.

[26] Crossman, Richard, *How Britain in Governed*, London, Labour Book Service, 1939.

[27] Crossman, Richard, *Socialism and the New Despotism*, Fabian Tract 298, 1956. The pamphlet was the text of a speech which Crossman had delivered in November 1955 to a Fabian Audience at the Livingstone Hall in Westminster.

[28] Crossman, Richard, *Socialism and the New Despotism*, p.4.

[29] Crossman, Richard, "Towards a Philosophy of Socialism", pp. 1-32.

[30] Crossman, Richard, *Socialism and the New Despotism*, pp. 5/6.

[31] Crossman, Richard, *Socialism and the New Despotism*, p.14.

[32] Crossman, Richard, *Socialism and the New Despotism*, p.13.

[33] Crossman, Richard, *Socialism and the New Despotism*, pp. 13-15.

[34] Crosland, Anthony, *The Future of Socialism*, London, Cape, 1956.

[35] Crossman, Richard, *Labour in the Affluent Society*, Fabian Tract 325, 1960.

[36] Crossman, Richard, *Socialism and the New Despotism,* pp. 12/3.

[37] Crossman, Richard, *Labour in the Affluent Society*, p.23.

[38] Crossman, Richard, *Labour in the Affluent Society*, p.17.

[39] Crossman, Richard, *Labour in the Affluent Society*.

[40] For an example of Crossman's attitude see Crossman, Richard, *The Diaries of a Cabinet Minister*, Vol. I, London, Hamish Hamilton and Jonathan Cape, 1975, p.29. Entry for Thursday 22nd October 1964.

[41] Crossman, Richard, *The Diaries of a Cabinet Minister*, Vol. II,, London, Hamish Hamilton and Jonathan Cape, 1976, p.566. Entry for Friday 10th November 1967.

[42] Crossman, Richard, *The Diaries of a Cabinet Minister*, Vol. III, London, Hamish Hamilton and Jonathan Cape, 1977, p.433. Entry for Wednesday 9th April 1969.

[43] Crossman, Richard, *Cabinet Diaries*, Vol. II, p.579. Entry for Sunday 15th October 1967.

[44] Crossman, Richard, *Cabinet Diaries*, Vol. III, p.45. Entry for Sunday 5th May 1968.

[45] Pimlott, Ben, *Harold Wilson,,* p.152.

[46] Crossman commented on Wilson and Brown's relationship when Brown resigned as Foreign Secretary. Crossman, Richard, *Cabinet Diaries*, Vol. II, p.715. Entry for Sunday 17th March 1968.

[47] Morgan, Janet (ed.), *Backbench Diaries*, p.186. Entry for Wednesday 3rd December 1952.

[48] Morgan, Janet (ed.), *Backbench Diaries*, p.972. Entry for Friday 8th February 1963.

[49] Pimlott, Ben, *Harold Wilson*, p.363.

[50] Williams, Marcia, *Inside Number 10*, London, Weidenfeld and Nicolson, 1972, p.313.

[51] Morgan, Janet (ed.), *Backbench Diaries*, p.972. Entry for 8th February 1963

[52] Pimlott, Ben, *Harold Wilson*, p.177.

[53] Healey, Denis, *The Time of My Life*, London, Michael Joseph, 1989, p.108.

[54] Crossman, Richard, "Towards a New Philosophy of Socialism".

[55] Healey, Denis, *The Time of My Life* p.108.

[56] Morrison, Herbert, *Socialisation and Transport*, London, Constable, 1933, p.141.

[57] Durbin, Evan, *The Politics of Democratic Socialism*, London, Routledge and Kegan Paul, 1940.

[58] Crosland, Anthony, *The Future of Socialism*.

[59] Crosland, Anthony, *The Future of Socialism*, p.97.

[60] Wright, Anthony, *Socialisms: Old and New,* 2nd Edition, London, Routledge, 1996, pp.82/3.

[61] Crosland, Anthony, *The Future of Socialism,* p.20.

[62] Crosland, Anthony, *The Future of Socialism*, p.496.

[63] Thorpe, Andrew, *A History of the British Labour Party*, p.137.

[64] Foote, Geoffrey, *The Labour Party's Political Thought*, London, Croom Helm, 1985, p.201.

[65] Thorpe, Andrew, *A History of the British Labour Party*, p.38.

[66] Thorpe, Andrew, *A History of the British Labour Party*, p.137.

[67] Pimlott, Ben, *Harold Wilson*, p.227.

[68] Morgan, Janet (ed.), *Backbench Diaries*, pp.818/9. Entry for Wednesday 2nd March 1960. For more discussion of nuclear weapons, see Chapter 4.

[69] Wright, Anthony, *Socialisms: Old and New,* p.ix. Introduction by Tony Blair.

[70] Jones, Tudor, *Remaking the Labour Party*, London, Routledge, 1996, p.20.

[71] Jones, Tudor, *Remaking the Labour Party*, p.20.

[72] Crossman, Richard, *Labour in the Affluent Society*, p.9.

[73] Crosland noted that 'the issue now is not whether, but how much and for what purpose, to plan.' Crosland, Anthony, *The Future of Socialism*, p.501.

[74] Foote, Geoffrey, *The Labour Party's Political Thought*, pp.165/6.

[75] Durbin, Evan, *The Politics of Democratic Socialism*, p.302.

[76] None of these individuals wrote about the creation of a DEA-style body or advocated it as a useful tool for economic planning.

[77] Crossman, Richard, *Cabinet Diaries*, Vol. I, p.117. Entry for Sunday 3rd January 1965.

[78] Tawney, R.H., *The Acquisitive Society*, London, Bell, 1921, p.187.

[79] Crosland, Anthony, *The Future of Socialism,* p.503.

[80] Crossman, Richard, *Socialism and the New Despotism*, p.6.

[81] Crossman, Richard, *Cabinet Diaries*, Vol. II, p.41. Entry for Monday 19th September 1966.

[82] Crosland, Anthony, "On the Left Again", *Encounter* XV/4, October 1960, p.9.

[83] Crosland, Anthony, *The Future of Socialism*, p.89.

[84] Tawney, R.H., *Equality*, 4th Edition, London, George Allen and Unwin, 1952, p.225.

[85] Bevan, Aneurin, *In Place of Fear*, London, William Heinemann, 1952, p.31.

[86] Foote, Geoffrey, *The Labour Party's Political Thought*, pp. 198/9.

[87] Durbin, Evan, *The Politics of Democratic Socialism*, p.300.

[88] Tawney, R.H., *Equality*, p.209.

[89] Morgan, Janet (ed.), *Backbench Diaries,* p.53, Entry for Monday 17th December 1951.

[90] Tawney, R.H., *Equality*, pp. 176/7.

[91] Crosland, Anthony, *The Conservative Enemy*, London, Cape, 1962, pp. 91/2.

[92] Crosland, Anthony, *The Future of Socialism*, p.466.

[93] Durbin, Evan, *The Politics of Democratic Socialism*, p.303.

[94] Tawney, R.H., *The Acquisitive Society*, p.225.

[95] Tawney criticised the current inheritance system as allowing 'a small minority of rich men [to] bequeath to their heirs a right to free quarters at the expense of their fellow man.' Tawney, R.H., *Equality*, p.12.

[96] Coates, David, *The Labour Party and the Struggle for Socialism*, London, Cambridge University Press, 1975, p.50.

[97] Morrison, Herbert, *Socialisation and Transport*, p.148.

[98] Crosland, Anthony, *The Future of Socialism*, p.359.

[99] Crossman noted that while he had no concrete proposals on how to implement this, Britain should look to the German example to see if any lessons could be learnt. Crossman, Richard, *Socialism and the New Despotism*, p.14.

[100] Crossman, Richard, *Socialism and the New Despotism*, p.2.

[101] Available on *http://news.bbc.co.uk/hi/english/static/vote2001/In_depth/election_battles/1945_camp.stm*. Accessed 01/09/03.

[102] Bevan, Aneurin, *In Place of Fear*, p.68.

[103] Crossman, Richard, Foot, Michael, Mikardo, Ian, *Keep Left*, pp. 17/8.

[104] Crossman, Richard, *How Britain is Governed*, p.9.

[105] Tawney, R.H., *Equality,* p.227.

[106] A useful example where Crossman considered all three issues can be found in Crossman, Richard, *Inside View*, London, Jonathan Cape, 1972.

[107] Durbin, Evan, *The Politics of Democratic Socialism*, p.235.

[108] Crosland, Anthony, *The Future of Socialism*, p.522.

[109] Crossman reports that he deliberately sat on the front bench 'to give support to Leo Abse, who was moving his ten-minute Bill on homosexual reform in order to prove there is a majority in favour of changing the law.' Crossman, Richard, *Cabinet Diaries*, Vol. I, p.561. Entry for Tuesday 5th July 1966.

[110] Crossman, Richard, *Socialism and the New Despotism*, p.7.

[111] Tawney, R.H., *Equality*, p.181.

[112] Tawney, R.H., *Equality*, p.217.

[113] Durbin, Evan, *The Politics of Democratic Socialism*, p.218.

[114] Crosland, Anthony, *The Future of Socialism*, p.382.

[115] Crossman, Richard, "Towards a New Philosophy of Socialism", p.24

[116] Morgan, Janet (ed.), *Backbench Diaries*, p.712. Entry for Wednesday 27th August 1958.

[117] Pimlott, Ben, *Harold Wilson*, p.181.

[118] Crossman, Richard, *Labour in the Affluent Society*, p.9. Italics as in the original document.

[119] Crossman, Richard (ed.), "Towards a Philosophy of Socialism", p.13.

[120] Pimlott, Ben, *Harold Wilson*, p.274.

121 Crossman, Richard, "Scientists in Whitehall" in Crossman, Richard, *Planning for Freedom*, London, Hamish Hamilton, 1965, p.141.

122 Jefferys, Kevin, *Anthony Crosland*, London, Richard Cohen, 1999, p.102.

123 Horner, David, "The Road to Scarborough" in Coopey, Richard, Fielding, Steve and Tiratsoo, Nick, *The Wilson Governments 1964*-1970, London, Pinter, 1993, p.62.

124 Marquand, David, *The Progressive Dilemma*, London, Heinemann, 1991. The chapter on Crossman is entitled "The Progressive as Gadfly".

125 Morgan, Janet (ed.), *Backbench Diaries*, p.615. Entry for Friday 4th October 1957.

126 Crossman, Richard, *Cabinet Diaries*, Vol. I.

127 Williams, Marcia, *Inside Number 10*, p.313.

128 Benn, Tony, *Against the Tide: Diaries 1973-76*, London, Arrow, 1989, p.639. Entry for Sunday 7th November 1976.

129 Crossman, Richard, *Cabinet Diaries*, Vol. II, p.428. Entry for Monday 17th July 1967.

130 Gwyn, William, "The Labour Party and the Threat of Bureaucracy", *Political Studies* 19, 1971, p.388.

131 Crossman, Richard, *Labour in the Affluent Society*, p.9.

132 Crossman, Richard, *Cabinet Diaries*, Vol. III, p.405. Entry for Sunday 9th March 1969.

133 Crossman, Richard, *Cabinet Diaries*, Vol. I, p.584. Entry for Sunday 24th July 1966.

134 Crossman Papers, Modern Records Centre, University of Warwick Library, MSS.154/26/840. Copy of the speeches given at Crossman's memorial service.

Chapter Four

1 Crossman's pre-occupation with Germany and wider foreign policy can be seen in his early speeches in the House of Commons, which were limited to foreign policy issues and particularly the future of Germany.

2 Crossman pointed out that his initial reaction to his appointment to the Commission was 'that Palestine had become a ticklish problem' for the Labour Government, but he was 'ignorant' about the issue. Crossman, Richard, *Palestine Mission: A Personal Record*, London, Hamish Hamilton, 1947, p.11.

3 Crossman, Richard, *Palestine Mission*, p.12.

4 Crossman, Richard, Foot, Michael and Mikardo, Ian, *Keep Left*, London, New Statesman and Nation, 1947.

5 The Keep Left group noted that 'whether we like it or not, we and the other nations of Western Europe are still dependent on America.' However, later in the pamphlet the group advocated turning away from the USA in favour of the USSR. Crossman, Richard, Foot, Michael and Mikardo, Ian, *Keep Left*, pp. 37 and 46.

6 'Working together, we [Europeans] are still strong enough to hold the balance of world-power, to halt the division into a Western and Eastern *bloc*.' Crossman, Richard, Foot, Michael and Mikardo, Ian, *Keep Left*, p.38.

7 An example of Crossman's feelings on this is given in Crossman, Richard, *The Diaries of a Cabinet Minister*, Vol. II, London, Hamish Hamilton and Jonathan Cape, 1976, p.51. Entry for Sunday 25th September 1966.

8 Crossman, Richard, *The Diaries of a Cabinet Minister*, Vol. II, pp.108/9. Entry for Friday 4th November 1966.

9 Gordon, Michael, *Conflict and Consensus in Labour's Foreign Policy 1914-1965*, Stanford, California, Stanford University Press, 1969, pp. 13-43.

10 Vickers, Rhiannon, *The Labour Party and the World Volume 1: The Evolution of Labour's Foreign Policy 1900-51*, Manchester, Manchester University Press, 2003, p.5.

11 Shaw, Eric, *British Socialist Approaches to International Affairs 1945-1951*, an unpublished MPhil from the University of Leeds, May 1974, p.29.

12 Shaw, Eric, *British Socialist Approaches*, p.3.

[13] Shaw, Eric, *British Socialist Approaches*, p.4.

[14] Shaw, Eric, *British Socialist Approaches*, p.7.

[15] Shaw, Eric, *British Socialist Approaches*, p.8.

[16] Shaw, Eric, *British Socialist Approaches*, p.7.

[17] Shaw, Eric, *British Socialist Approaches*, pp. 21-29.

[18] Crossman, Richard, Foot, Michael and Mikardo, Ian, *Keep Left*, p.38.

[19] National Archive FCO 17/575, *Richard Crossman Interview about Ernest Bevin on Harlech Television 1967/8*.

[20] Vickers, Rhiannon, *The Labour Party and the World*, p.5.

[21] Shaw, Eric, *British Socialist Approaches*, p.35.

[22] Shaw, Eric, *British Socialist Approaches*, pp.144/5.

[23] Pelling, Henry, *America and the British Left*, London, A and C Black, 1956, p.151.

[24] Vickers, Rhiannon, *The Labour Party and the World*, p.166.

[25] Sanders, David, *Losing an Empire, Finding a Role: British Foreign Policy Since 1945*, Basingstoke, Macmillan Education, 1990, p.97.

[26] Vickers, Rhiannon, *The Labour Party and the World*, p.167.

[27] Sanders, David, *Losing an Empire, Finding a Role*, pp. 78/9.

[28] Bullock, Alan, *Ernest Bevin: Foreign Secretary 1945-51*, London and New York, Norton, 1983, pp. 46/7.

[29] Bullock, Alan, *Ernest Bevin: Foreign Secretary*, pp. 44/5.

[30] Gorney, Joseph, *The British Labour Movement and Zionism 1917-48*, London, Frank Cass, 1983, pp. 214-221.

[31] Bullock describes Bevin's achievement as having 'brought the Americans off the sidelines and involved them in finding a solution to the problem.' Bullock, Alan, *Ernest Bevin: Foreign Secretary*, p.179.

[32] Crossman, Richard, 'Americans, Jews and Arabs', *New Statesman*, 32, 13th July 1946, p.22.

[33] Louis, William Roger, *The British Empire in the Middle East 1945-51*, Oxford, Clarendon Press, 1984, pp. 392/3.

[34] Crossman, Richard, *Palestine Mission*, p.12.

[35] Hector McNeil indicated that the government wanted to 'try you [Crossman] out'. Crossman, Richard, *Palestine Mission*, p.12.

[36] National Archive PREM 8/302, *Mr Crossman MP Sent Memo on the Palestine Report on the Anglo-American Commission following the interview with the Prime Minister 1946*. Letter from Crossman to Attlee dated 7th May 1946. Underlining as in original document.

[37] 'At a lunch given to the committee in London, the Foreign Secretary stated unequivocally that, if the committee reached unanimity, he himself would carry the report into effect.' National Archive PREM 8/302, *Mr Crossman MP Sent Memo on the Palestine Report on the Anglo-American Commission following the interview with the Prime Minister 1946*

[38] Cohen, Michael J., *Palestine and the Great Powers 1945-48*, Princeton, New Jersey and Guildford, Surrey, Princeton University Press, 1982, p.107.

[39] Bullock, Alan, *Ernest Bevin: Foreign Secretary*, p.305.

[40] Crossman, Richard, *Palestine Mission*, p.197. For more details of this see Chapter 8 "After the Report".

[41] Bullock, Alan, *Ernest Bevin: Foreign Secretary*, p.306.

[42] Crossman, Richard, "The Case for Partition", *New Statesman* 32, 14th September 1946, p.184.

[43] National Archive PREM 8/302, *Mr Crossman MP Sent Memo on the Palestine Report on the Anglo-American Commission following the interview with the Prime Minister 1946*. Letter from Crossman to Attlee dated 7th May 1946.

[44] Morgan, Janet (ed.), *Backbench Diaries*, p.326. Entry for 6th May 1954.

[45] Bullock, Alan, *Ernest Bevin: Foreign Secretary*, pp. 78/9.

[46] Bevin did have some limited experience of overseas relations due to his Trade Union links with overseas unions in both East and West. For further information on the career of Bevin as Foreign Secretary, a key publication is Bullock, Alan, *Ernest Bevin: Foreign Secretary*.

[47] National Archive PREM 8/302, *Mr Crossman MP Sent Memo on the Palestine Report on the Anglo-American Commission following the interview with the Prime Minister 1946*. Letter from Bevin to Attlee dated 27th September 1946.

[48] *Clem Attlee: The Granada Historical Records Interview*, Panther Record, 1967, p.39.

[49] Donoughue, Bernard, *Downing Street Diary: With Harold Wilson in No. 10*, London, Cape, 2005, p.271. Entry for 2nd January 1975.

[50] Crossman Papers, Modern Records Centre, University of Warwick Library, MSS.154/3/BR/3/12-32. *The Open Mind*, transcript of a television show which Crossman took part in, entitled "How Vital is Zionism for American Jewry?" On NBC television, Saturday 28th January 1961.

[51] Crossman, Richard, "A Date for India – Why not for Palestine?" *Sunday Pictorial*, 23rd February 1947, as quoted in *New Statesman Special Edition*, reproduction of articles from other publications due to fuel crisis, 33, February 1947, p.10.

[52] Crossman, Richard, "A Date for India – Why not for Palestine?" p.10.

[53] Bullock, Alan, *Ernest Bevin: Foreign Secretary*, p.110.

[54] Crossman, Richard, "How it Looks in Palestine", *New Statesman*, 37, 15th January 1949, p.47.

[55] Crossman, Richard, "How it Looks in Palestine", *New Statesman*, 37, 15th January 1949, p.48.

[56] Crossman, Richard, "Israel and Jordan IV: Britain's Role", *New Statesman*, 41, 10th March 1951, p.269.

[57] Crossman, Richard, "Israel and Jordan I: The Wounds of War", *New Statesman*, 41, 10th February 1951, pp. 148/9.

[58] For example, Crossman, Richard, "Israel and the Arabs", *New Statesman*, 45, 14th February 1953, pp. 168/9. Crossman, Richard, "Israel and the Arabs", *New Statesman*, 46, 24th October 1953, pp. 476/7. Crossman, Richard, "Gaza – One Key to Peace", *New Statesman*, 53, 12th January 1957, pp. 32/3.

[59] Crossman, Richard, *A Nation Reborn: The Israel of Weizmann, Bevin and Ben-Gurion*, London, Hamish Hamilton, 1960, p.118.

[60] Crossman, Richard, *A Nation Reborn*, p.113. Crossman discussed in his third lecture the issue of Israel gaining NATO membership and its external alliances.

[61] Crossman Papers, MSS.154/10/52. Pinner, Hayim, "An Appreciation: R.H.S. Crossman, friend of Israel Par Excellence", *Jewish Vanguard*, 24th April 1974, p.7. It should be noted that Crossman did not note that he had held that position, either in his diaries or in other publications and the Labour Friends of Israel have no record of this being the case either. This appears to have been a case of over-enthusiasm.

[62] Bullock, Alan, *Ernest Bevin: Foreign Secretary*, pp. 78/9.

[63] Bullock, Alan, *Ernest Bevin: Foreign Secretary*, p.64.

[64] Bullock, Alan, *Ernest Bevin: Foreign Secretary*, p.95.

[65] Bullock, Alan, *Ernest Bevin: Foreign Secretary*, p.98.

[66] Crossman, Richard, "Politics at Lake Success", *New Statesman*, 34, 25th October 1947, p.64.

[67] Bullock, Alan, *Ernest Bevin: Foreign Secretary*, p.69.

[68] Crossman, Richard, "Know Thine Enemy", *New Statesman*, 41, 21st April 1951, p.453. Speaking in 1967/8, Crossman stated that the group of socialists he had associated with had hoped that a socialist Europe could mediate between the USA and the USSR. National Archive FCO 17/575, *Richard Crossman Interview about Ernest Bevin on Harlech Television 1967/8*.

[69] Crossman, Foot and Mikardo, *Keep Left.*

[70] Mark Wickham-Jones argued that the Keep Left group was the origin of the Bevanites. Wickham-Jones, Mark, *Economic Strategy and the Labour Party: Politics and Policy Making 1970-83*, Basingstoke, Macmillan, 1996, p.38.

[71] Crossman, Richard, "Are the French Impossible?" *New Statesman*, 32, 21st December 1946, p.458.

[72] Crossman, Foot and Mikardo, *Keep Left*, p.35.

[73] Crossman, Foot and Mikardo, *Keep Left*, p.41.

[74] Crossman, Foot and Mikardo, *Keep Left*, p.33.

[75] Crossman Papers, MSS.154/3/BR/3/1-7. "Grossbritanniens Stellung Zu Europa Und Der EDC", *Sudwestdeutscher Rundfunk*, 29th April 1953.

[76] Bullock, Alan, *Ernest Bevin: Foreign Secretary*, p.191.

[77] Crossman Papers, MSS.154/3/LIT/8/33-36. "Where do we Stand", a Keep Left Group paper written by Richard Crossman, 8th December 1950.

[78] Crossman, Richard, "The Great Debate II", *New Statesman*, 34, 22nd November 1947, p.406.

[79] Crossman, Richard, "Can We Cut Commitments?" *New Statesman*, 45, 3rd January 1953, p.5.

[80] Crossman, Richard, *Cabinet Diaries*, Vol. II, pp.155/6. Entry for Friday 9th December 1966.

[81] Crossman, Richard, "Are the French Impossible?" p.458.

[82] Crossman, Richard, "The Case for German Neutralisation", *New Statesman*, 48, 4th September 1954, p.253.

[83] Bullock, Alan, *Ernest Bevin: Foreign Secretary*, p.312.

[84] Crossman, Foot and Mikardo, *Keep Left*, p.46.

[85] Crossman, Richard, "Interim Balance Sheet", *New Statesman*, 29, 12th May 1945, p.302.

[86] Crossman, Foot and Mikardo, *Keep Left*, p.42.

[87] A full account of the blockade is available in Chapter 14, "Berlin Blockade, Israel Proclaimed" in Bullock, Alan, *Ernest Bevin: Foreign Secretary*, p.549.

[88] Crossman, Richard, "The Case for German Neutralisation", p.253.

[89] Crossman Papers, MSS.154/4/PAM/6. *It Need Not Happen: The Alternative to German Rearmament*, a Tribune pamphlet signed by Aneurin Bevan, Barbara Castle, Richard Crossman, Tom Driberg, Ian Mikardo and Harold Wilson, London, Tribune Publications, 1954.

[90] Crossman, Richard, "The Case for German Neutralisation", p.253.

[91] Crossman Papers, MSS.154/3/BR/3/1-7. "Grossbritanniens Stellung Zu Europa Und Der EDC".

[92] Crossman Papers, MSS.154/4/PAM/5. *Should Britain Join a North Atlantic Union?* 31st August 1952. Transcript of an NBC radio discussion.

[93] Dell, Edmund, *The Schuman Plan and the British Abdication of Leadership in Europe*, Oxford, Oxford University Press, 1995, pp. 8/9.

[94] Dell, Edmund, *The Schuman Plan*, p.64.

[95] Dell, Edmund, *The Schuman Plan*, pp. 9 and 48.

[96] Dell, Edmund, *The Schuman Plan*, p.276.

[97] Dell, Edmund, *The Schuman Plan*, p.33.

[98] Crossman, Richard, "World View", *Sunday Pictorial*, 29th August 1948.

[99] Crossman Papers, MSS.154/3/BR/3/80-85. *London Letter*, a broadcast on Italian Radio on 16th July 1962.

[100] The incorporation of Commonwealth countries into the ECSC was an issue which the Foreign Office believed could be accommodated within an agreement. Dell, Edmund, *The Schuman Plan*, p.277.

[101] Crossman Papers, MSS.154/10/23. Crossman, Richard, "Policies for Socialists", *The New Leader*, 6th August 1956, p.13.

[102] Crossman Papers, MSS.154/3/BR/3/80-85. *London Letter.*

[103] Crossman Papers, MSS.154/3/MIS/26/141. Letter from Crossman to The Duchess of Bedford dated 14th September 1972. In this Crossman writes 'I am afraid I regard January 1 next year as a black day in our history…'

[104] Crossman, Richard, *Cabinet Diaries*, Vol. II, p.188. Entry for Friday 6th January 1967.

[105] Crossman, Richard, *Cabinet Diaries,* Vol. III, London, Hamish Hamilton and Jonathan Cape, 1977, p.225. Entry for Wednesday 16th October 1968.

[106] Crossman, Richard, *Cabinet Diaries,* Vol. III, p.642. Entry for Sunday 14th September 1969.

[107] Crossman Papers, MSS.154/3/BR/3/9-11. No title, though this appears to be the transcript of a report given by Crossman on a German radio Station dated 25th January 1957.

[108] Crossman Papers, MSS.154/3/GDR/16-17. Copy of a questionnaire produced by the Committee for the Recognition of the German Democratic Republic, authored by Crossman and dated 5th July 1971.

[109] Crossman Papers, MSS.154/3/GDR/32. Letter from Crossman to Christopher Tugendhat MP asking him to join the Committee for the Recognition of the German Republic, dated 28th October 1971. Crossman states that 'this country should do something in its own economic interest to improve our export possibilities to the GDR.'

[110] Crossman Papers, MSS.154/3/BR/3/80-85. *London Letter.*

[111] Crossman Papers, MSS.154/10/19. *Prospects for Peace*, a press release of a Fabian Lecture delivered on 15th November 1949 by Crossman. Crossman indicated that 'it is high time that we all stopped pretending that Western Europe can be independent of American Aid by 1952.'

[112] Evidence of his changing views can be seen in a 1948 House of Commons speech when Crossman admitted 'I will be frank, my own views about America have changed a great deal in the last six months.' *House of Commons Debates*, 23rd January 1948, col. 566.

[113] Hennessy noted that at the end of the Second World War '…the number of people in the United Kingdom who knew how far the intensely secret combined US, UK and Canadian atomic weapon programme had progressed was limited to a tiny circle around Winston Churchill.' Hennessy, Peter, *The Secret State: Whitehall and the Cold War*, London, Allen Lane and the Penguin Press, 2002, p.xi.

[114] A brief outline of these difficulties are available in Williams, Phillip, *Hugh Gaitskell*, London, Cape, 1979, p.574.

[115] Bullock, Alan, *Ernest Bevin: Foreign Secretary*, p.57.

[116] House of Commons debate, 14th March 1955, col. 999.

[117] Hennessy, Peter, *The Secret State*, p.49.

[118] Crossman, Richard, and Wigg, George, "The Dilemma of the H-Bomb", *New Statesman,* 49, 26th February 1955, p.268.

[119] Crossman, Richard, "If We Banned that Bomb?", *Sunday Pictorial*, 30th July 1950.

[120] House of Commons, 5th March 1953, col. 658.

[121] This was not a view that Crossman maintained, as argued below. Crossman, Richard, "Should we Make Atom Bombs?", *Sunday Pictorial*, 24th July 1949.

[122] The McMahon Act of 1946 prevented the USA collaborating with any other country, including the UK and Canada. Hennessy, Hennessy, Peter, *The Secret State*, p.47.

[123] Sanders, David, *Losing an Empire, Finding a Role*, p.236.

[124] Crossman Papers, MSS.154/10/18. Text of a speech made by RHSC at Central Hall on 11th April 1947, p.5.

[125] Crossman, Richard, "Should we Make Atom Bombs?", *Sunday Pictorial*, 24th July 1949.

126 Manchester Labour Party Archive, Defence Sub-Committee file, folder 7, *Disarmament Sub-Committee Correspondence 1958-9*, p.3.

127 Manchester Labour Party Archive, Defence Sub-Committee file, folder 7, *Disarmament Sub-Committee Correspondence 1958-*9, document dated 24th July 1949.

128 Crossman, Richard and Wigg, George, "The Dilemma of the H-Bomb", p.269.

129 Williams, Phillip, *Hugh Gaitskell*, p.393.

130 Howard, Anthony, *Crossman: The Pursuit of Power*, London, Jonathan Cape, 1990, p.213.

131 The documents relating to this committee are held at the Manchester Labour Party Archive and demonstrate Crossman's lack of attendance.

132 The article, "The Dilemma of the H-Bomb", outlined the arguments for and against withdrawing from NATO and renouncing nuclear weapons but with no indication of how to communicate this more widely.

133 Williams, Phillip, *Hugh Gaitskell*, p.602.

134 The Labour Party, *Your Personal Guide to the Future Labour Offers You*, 1958.

135 Williams, Phillip, *Hugh Gaitskell*, p.575.

136 Crossman, Richard, "Grotius on Atomic War" in Crossman, Richard, *Planning for Freedom*, London, Hamish Hamilton, 1965, p.233.

137 Crossman, Richard and Wigg, George, "Dilemma of the H-Bomb", p.269.

138 Williams, Phillip, *Hugh Gaitskell*, p.602.

139 Williams, Phillip, *Hugh Gaitskell*, p.589.

140 Morgan, Janet (ed.), *Backbench Diaries*, p.856. Entry for Wednesday 1st June 1960.

141 Crossman, Richard, *Cabinet Diaries*, Vol. III, p.642. Entry for Sunday 14th September 1969.

142 Crossman Papers, MSS.154/4/PAM/5. *Should Britain Join a North Atlantic Union?* An NBC radio broadcast by Crossman delivered on 31st August 1952.

143 Crossman, Richard, "Towards a Philosophy of Socialism" in Crossman, Richard, *New Fabian Essays*, London, Turnstile Press, 1952, p.13.

Chapter Five

1 Theakston, Kevin, *The Labour Party and Whitehall*, London, Routledge, 1992, p.4.

2 Crossman, Richard, *The Diaries of a Cabinet Minister*, Vol. II, London, Hamish Hamilton and Jonathan Cape, 1976, p.101. Entry for Wednesday 19th June 1968.

3 Crossman, Richard, *How Britain is Governed*, London, Labour Book Service, 1939, p.29.

4 Crossman, Richard, *How Britain is Governed*, p.31.

5 Crossman, Richard, "Introduction" in Bagehot, Walter, *The English Constitution*, Glasgow, Fontana/Collins, 1963, p.10.

6 Attlee, Clement, *The Labour Party in Perspective*, London, Gollancz, 1937, p.154.

7 Crossman, Richard, *The Diaries of a Cabinet Minister*, Vol. I, London, Hamish Hamilton and Jonathan Cape, 1975, p.433. Entry for Sunday 23rd January 1966.

8 Bogdanor, Vernon, "Labour and the Constitution, Part One: The Record" in Brivati, Brian and Bale, Tim, *New Labour in Power: Precedents and Prospects*, London, Routledge, 1997, p.112.

9 Bogdanor, Vernon, "Labour and the Constitution", p.112.

10 Bogdanor, Vernon, "Labour and the Constitution", p.115.

11 Bogdanor, Vernon, "Labour and the Constitution", p.173.

12 Bogdanor, Vernon, "Labour and the Constitution", p.173.

13 Taylor, Miles, "Labour and the Constitution" in Tanner, Duncan, Thane, Pat and Tiratsoo, Nick, *Labour's First Century*, Cambridge, Cambridge University Press, 2000, p.166.

14 Taylor, Miles, "Labour and the Constitution", p.169.

15 Theakston, Kevin, *The Labour Party and Whitehall*, p.4.

[16] Theakston, Kevin, *The Labour Party and Whitehall,* p.111.

[17] Theakston, Kevin, "Prime Ministers and the Constitution: Attlee to Blair", *Parliamentary Affairs,* 58/1, January 2005, p.17.

[18] Attlee, Clement, *The Labour Party in Perspective,* p.114.

[19] Attlee, Clement, *The Labour Party in Perspective,* p.139.

[20] Attlee, Clement, *The Labour Party in Perspective,* p.169.

[21] Burridge, Trevor, *Clement Attlee: A Political Biography,* London, Cape, 1985, p.318.

[22] Theakston, Kevin, *The Labour Party and Whitehall,* p.168.

[23] Crossman, Richard, *Cabinet Diaries,* Vol. II, p.130. Entry for Thursday 17th November 1966.

[24] Laski, Harold, *Parliamentary Government in England,* London, George Allen and Unwin, 1938, p.118.

[25] Gwyn, William, "The Labour Party and the Threat of Bureaucracy", *Political Studies,* 19, 1971, p.384.

[26] Gwyn, William, "The Labour Party and the Threat of Bureaucracy", p.385.

[27] Gwyn, William, "The Labour Party and the Threat of Bureaucracy", p.386.

[28] Gwyn, William, "The Labour Party and the Threat of Bureaucracy", p.391. Gwyn used evidence from both Jenkins and Crosland to show their support for liberty of the individual regardless of where control may emanate from.

[29] Crossman stated 'In practice, therefore, a Government is no longer fully responsible to Parliament.' Crossman, Richard, *Socialism and the New Despotism,* Fabian Tract 298, 1956, p.18.

[30] Gwyn, William, "The Labour Party and the Threat of Bureaucracy", p.391.

[31] Gwyn, William, "The Labour Party and the Threat of Bureaucracy", p.388.

[32] Theakston, Kevin, *The Labour Party and Whitehall,* p.11.

[33] Theakston, Kevin, *The Labour Party and Whitehall,* pp.11/12.

[34] Theakston, Kevin, *The Labour Party and Whitehall,* p.12.

[35] Webb, Beatrice and Webb, Sidney, *A Constitution for the Socialist Commonwealth of Great Britain,* London, Longman, Green and Co., 1920

[36] Webb, Beatrice and Webb, Sidney, *A Constitution for the Socialist Commonwealth,* p.118.

[37] Webb, Beatrice and Webb, Sidney, *A Constitution for the Socialist Commonwealth,* p.67.

[38] Webb, Beatrice and Webb, Sidney, *A Constitution for the Socialist Commonwealth,* p.69.

[39] Webb, Beatrice and Webb, Sidney, *A Constitution for the Socialist Commonwealth,* p.69.

[40] Muir, Ramsey, *How Britain is Governed,* London, R.R. Smith, 1930.

[41] Crossman, Richard, *How Britain is Governed,* p.7.

[42] Crossman, Richard, *How Britain is Governed,* p.29. Muir, Ramsey, *How Britain is Governed,* p.63.

[43] Theakston, Kevin, "Richard Crossman: The Diaries of a Cabinet Minister", *Public Administration and Policy,* 18/4, Winter 2003, p.31.

[44] Laski, Harold, *Parliamentary Government,* p.115.

[45] Laski, Harold, *Parliamentary Government,* p.43.

[46] Laski, Harold, *Parliamentary Government,* p.74.

[47] Hanson, A.H., "The Labour Party and the House of Commons", in Hanson, A. H., *Planning and the Politicians and Other Essays,* London, Routledge and Kegan Paul, 1969, p.65. This article initially appeared in *Parliamentary Affairs,* Autumn 1957 and Winter 1957/8.

[48] Hanson, A.H., "The Purpose of Parliament" in Hanson, A. H., *Planning and the Politicians and Other Essays,* p.12. This article initially appeared in *Parliamentary Affairs,* Summer 1964.

[49] Hanson, A.H., "The Labour Party and the House of Commons" in Hanson, A. H., *Planning and the Politicians and Other Essays,* p.65.

[50] Crossman, Richard, *Socialism and the New Despotism,* pp. 15-24.

51 Hewart, Gordon, *The New Despotism*, London, Ernest Benn Ltd., 1929.

52 Further explanation of Lord Hewart's use of this term is available in Gwyn, William, "The Labour Party and the Threat of Bureaucracy", p.390.

53 Crossman, Richard, *Socialism and the New Despotism*, p.15.

54 Crossman, Richard, *Socialism and the New Despotism*, p.19.

55 Crossman, Richard, *Socialism and the New Despotism*, p.19.

56 Crossman, Richard, *How Britain is Governed*, p.70.

57 Drucker, H., *Doctrine and Ethos in the Labour Party*, London and Boston, George Allen and Unwin, 1979.

58 Drucker, H., *Doctrine and Ethos*, p.97.

59 Drucker, H., *Doctrine and Ethos*, p.99.

60 For an example of this see Crossman, Richard, *Cabinet Diaries*, Vol. I, p.333. Entry for Wednesday 22nd September 1965.

61 Castle, Barbara, *The Castle Diaries 1964-76*, London, Papermac, Paperback Edition, 1990, pp.454/5. Entry for Wednesday 24th April 1974.

62 Castle, Barbara, "Mandarin Power", *The Sunday Times*, 10th June 1973.

63 Castle, Barbara, "Mandarin Power", pp. 17-19.

64 Benn, Tony, *Out of the Wilderness: Diaries 1963-67*, London, Arrow, 1989, p.184. Entry for Thursday 12th November 1964.

65 Benn, Tony, *Out of the Wilderness*, p.209. Entry for Monday 25th January 1965.

66 Benn, Tony, *Out of the Wilderness*, p.222. Entry for Thursday 18th February 1965.

67 Gordon-Walker, Patrick, *The Cabinet*, Revised Edition, London, Fontana, 1972. Morrison, Herbert, *Government and Parliament: A Survey from the Inside*, 2nd Edition, London, Oxford University Press, 1959.

68 Gordon-Walker, Patrick, *The Cabinet*, p.66.

69 Crossman, Richard, *Cabinet Diaries*, Vol. II, p.211. Entry for Thursday 26th January 1967.

70 Crossman Papers, Warwick Modern Records Centre, MS154/3/LPO/19/24-25. "Transcript of an Interview", 6th November 1967 in Taylor, Miles, "The Labour Party and the Constitution", p.167.

71 Crossman, Richard, *Cabinet Diaries*, Vol. II, p.211. Entry for Thursday 26th January 1967.

72 Crossman, Richard, *Socialism and the New Despotism*, p.16.

73 Crossman, Richard, *Socialism and the New Despotism*, p.16.

74 Crossman, Richard, *Cabinet Diaries*, Vol. I, p.31. Entry for Tuesday 27th October 1964.

75 Crossman, Richard, *Socialism and the New Despotism*, p.16.

76 Crossman, Richard, *How Britain is Governed*, p.72.

77 Laski, Harold, *Parliamentary Government*, p.302.

78 Laski, Harold, *Parliamentary Government*, pp.303/4.

79 National Archive BA 1/6, *Civil Service Department: Committee on the Civil Service, Fulton Committee). Minutes, Papers and Report 1966-69*.

80 Laski, Harold, *Parliamentary Government*, p.313.

81 Laski, Harold, *Parliamentary Government*, p.329. Crossman argued that reform would awaken resistance within the service. Crossman, Richard, *Socialism and the New Despotism*, p.16.

82 Laski, Harold, *Parliamentary Government*, p.313.

83 Laski, Harold, *Parliamentary Government*, p.326.

84 Laski, Harold, *Parliamentary Government*, p.326.

85 'There is no lack at all in the Civil Service of energy and devotion, of selflessness and public spirit.' Laski, Harold, *Parliamentary Government*, p.329.

86 Crossman, Richard, *How Britain is Governed*, p.69.

87 Crossman, Richard, *How Britain is Governed*, p.71.

88 Bridges, Edward, *Portrait of a Profession: The Civil Service Tradition*, Rede Lecture, Cambridge, Cambridge University Press, 1950, p.15.

89 Crossman, Richard, *Socialism and the New Despotism*, p.15,

[90] Crossman, Richard, *Socialism and the New Despotism*, p.16.

[91] Crossman, Richard, *Socialism and the New Despotism*, p.16.

[92] Crossman, Richard, *Inside View: Three Lectures on Prime Ministerial Government*, London, Jonathan Cape, 1972, p.9.

[93] Theakston, Kevin, "Evelyn Sharp (1903-85)", *Contemporary Record*, 7/1, Summer 1993, p.137.

[94] Crossman, Richard, *Cabinet Diaries*, Vol. I, p.66. Entry for Friday 20th November 1964.

[95] Crossman, Richard, *Cabinet Diaries*, Vol. I, p.614. Entry for Wednesday 24th August 1966.

[96] Crossman stated quite openly in his diaries 'About this job I knew virtually nothing.' Crossman, Richard, *Cabinet Diaries*, Vol. I, p.12.

[97] Crossman, Richard, *Inside View*, p.15.

[98] Crossman, Richard, *Cabinet Diaries,* Vol. I, p.21. Entry for Thursday 22nd October 1964.

[99] Crossman, Richard, *Cabinet Diaries*, Vol. I, p.21. Entry for Thursday 22nd October 1964.

[100] Crossman, Richard, *Cabinet Diaries*, Vol. I, p.614. Entry for Wednesday 24th August 1966.

[101] Crossman, Richard, *Cabinet Diaries*, Vol. I, p.614. Entry for Wednesday 24th August 1966.

[102] Jenkins, Simon, "Dame Evelyn Hits Back", *The Sunday Times*, 5th October 1975, p.17.

[103] For an example of Crossman's concerns regarding the replacement of Dame Evelyn Sharp see Crossman, Richard, *Cabinet Diaries*, Vol. I, p.470. Entry for Thursday 3rd March 1966.

[104] Fry, Geoffrey, *Reforming the Civil Service: The Fulton Committee on the British Civil Service of 1966-68*, Edinburgh, Edinburgh University Press, 1993, p.31. Quoted from an interview which the author held with Michael Simons in 1989.

[105] Crossman, Richard, *Cabinet Diaries*, Vol. II, p.200. Entry for Tuesday 17th January 1967.

[106] Balogh, Thomas, "The Apotheosis of the Dilettante: The Establishment of Mandarins" in Thomas, Hugh (ed.), *Crisis in the Civil Service*, London, Blond, 1968.

[107] Balogh, Thomas, "The Apotheosis of the Dilettante", p.17.

[108] Balogh, Thomas, "The Apotheosis of the Dilettante", p.18.

[109] Balogh, Thomas, "The Apotheosis of the Dilettante", p.25.

[110] Crossman, Richard, *How Britain is Governed*, p.71.

[111] Crossman, Richard, *Cabinet Diaries,* Vol. II, p.200. Entry for Tuesday 17th January 1967.

[112] National Archive BA 1/6, *Civil Service Department: Committee on the Civil Service (Fulton Committee). Minutes, Papers and Report 1966-69.*

[113] Crossman, Richard, *Cabinet Diaries,* Vol. II, p.200. Entry for Tuesday 17th January 1967.

[114] Fry, Geoffrey, *Reforming the Civil Service*, p.31. Quoted from an interview which the author held with Michael Simons in 1989.

[115] Crossman, Richard, *Cabinet Diaries*, Vol. III, London, Hamish Hamilton and Jonathan Cape, 1977, p.78. Entry for Sunday 26th May 1968. Crossman had alluded to this in his evidence to the Fulton Committee. National Archive, BA 1/6, *Civil Service Department: Committee on the Civil Service (Fulton Committee). Minutes, Papers and Report 1966-69.*

[116] Crossman, Richard, *Cabinet Diaries*, Vol. III, p.107. Entry for Tuesday 25th June 1968.

[117] Crossman, Richard, *Inside View*, p.15.

[118] For an example of this see Crossman's account of the mortgage scheme in Crossman, Richard, *Cabinet Diaries*, Vol. I, p.617. Entry for Wednesday 24th August 1966.

[119] Crossman, Richard, *Inside View,* p.77.

[120] For an example of Crossman's arguments and strong attitude towards his civil servants see Crossman, Richard, *Cabinet Diaries*, Vol. I, p.333. Entry for Wednesday 22nd September 1965.

[121] Crossman, Richard, *How Britain is Governed*, p.45. Jennings, W. Ivor, *Parliamentary Reform*, London, Gollancz for the New Fabian Research Bureau, 1934.

[122] Jennings, W. Ivor, *The British Constitution*, 4th Edition, London, Cambridge University Press, 1961.

[123] Bridges, Edward, *Portrait of a Profession*, p.19.

[124] Bridges, Edward, *Portrait of a Profession*, p.30.

[125] Bridges, Edward, *Portrait of a Profession*, p.29.

[126] Bridges, Edward, *Portrait of a Profession*, p.26.

[127] Crossman, Richard, *Cabinet Diaries*, Vol. I, p.274. Entry for Saturday 17th July 1965.

[128] Crossman, Richard, *Cabinet Diaries*, Vol. I, p.40. Entry for Sunday 3rd April 1966.

[129] Theakston, Kevin, *The Labour Party and Whitehall*, p.x.

[130] Crossman, Richard, *Inside View*, p.101.

[131] Laski, Harold, *Parliamentary Government*, p.294.

[132] Morrison, Herbert, *Government and Parliament*, p.313.

[133] Crossman, Richard, *Cabinet Diaries*, Vol. I, p.627. Entry for Thursday 11th August 1966.

[134] Mackintosh, John, *The British Cabinet*, London, Stevens, 1962.

[135] Mackintosh, John, *The British Cabinet* p.451.

[136] Mackintosh, John, *The British Cabinet* p.385.

[137] Crossman, Richard, "Retreat from Democracy", *The Guardian*, 6th June 1962, p.24.

[138] Crossman, Richard, "Retreat from Democracy", p.24.

[139] Crossman, Richard, "Retreat from Democracy", p.24.

[140] Crossman, Richard, "Retreat from Democracy", p.24.

[141] Crossman, Richard, "Retreat from Democracy", p.24.

[142] Crossman, Richard, *Cabinet Diaries*, Vol. I, p.29. Entry for Thursday 22nd October 1964.

[143] Crossman, Richard, *Cabinet Diaries*, Vol. I, p.68. Entry for Sunday 11th November 1964.

[144] Crossman, Richard, *Cabinet Diaries*, Vol. I, p.80. Entry for Thursday 3rd December 1964.

[145] Crossman, Richard, *Cabinet Diaries*, Vol. I, p.201. Entry for Sunday 18th April 1965. Crossman stated that 'this PM very much likes fixing things up privately with Ministers by bilateral discussions if he possibly can. On the other hand, he is extremely conventional in his desire to make the cabinet system work in the traditional way.'

[146] Crossman Papers, MSS.154/8/92. Photocopied typescripts of the first and second volume of the Cabinet Diaries 13th June 1966 to 23rd September 1966. Entry for 24th July 1966 (G.837).

[147] Crossman, Richard, *Cabinet Diaries*, Vol. II, p.380. Entry for Tuesday 13th June 1967.

[148] Crossman, Richard, *Cabinet Diaries*, Vol. II, p.466. Entry for Thursday 7th September 1967.

[149] Crossman, Richard, *Inside View*, p.7.

[150] Crossman, Richard, *Inside View*, pp.8/9.

[151] Crossman, Richard, *Inside View*, p.64.

[152] Crossman, Richard, *Inside View*, p.67.

[153] Crossman, Richard, *Socialism and the New Despotism*, p.18.

[154] Crossman, Richard, *Socialism and the New Despotism* p.18.

[155] Crossman, Richard, *Socialism and the New Despotism* p.19.

[156] Crossman, Richard, *Socialism and the New Despotism* p.19.

[157] Crossman, Richard, *Socialism and the New Despotism*, p.23.

[158] Crossman, Richard, *Inside View*, p.94.

[159] National Archive PREM 13/2528, *File on Fulton Committee and Official Secrets Act*. Memo from Crossman to Wilson dated 20/03/1969.

[160] Crossman, Richard, *Inside View*, p.94.

[161] Crossman, Richard, *Inside View*, p.94.

[162] Crossman, Richard, *Cabinet Diaries*, Vol. III, p.101. Entry for Wednesday 19th June 1968.

[163] Crossman, Richard, *How Britain is Governed*, p.50.

[164] Crosland, Anthony, *The Future of Socialism*, London, Cape, 1956.

[165] Crossman, Richard, *Cabinet Diaries*, Vol. I, p.608. Entry for Wednesday 10th August 1966.

[166] Crick, Bernard, *The Reform of Parliament*, 2nd Edition, London, Cape, 1968, p.210.

[167] National Archive, HO 392/39, *Preparation of White Paper on House of Lords Reform: Drafts 1968*. Wilson's agreement to this policy of cross-party talks can be seen in these documents.

[168] Morgan, Janet, *The House of Lords and the Labour Government 1964-70*, Oxford, Clarendon Press, 1975, p.190.

[169] Morgan, Janet, *The House of Lords*, p.192.

[170] Morgan, Janet, *The House of Lords*, p.188.

[171] Crossman, Richard, *Cabinet Diaries*, Vol. II, pp.135/6. Entry for Thursday 24th November 1966.

[172] Crossman, Richard, *Cabinet Diaries*, Vol. II, pp.253/4. Entry for Thursday 23rd February 1967.

[173] Crossman, Richard, *Cabinet Diaries*, Vol. II, p.672. Entry for Thursday 8th February 1968.

[174] Crossman, Richard, *Socialism and the New Despotism*, p.19.

[175] Crossman, Richard, *Socialism and the New Despotism*, p.19.

[176] National Archive BA 1/6, *Civil Service Department: Committee on the Civil Service (Fulton Committee). Minutes, Papers and Report 1966-69*.

[177] Crossman, Richard, *Cabinet Diaries*, Vol. II, p.235. Entry for Monday 13th February 1967.

[178] Howard, Anthony, *Crossman: The Pursuit of Power*, London, Jonathan Cape, 1990, p.281.

[179] Crossman, Richard, *Cabinet Diaries*, Vol. II, p.347. Entry for Tuesday 9th May 1967.

[180] Crossman, Richard, *Cabinet Diaries*, Vol. II, pp.223/4. Entry for Friday 3rd February 1967.

[181] Crossman noted a discussion about these difficulties with backbench MPs. See Crossman, Richard, *Cabinet Diaries*, Vol. II, p.235. Entry for Monday 13th February 1967.

[182] For an example of this see Crossman, Richard, *Cabinet Diaries*, Vol. II, pp.219/20. Entry for Thursday 2nd February 1967.

[183] Crossman, Richard, *Cabinet Diaries*, Vol. II, p.283. Entry for Monday 2nd March 1967.

[184] Crick, Bernard, *The Reform of Parliament*, p.230.

[185] 'It [the Privy Council meeting] is the most idiotic flummery and I must admit that I feel morally superior to my colleagues in despising it.' Crossman, Richard, *Cabinet Diaries*, Vol. I, p.257. Entry for Sunday 27th June 1965.

[186] Pimlott, Ben, *The Queen: A Biography of Elizabeth II*, London, HarperCollins, 1996, p.366.

[187] Crossman, Richard, *How Britain is Governed*, pp.56/7.

[188] Crossman, Richard, "Introduction" in Bagehot, Walter, *The English Constitution*, Glasgow, Fontana/Collins, 1963, pp. 24-6.

[189] Crossman, Richard, *Cabinet Diaries*, Vol. I, p.29. Entry for Thursday 22nd October 1964.

[190] Pimlott, Ben, *The Queen*, p.367.

[191] Crossman, Richard, *Cabinet Diaries*, Vol. I, p.611. Entry for Thursday 11th August 1966.

[192] Crossman, Richard, *Cabinet Diaries*, Vol. II, p.44. Entry for Tuesday 20th September 1966.

[193] Crossman, Richard, *Cabinet Diaries*, Vol. II, p.490. Entry for Friday 22nd September 1967.

[194] Crossman, Richard, *Cabinet Diaries*, Vol. I, p.11.

[195] Crossman, Richard, *Inside View*, p.94.

[196] Crossman, Richard, *Inside View*, p.77.

[197] Crossman, Richard, *Inside View*, p.102.

[198] Crossman, Richard, *Cabinet Diaries*, Vol. I, p.11.

Chapter Six

[1] David Judge noted the difference between a full-time and a part-time MP in his 1981 study *Backbench Specialisation in the House of Commons*, London, Heinemann Educational, 1981, pp. 84/5.

[2] This impression is highlighted by David Marquand's description of Crossman as "The Progressive as Gadfly". Marquand, David, *The Progressive Dilemma*, Revised Edition, London, Heinemann, 1992, pp. 137-146.

[3] Crosland, Anthony, *The Future of Socialism*, London, Cape, 1956, p.30.

[4] Ian Mikardo described Crossman as 'a towering intellect.' Mikardo, Ian, *Back-Bencher*, London, Weidenfeld and Nicolson, 1988, p.91.

[5] Crossman named the oil and chemical industries as prime for nationalisation. Morgan, Janet (ed.), *The Backbench Diaries of Richard Crossman,* London, Hamish Hamilton and Jonathan Cape, 1981, p.53, Entry for Monday 17th December 1951.

[6] Crossman, Richard, *Labour in the Affluent Society*, Fabian Tract 325, 1960, p.16.

[7] While Crossman argued that 'the nations of the Western world will be unable to strengthen themselves by developing adequate public services until the public sector becomes the dominant sector in our economies', he failed to outline how this might be achieved. Crossman, Richard, *Labour in the Affluent Society*, p.22.

[8] Crossman, Richard, *Socialism and the New Despotism*, Fabian Tract 298, 1956, p.3.

[9] Crossman, Richard, *Labour in the Affluent Society*.

[10] Crossman Papers, Modern Records Centre, University of Warwick Library, MSS.154/10/52. Isaacs, David, "Crossman Brilliance Not Used to the Best Advantage", *The Coventry Evening Telegraph*, 6th April 1974, p.10.

[11] Gwyn, William, "The Labour Party and the Threat of Bureaucracy", *Political Studies*, 19, 1971, pp. 395/6.

[12] Gwyn, William, "The Labour Party and the Threat of Bureaucracy", pp.387 and 391.

[13] Gwyn, William, "The Labour Party and the Threat of Bureaucracy", p.390.

[14] Gwyn, William, "The Labour Party and the Threat of Bureaucracy", pp. 388/9.

[15] Crossman, Richard, *The Diaries of a Cabinet Minister*, Vol. II, London, Hamish Hamilton and Jonathan Cape, 1976, p.190. Entry for Sunday 8th January 1967.

[16] Crossman, Richard, *The Diaries of a Cabinet Minister*, Vol. I, London, Hamish Hamilton and Jonathan Cape, 1975, p.377. Entry for Sunday 14th November 1965.

[17] Crossman, Richard, *The Diaries of a Cabinet Minister*, Vol. III, London, Hamish Hamilton and Jonathan Cape, 1977, pp. 298/9. Entry for Tuesday 24th December-Friday 27th December 1968.

[18] Crossman, Richard, *Cabinet Diaries*, Vol. II, p.627. Entry for Sunday 31st December 1967.

[19] Crossman, Richard, *Cabinet Diaries*, Vol. II, p.780. Entry for Sunday 14th April 1968.

[20] Crossman, Richard, *Cabinet Diaries*, Vol. III, p.45. Entry for Sunday 5th May 1968.

[21] Crossman, Richard, *Cabinet Diaries*, Vol. I, p.230. Entry for Wednesday 26th May 1965.

[22] Crossman, Richard, *Cabinet Diaries*, Vol. I., p.257. Entry for Sunday 27th June 1965.

[23] Crossman, Richard, *Cabinet Diaries*, Vol. II, p.617. Entry for Thursday 21st December 1967.

[24] Healey, Denis, *The Time of My Life*, London, Michael Joseph, 1989, p.108.

[25] Crossman, Richard, *Cabinet Diaries*, Vol. III, p.328 and p.566. Entries for Wednesday 15th January 1969 and Sunday 13th July 1969.

[26] Crossman spoke exclusively on foreign affairs and defence issues at the Labour Party Conferences until 1954, failing to participate in debates on domestic issues.

[27] Desai, Radhika, *Intellectuals and Socialism*, London, Lawrence and Wishart Ltd., 1994, p.101.

[28] Crossman, Richard, Foot, Michael and Mikardo, Ian, *Keep Left*, London, New Statesman and Nation, 1947, p.40.

[29] Crossman, Richard, Foot, Michael and Mikardo, Ian, *Keep Left*.

[30] Pelling argued that the change of governments in France and Italy coupled with Marshall aid forced the third force policy to collapse. Pelling, Henry, *America and the British Left*, London, A and C Black, 1956, p.151.

[31] Crossman, Richard, *Cabinet Diaries*, Vol. II, p.188. Entry for Friday 6th January 1967.

[32] Crossman, Richard, *Cabinet Diaries*, Vol. III, p.642. Entry for 14th September 1969.

[33] Crossman Papers, MSS.154/3/MIS/26/141 – Letter from Crossman to The Duchess of Bedford dated 14th September 1972.

[34] Pelling, Henry, *America and the British Left*, p.151.

[35] Pelling, Henry, *America and the British Left*, p.152.

[36] Crossman, Richard and Younger, Kenneth, *Socialist Foreign Policy*, Fabian Tract 287, London, Fabian Publications and Vincent Gollancz, April 1951, p.7.

[37] Crossman, Richard, *A Nation Reborn: The Israel of Weizmann, Bevin and Ben-Gurion*, London, Hamish Hamilton, 1960.

[38] Crossman, Richard, *Cabinet Diaries*, Vol. II, p.358. Entry for Monday 29th May 1967.

[39] Crossman, Richard, *How Britain is Governed*, Labour Book Service, 1939.

[40] Crossman, Richard, *Socialism and the New Despotism*.

[41] Crossman, Richard, "Introduction" in Bagehot, Walter, *The English Constitution*, Glasgow, Fontana/Collins, 1963. Mackintosh, John, *The British Cabinet*, London, Stevens, 1962.

[42] Crossman, Richard, *Cabinet Diaries*, Vol. I, p.11.

[43] Crossman, Richard, *Inside View*, London, Jonathan Cape, 1972.

[44] Dame Evelyn noted that while he had 'been interested in politics for so long, as a member of the House of Commons, and been so totally unaware of the apparatus of government was astonishing.' Jenkins, Simon, "Dame Evelyn Hits Back", *The Sunday Times*, 5th October 1975, p.17.

[45] Crossman, Richard, *Inside View*, p.94.

[46] Crossman, Richard, *Inside View*, p.94.

[47] Mikardo, Ian, *Back-Bencher*, p.152.

[48] Crossman, Richard, *Inside View*, p.77.

[49] Crossman, Richard, *Inside View*, p.102.

[50] Crossman argued that Bevin's 'vanity was very easily played on by the extremely charming and loyal civil servants who looked after him.' National Archive FCO 17/575, *Richard Crossman Interview about Ernest Bevin on Harlech Television 1967/8*.

[51] Crossman, Richard and Foot, Michael, *A Palestine Munich?*, London, Gollancz, 1946, pp. 14/5.

[52] Crossman, Richard, *How Britain is Governed*, p.70.

[53] Laski, Harold. *Parliamentary Government in England*, London, George Allen and Unwin, 1938, p.329.

[54] Drucker, H. M., *Doctrine and Ethos in the Labour Party*, London and Boston, George Allen and Unwin, 1979, p.99.

[55] Foot, Michael, *Aneurin Bevan 1945-60*, Vol. II, London, Davis-Poynter, 1973, p.40.

[56] Drucker, H. M., *Doctrine and Ethos*, p.99.

[57] Crossman recounted in his diaries how he was reprimanded by Peter Lederer, who told him 'You treated the civil servants appallingly. You dressed them down and didn't give them a chance to speak. I wouldn't like to have been treated in that way.' Crossman, Richard, *Cabinet Diaries*, Vol. I, p.333. Entry for Friday 17th September 1965.

[58] For details of the testimonies of Roy Jenkins, Anthony Crosland, Denis Healey and others see Fry, Geoffrey, *Reforming the Civil Service*, Edinburgh, Edinburgh University Press, 1993, pp. 106-8. Also see National Archive, B1 series.

[59] Crossman noted the under-staffing in the planning division and the problems this caused. 'Here I found when I arrived that eight or nine months was acceptable as a responsible time for a planning appeal to wait in the ministry before a decision. There was an extraordinary sense of timelessness in that division.' Crossman, Richard, *Cabinet Diaries*, Vol. I, p.615. Entry for Wednesday 24th August 1966.

[60] Crossman, Richard, *Inside View*, p.101.

[61] Crossman Papers, MSS.154/3/LPO/4/28 - Letter from Crossman to Peter Meyer dated 10th January 1967.

[62] Tanner, Duncan, *Richard Crossman, the Labour Party and the Constitution*, p.10. This was a paper delivered at Manchester Metropolitan University on 5th November 2004.

[63] This was an answer that Duncan Tanner gave to a question from the author at a conference at Manchester Metropolitan University on 5th November 2004.

[64] Desai, Radhika, *Intellectuals and Socialism*, pp. 6 and 67.

[65] Ziegler, Philip, *Wilson*, London, Weidenfeld and Nicolson, 1993, p.42.

[66] Pimlott, Ben, *Harold Wilson*, London, HarperCollins, 1992, p.106.

[67] Goodman, Geoffrey, "Harold Wilson: Leading Labour Before Pipe Dreams", *The Guardian*, 25th May 1995, p.14.

[68] Desai, Radhika, *Intellectuals and Socialism*, p.3.

[69] Crossman, Richard, "Introduction" in Koestler, Arthur et al., *The God That Failed*, 2nd Impression, London, Hamish Hamilton, 1960, p.8.

[70] Crossman, Richard, *Cabinet Diaries*, Vol. III, p.677. Entry for Saturday 10th October 1969.

[71] Young, Hugo, *One of Us: A biography of Mrs Thatcher*, London, Macmillan, 1989, p.43.

[72] English, Richard and Kenny, Michael, "Public Intellectuals and the Question of British Decline", *British Journal of Politics and International Relations*, 3/3, October 2001, p.260.

[73] Miliband, Ralph, "Harold Laski: An Exemplary Public Intellectual", *New Left Review*, 200, July/Aug 1993.

[74] Desai, Radhika, *Intellectuals and Socialism*, p.100.

[75] Crossman, Richard, "Introduction" in Koestler, Arthur et al., *The God That Failed*, p.7.

[76] Rosen, Greg, "John P. Mackintosh: His Achievements and Legacy", *Political Quarterly*, 70/2, April 1999, p.211.

[77] Crosland, Anthony, *The Future of Socialism*.

[78] Jones, Tudor, *Rethinking the Labour Party: From Gaitskell to Blair*, London, Routledge, 1996, p.156.

[79] Mikardo, Ian, *Back-Bencher*, p.152.

[80] Mikardo, Ian, *Back-Bencher*, p.100.

[81] Denham, Andrew and Garnett, Mark, *Keith Joseph*, Chesham, Acumen, 2001, p.196.

[82] An example of Crossman's redrafting and rethinking of draft documents, utilising outside experts, can be seen in Crossman, Richard, *Cabinet Diaries*, Vol. I, p.63. Entry for Thursday 19th November 1964.

[83] Jefferys, Kevin, *Anthony Crosland*, London, Richard Cohen, 1999, p.172.

[84] Denham, Andrew and Garnett, Mark, "The Nature and Impact of Think Tanks in Contemporary Britain", *Contemporary British History*, 10/1, Spring 1996, p.45.

[85] This disclaimer is from Crossman, Richard, *Socialism and the New Despotism*.

[86] Denham, Andrew and Garnett, Mark, *Keith Joseph*, p.139.

[87] Denham, Andrew and Garnett, Mark, *Keith Joseph*, p.140.

[88] Crosland, Susan, *Tony Crosland*, Sevenoaks, Hodder and Stoughton, 1983, p.66.

[89] Crossman Papers, MSS.154/10/52. Isaacs, David, "Crossman Brilliance Not Used to the Best Advantage", *Coventry Evening Telegraph*, 6th April 1974, p.10.

[90] Miliband, Ralph, "Harold Laski: An Exemplary Public Intellectual", p.176.

[91] Kramnick, Isaac and Sheerman, Barry, *Harold Laski: A Life on the Left*, London, Hamish Hamilton, 1993, p.481.

[92] Jenkins, Simon, "Dame Evelyn Hits Back", p.17.

[93] Jefferys, Kevin, *Anthony Crosland*, p.102.

[94] Denham, Andrew and Garnett, Mark, *Keith Joseph*, p.89.

[95] 'She [Dame Evelyn Sharp] is still living in the era of Keith Joseph – a fine soul who didn't like rough questioning and needed her protection. I don't see any point in Question Time unless it is rough.' Crossman, Richard, *Cabinet Diaries*, Vol. I, p.146. Entry for Tuesday 2nd February 1965.

[96] Denham, Andrew and Garnett, Mark, *Keith Joseph* p.197.

[97] Kramnick, Isaac and Sheerman, Barry, *Harold Laski*, p.585.

[98] Newman, Michael, *Harold Laski: A Political Biography*, Basingstoke, Macmillan, 1993, p.152.

[99] Jefferys, Kevin, *Anthony Crosland*, p.49.

[100] Jefferys, Kevin, *Anthony Crosland*, p.77.

[101] Denham, Andrew and Garnett, Mark, *Keith Joseph*, p.125.

[102] Marquand, David, *The Progressive Dilemma*. The chapter on Crossman is entitled "The Progressive as Gadfly".

[103] Healey, Denis, *The Time of My Life*, p.108.

[104] Mikardo, Ian, *Back-Bencher*, p.152.

[105] Judge, David, *Backbench Specialisation in the House of Commons*.

[106] Judge, David, *Backbench Specialisation in the House of Commons*, p.66.

[107] Judge, David, *Backbench Specialisation in the House of Commons*, pp.81/2.

[108] Philip Williams noted that 'when he [Gaitskell] became leader, foreign affairs replaced finance as his main single preoccupation.' Williams, Philip, *Hugh Gaitskell*, London, Cape, 1979, p.393.

[109] Williams, Philip (ed.), *The Diaries of Hugh Gaitskell 1945-56*, London, Cape, 1983, p.464. Entry for Friday 9th March 1956.

[110] Crossman, Richard, *Cabinet Diaries*, Vol. I, p.189. Entry for Tuesday 30th March 1965.

[111] Jenkins, Simon, "Dame Evelyn Hits Back", p.17.

[112] Foote, Geoffrey, *The Labour Party's Political Thought: A History*, London, Croom Helm, 1985.

[113] Wright, Anthony, *British Socialism: Socialist Thought From the 1880's to 1960's*, London and New York, Longman, 1983.

[114] Jones, Tudor, *Rethinking the Labour Party*.

[115] Crossman, Richard, *New Fabian Essays*, London, Turnstile Press, 1952.

[116] Jones, Tudor, *Rethinking the Labour Party*, pp.28/9.

[117] Thorpe, Andrew, *A History of the British Labour Party*, 2nd Edition, Basingstoke, Palgrave, 2001.

[118] Pelling, Henry and Reid, Alistair J., *A Short History of the Labour Party*, 12th Edition, Basingstoke, Palgrave Macmillan, 2005.

[119] Jefferys, Kevin, *The Labour Party Since 1945*, London, Palgrave Macmillan, 1993.

[120] Brivati, Brian and Heffernan, Richard (eds.), *The Labour Party: A Centenary History*, Basingstoke, Macmillan, 2000.

[121] Benn, Tony, *Against the Tide: Diaries 1973-76*, London, Arrow, 1989, p.639. Entry for Sunday 7th November 1976.

[122] Crossman, Richard, *Labour in the Affluent Society*, p.18.

[123] Crossman, Richard, *Labour in the Affluent Society*, p.24.

[124] For a fuller account of the views of many prominent Labour MPs and Ministers see Gorny, Joseph, *The British Labour Movement and Zionism 1917-1948*, London, Frank Cass, 1983, pp. 214-234.

[125] Crossman published his account of his time on the Anglo-American commission in *Palestine Mission*.

[126] Louis, William Roger, *The British Empire in the Middle East 1945-51*, Oxford, Clarendon Press, 1984, p.417.

[127] For Crossman's own account of Bevin's speech see Crossman, Richard, "A Margate Diary", *New Statesman,* 33, 7th June 1947, p.408. Labour Party Conference Annual Report 1947, p.179.

[128] Pelling, Henry, *America and the British Left,* p.151.

[129] The work of the Keep Left group has been considered to varying degrees by several authors on foreign policy. See Gordon, Michael, *Conflict and Consensus in Labour's Foreign Policy 1914-65*, Stanford, California, Stanford University Press, 1969, and Vickers, Rhiannon, *The Labour Party and the World Volume 1: The Evolution of Labour's Foreign Policy 1900-51*, Manchester, Manchester University Press, 2003.

[130] Gorny, Joseph, *The British Labour Movement and* Zionism, p.233.

[131] Crossman Papers, MSS.154/4/PAM/6. Bevan, Aneurin, Castle, Barbara, Crossman, Richard, Driberg, Tom, Mikardo, Ian, Wilson, Harold, *It Need Not Happen: The Alternative to German Rearmament,* London, Tribune Pamphlet, 1954.

[132] Crossman Papers, MSS.154/4/PAM/6. Bevan, Aneurin, Castle, Barbara, Crossman, Richard, Driberg, Tom, Mikardo, Ian, Wilson, Harold, *It Need Not Happen,* p.18.

[133] Taylor, Miles, "Labour and the Constitution" in Tanner, Duncan, Thane, Pat and Tiratsoo, Nick, *Labour's First Century,* Cambridge, Cambridge University Press, 2000, p.173.

[134] Crossman, Richard, "Introduction" in Bagehot, Walter, *The English Constitution.*

[135] Berkeley, Humphrey, *The Power of the Prime Minister,* London, Allen and Unwin, 1968, p.89.

[136] Crossman Papers, MSS.154/8/92 – Photocopied typescript of the unpublished first and second volumes of the Cabinet Diaries 13th June 1966 to 23rd September 1966. Entry for 24th July 1966 (G.837).

[137] Crossman, Richard, *Inside View.*

[138] Theakston, Kevin, *The Labour Party and Whitehall,* London, Routledge, 1992, p.168.

[139] Theakston, Kevin, *The Labour Party and Whitehall,* p.x.

[140] Crossman, Richard, *Cabinet Diaries,* Vol. I, p.11.

[141] Benn, Tony, *Out of the Wilderness: Diaries 1963-67,* London, Arrow, 1989. Castle, Barbara, *The Castle Diaries 1974-76,* London, Weidenfeld and Nicolson, 1980. Clarke, Alan, *Diaries,* London, Weidenfeld and Nicolson, 1993.

[142] Castle, Barbara, *The Castle Diaries 1964-76,* Paperback edition, London, Papermac, 1990, p.viii.

[143] Details of the court battle can be found in Young, Hugo, *The Crossman Affair,* London, Hamilton and Cape for the Sunday Times, 1976.

[144] Wilson, Harold, "The Desire to Educate", *The Listener,* 5th January 1978, p.4.

[145] Benn, Tony, *Against the Tide,* p.660. Entry for Sunday 28th November 1976.

[146] Judge, David, *Backbench Specialisation in the House of Commons,* p.186.

[147] Crossman, Papers, MSS.154/3/BR/2/4-18. Transcript of *A Chance to Meet* with Cliff Michelmore, BBC programme, no date but appears to be 4th April 1970.

[148] Crossman, Richard, "My Father", *The Sunday Telegraph,* 16th December 1962.

[149] Kogan, Maurice, Boyle, Edward and Crosland, Anthony, *The Politics of Education,* London, Harmondsworth, Penguin, 1971, p.183.

[150] Crossman, Richard, *Inside View,* p.77. Jenkins, Simon, "Dame Evelyn Hits Back", p.17.

[151] Drucker, H. M., *Doctrine and Ethos,* p.99.

[152] 'He [Oliver Cox] sat down and lectured me on being a good European. I found myself saying, 'Look, I'm not concerned with Europe now,' and I realized how departmentalized I have already become and how little the role I am playing in foreign affairs.' Crossman, Richard, *Cabinet Diaries,* Vol. I, p.146. Entry for Monday 1st February 1965.

[153] Healey, Denis, *The Time of My Life,* p.330.

Bibliography

This bibliography contains two categories of material. The first category are those sources which have been directly used or quoted from in this biography. The second category are materials which have informed my thinking and understanding of Crossman and the wider Labour Party but are not directly quoted from in this biography.

Crossman's own Publications

Crossman's individual articles are not listed here though the newspapers in which they appeared are listed.

Crossman, Richard, *Plato Today,* London, George Allen and Unwin, 1937.

Crossman, Richard, *How Britain in Governed,* London, Labour Book Service, 1939.

Crossman, Richard, *Government and the Governed,* London, Christophers, 1940.

Crossman, Richard and Foot, Michael, *A Palestine Munich?* London, Gollancz, 1946.

Crossman, Richard, *Palestine Mission: A Personal Record,* London, Hamish Hamilton, 1947.

Crossman, Richard, Foot, Michael and Mikardo, Ian, *Keep Left,* London, New Statesman and Nation, 1947.

Crossman, Richard, *Keeping Left,* London, New Statesman and Nation, 1950.

Crossman, Richard, *Socialist Values in a Changing Civilisation*, Fabian Tract No. 286, London, April 1951.

Crossman, Richard and Younger, Kenneth, *Socialist Foreign Policy*, Fabian Pamphlet No. 287, London, Fabian Publications and Vincent Gollancz, 1951.

Crossman, Richard (ed.), *New Fabian Essays*, London, Turnstile Press, 1952.

Crossman, Richard, *Socialism and the New Despotism*, Fabian Tract 298, London, February 1956.

Crossman, Richard, *The Charm of Politics and Other Essays in Political Criticism*, London, Hamish Hamilton, 1958.

Crossman, Richard, *Labour in the Affluent Society*, Fabian Tract 325, London, June 1960.

Crossman, Richard, *A Nation Reborn: The Israel of Weizmann, Bevin and Ben-Gurion*, London, Hamish Hamilton, 1960.

Crossman, Richard, *Planning for Freedom*, London, Hamish Hamilton, 1965.

Crossman, Richard, *Socialism and Affluence*, London, May 1967.

Crossman, Richard, *Inside View: Three Lectures on Prime Ministerial Government*, London, Jonathan Cape, 1972.

Crossman, Richard, *The Diaries of a Cabinet Minister: Minister of Housing 1964-66*, Vol. I, London, Hamish Hamilton and Jonathan Cape, 1975.
Crossman, Richard, *The Diaries of a Cabinet Minister: Lord President of the Council and Leader of the House of Commons 1966-68*, Vol. II, London, Hamish Hamilton and Jonathan Cape, 1976.
Crossman, Richard, *The Diaries of a Cabinet Minister: Secretary of State for Social Services 1968-70*, Vol. III, London, Hamish Hamilton and Jonathan Cape, 1977.

Primary Sources

Clem Attlee: The Granada Historical Records Interview, Panther Record, 1967.
The Crossman Papers, Modern Records Centre, University of Warwick.
The Labour Archives, University of Manchester.
National Archive, Kew, London.

Secondary Sources

Aaron, Daniel, *Studies in Biography*, Cambridge Massachusetts, Harvard University Press, 1978.
Annan, Noel, *Our Age*, London, Weidenfeld and Nicolson, 1990.
Attlee, Clement, *The Labour Party in Perspective*, London, Gollancz, 1937.
Backscheider, Paula, *Reflections in Biography*, Oxford, Oxford University Press, 1999.
Bagehot, Walter, *The English Constitution*, Glasgow, Fontana/Collins, 1963.
Batchelor, John (ed.), *The Art of Literary Biography*, Oxford, Clarendon Press, 1995.
Bealey, Frank (ed.), *The Social and Political Thought of the British Labour Party*, London, Weidenfeld and Nicolson, 1970.
Beloff, Max, *The Intellectual in Politics and Other Essays*, London, Weidenfeld and Nicolson, 1970.
Beloff, Max and Peele, Gillian (eds.), *The Government of the UK: Political Authority in a Changing Society*, 2nd Edition, London, Weidenfeld and Nicolson, 1985.
Benn, Tony, *Out of the Wilderness: Diaries 1963-67*, London, Arrow, 1989.
Benn, Tony, *Office Without Power: Diaries 1968-72*, London, Arrow, 1989.
Benn, Tony, *Against the Tide: Diaries 1973-76*, London, Arrow, 1989.
Berkeley, Humphrey, *The Power of the Prime Minister*, London, Allen and Unwin, 1968.
Berrington, Hugh, *Backbench Opinion in the House of Commons 1945-55*, Oxford, Pergamon, 1973.
Bevan, Aneurin, *In Place of Fear*, London, William Heinemann, 1952.
Bridges, Edward, *Portrait of a Profession: The Civil Service Tradition*, Cambridge, Cambridge University Press, 1950.
Brivati, Brian and Bale, Tim, *New Labour in Power: Precedents and Prospects*, London, Routledge, 1997.
Brivati, Brian and Heffernan, Richard, *The Labour Party: A Centenary History*, Basingstoke, Macmillan, 2000.
Brivati, Brian, *Hugh Gaitskell*, London, Richard Cohen, 1996.
Brym, Robert, *Intellectuals and Politics*, London, George Allen and Unwin, 1980.
Bullock, Alan, *The Life and Times of Ernest Bevin*, Vol. I, London, Heinemann, 1960.
Bullock, Alan, *The Life and Times of Ernest Bevin*, Vol. II, London, Heinemann, 1967.
Bullock, Alan, *Ernest Bevin: Foreign Secretary 1945-51*, London and New York, Norton, 1983.
Burridge, Trevor, *Clement Attlee: A Political Biography*, London, Cape, 1985.
Castle, Barbara, *The Castle Diaries 1974-76*, London, Weidenfeld and Nicolson, 1980.
Castle Barbara, *The Castle Diaries 1964-70*, London, Weidenfeld and Nicolson, 1984.
Castle, Barbara, *The Castle Diaries 1964-76*, Paperback edition, London, Papermac, 1990.

Catlin, George and Durbin, Evan (ed.), *War and Democracy: Essays on the Causes and Prevention of War*, London, Kegan Paul and Co., 1938.

Catterall, Peter and Jones, Harriet, *Understanding Documents and Sources*, Oxford, Heinemann, 1994.

Chapman, Brian, *The Profession of Government*, London, Unwin University Books, 1971.

Charmley, John and Homberger, Eric (eds.), *The Troubled Face of Biography*, Basingstoke, Macmillan, 1988.

Clarke, Peter, *Liberals and Social Democrats*, Cambridge and New York, Cambridge University Press, 1978.

Coates, David, *The Labour Party and the Struggle for Socialism*, London, Cambridge University Press, 1975.

Coopey, Richard, Fielding Steve and Tiratsoo, Nick, *The Wilson Governments 1964-70*, London, Pinter, 1993.

Cohen, Michael J., *Palestine and the Great Powers 1945-48*, Princeton, New Jersey and Guildford, Surrey, Princeton University Press, 1982.

Crick, Bernard, *George Orwell: A Life*, London, Secker and Warberg, 1980.

Crick, Bernard, *The Reform of Parliament*, 2nd Edition, London, Weidenfeld and Nicolson, 1968.

Crosland, Anthony, *The Future of Socialism*, London, Cape, 1956.

Crosland, Anthony, *The Conservative Enemy*, London, Cape, 1962.

Crosland, Anthony, *Socialism Now and Other Essays*, London, Cape, 1974.

Crosland, Susan, *Tony Crosland*, Sevenoaks, Hodder and Stoughton, 1983.

Dalyell, Tam, *Dick Crossman: A Portrait*, London, Weidenfeld and Nicolson, 1989.

Dell, Edmund, *The Schuman Plan and the British Abdication of Leadership in Europe*, Oxford, Oxford University Press, 1995.

Denham, Andrew and Garnett, Mark, *Keith Joseph*, Chesham, Acumen, 2001.

Desai, Radhika, *Intellectuals and Socialism: 'Social Democrats' and the Labour Party*, London, Lawrence and Wishart Limited, 1994.

Dietze, Gottfried (ed.), *Essays on the American Constitution*, Englewood Cliffs, New Jersey, Prentice-Hall, 1964.

Donoughue, Bernard, *Downing Street Diary: With Harold Wilson in No. 10*, London, Cape, 2005.

Drucker, H.M., *Doctrine and Ethos in the Labour Party*, London and Boston, George Allen and Unwin, 1979.

Duff, Peggy, *Left, Left, Left: A Personal Account of Six Protest Campaigns 1945-65*, London, Allison and Busby, 1971.

Durbin, Evan, *The Politics of Democratic Socialism*, 5th Impression, London, Routledge and Kegan Paul, 1957.

Durfee, Mary and Rosenau, James, *Thinking Theory Thoroughly*, London, Bolder, 1995.

Edel, Leon, *Literary Biography*, London, R. Hart-Davis, 1957.

Egerton, George, *Political Memoir: Essays on the Politics of Memory*, London and Portland, Oregon, Frank Cass, 1994.

Fielding, Steven (ed.), *The Labour Party: 'Socialism' and Society since 1951*, Manchester and New York, Manchester University Press, 1997.

Foot, Michael, *Aneurin Bevan: A Biography*, Vol. I, London, Macgibbon and Kee, 1962.

Foot, Michael, *Aneurin Bevan: A Biography*, Vol. II, London, Davis-Poynter, 1973.

Foot, Michael, *Loyalists and Loners*, London, Collins, 1986.

Foote, Geoffrey, *The Labour Party's Political Thought*, London, Croom Helm, 1985.

Francis, Martin, *Ideas and Politics under Labour 1945-1951*, Manchester, Manchester University Press, 1997.

Freeden, Michael, *Ideologies and Political Theory: A Conceptual Approach,* Oxford, Clarendon Press, 1996.

Fry, Geoffrey, *Reforming the Civil Service: The Fulton Committee on the British Civil Service of 1966-68,* Edinburgh, Edinburgh University Press, 1993.

Galbraith, John, *The Affluent Society,* New York, New American Library, 1958.

Gamble, Andrew and Wright, Anthony (ed.), *The New Social Democracy,* Malden, Massachusetts, Blackwell Publishers, 1999.

Gash, Norman, *Pillars of Government and Other Essays on State and Society c.1770-c.1880,* London, Edward Arnold, 1986.

Gittings, Robert, *The Nature of Biography,* London, Heinemann, 1978.

Gordon, Michael, *Conflict and Consensus in Labour's Foreign Policy 1914-1965,* Stanford, California, Stanford University Press, 1969.

Gordon-Walker, Patrick, *The Cabinet,* Revised Edition, London, Fontana, 1972.

Gorny, Joseph, *The British Labour Movement and Zionism 1917-48,* London, Frank Cass, 1983.

Groom, A.J.R., *British Thinking about Nuclear Weapons,* London, Frances Pinter, 1974.

Halcrow, Morrison, *Keith Joseph: A Single Mind,* Basingstoke, Macmillan, 1989.

Hamilton, Alastair, *The Appeal of Fascism: A Study of Intellectuals and Fascism 1919-45,* London, Blond, 1971.

Hanson, A.H., *Planning and the Politicians and Other Essays,* London, Routledge and Kegan Paul, 1969.

Harris, Jose, *William Beveridge: A Biography,* Oxford, Clarendon Press, 1977.

Harris, Kenneth, *Attlee,* London, Weidenfeld and Nicolson, 1982.

Headey, Bruce, *British Cabinet Ministers,* London, George Allen and Unwin, 1974.

Healey, Denis, *The Time of My Life,* London, Michael Joseph, 1989.

Hennessy, Peter, *Cabinet,* Oxford, Basil Blackwell, 1986.

Hennessy, Peter, *The Secret State: Whitehall and the Cold War,* London, Allen Lane and the Penguin Press, 2002.

Hewart, Gordon, *The New Despotism,* London, Ernest Benn Ltd., 1929.

Hinton, James, *Labour and Socialism: A History of the British Labour Movement 1867-1974,* Brighton, Wheatsheaf Books, 1983.

Howard, Anthony (ed.), *The Crossman Diaries,* London, Cape and Hamish Hamilton, 1979.

Howard, Anthony, *Crossman: The Pursuit of Power,* London, Jonathan Cape 1990.

Howe, Stephen, *Anti-Colonialism in British Politics: The Left and the End of Empire 1918-1964,* Oxford, Clarendon Press, 1993.

Howell, David, *British Social Democracy: A Study in Development and Decay,* London, Croom Helm, 1976.

Jefferys, Kevin, *The Labour Party since 1945,* London, Palgrave Macmillan, 1993.

Jefferys, Kevin, *Anthony Crosland,* London, Richard Cohen, 1999.

Jefferys, Kevin (ed.), *Labour Forces: From Ernest Bevin to Gordon Brown,* London, I.B.Tauris, 2002.

Jenkins, Mark, *Bevanism: Labour's High Tide; The Cold War and the Democratic Mass Movement,* Nottingham, Spokesman, 1979.

Jenkins, Roy, *Portraits and Miniatures,* London, Macmillan, 1993.

Jennings, W. Ivor, *The British Constitution,* 4th Edition, London, Cambridge University Press, 1961.

Jennings, W. Ivor, *Parliamentary Reform,* London, Gollancz and the New Fabian Research Bureau, 1934.

Joll, James, *Intellectuals in Politics,* London, Weidenfeld and Nicolson, 1960.

Jones, Barry and Keating, Michael (eds.), *Labour and the British State,* Oxford, Clarendon Press, 1985.

Jones, Tudor, *Remaking the Labour Party: From Gaitskell to Blair,* London, Routledge, 1996.

Jordan, Grant, *The British Administrative System: Principles versus Practice,* London, Routledge, 1994.

Judge, David, *Backbench Specialisms in the House of Commons,* London, Heinemann Educational, 1981.

Kedourie, Elie, *The Crossman Confessions and Other Essays in Politics, History and Religion,* London, Mansell, 1984.

Koestler, Arthur, *The God That Failed,* 2nd Impression, London, Hamish Hamilton, 1960.

King, Anthony, *The British Prime Minister,* 2nd Edition, Basingstoke, Macmillan, 1985.

Kogan, Maurice, Boyle, Edward and Crosland, Anthony, *The Politics of Education,* Harmonsdworth, Penguin, 1971.

Kramnick, Isaac and Sheerman, Barry, *Harold Laski: A Life on the Left,* London, Hamish Hamilton, 1993.

Laski, Harold, *Parliamentary Government in England,* London, George Allen and Unwin, 1938.

Leonard, Dick (ed.), *Crosland and New Labour,* Basingstoke, Macmillan, 1999.

Lipsey, David and Leonard, Dick (ed.), *The Socialist Agenda: Crosland's Legacy,* London, Cape, 1981.

Louis, William Roger, *The British Empire in the Middle East 1945-51: Arab Nationalism, the United States and Postwar Imperialism,* Oxford, Clarendon Press, 1984.

Louis, William Roger (ed.), *More Adventures with Britannia: Personalities, Politics and Culture in Britain,* London, I.B.Tauris, 1998.

Mackintosh, John, *The British Cabinet,* London, Stevens, 1962.

Marquand, David, *The Progressive Dilemma,* London, Heinemann, 1991.

Marquand, David, *The Progressive Dilemma,* Revised edition, London, Heinemann, 1992.

Marquand, David, *The New Reckoning: Capitalism, States and Citizens,* London, Cambridge, Polity Press in Association with the New Statesman, 1997.

Martin, David and Rubinstein, David (eds.), *Ideology and the Labour Movement: Essays Presented to John Saville,* London, Croom Helm, 1979.

Marwick, Arthur, *The Nature of History,* 3rd Edition, Basingstoke, Macmillan Education, 1989.

Matthew, H.C.G. and Harrison, Brian, *Oxford Dictionary of National Biography,* 14, Oxford, Oxford University Press, 2004.

MacLeod, Roy (ed.), *Government and Expertise: Specialists, Administrators and Professionals 1860-1919,* Cambridge, Cambridge University Press, 1988.

Meehan, Eugene, *The British Left Wing and Foreign Policy: A Study of the Influence of Ideology,* New Jersey, Rutgers University Press, 1960.

Mikardo, Ian, *Back-bencher,* London, Weidenfeld and Nicolson, 1988.

Miller, Kenneth, *Socialism and Foreign Policy: Theory and Practice in Britain to 1931,* The Hague, Martinus Nijhoff, 1967.

Miliband, Ralph, *Parliamentary Socialism: A Study in the Politics of Labour,* 2nd Edition, London, Merlin Press, 1972.

Minkin, Lewis, *The Labour Party Conference; A Study in the Politics of Intra-Party Democracy,* London, Allen Lane, 1978.

Minkin, Lewis, *The Contentious Alliance; Trade Unions and the Labour Party,* Edinburgh, Edinburgh University Press, 1991.

Morgan, Janet, *The House of Lords and the Labour Government 1964-70,* Oxford, Clarendon Press, 1975.

Morgan, Janet (ed.), *The Backbench Diaries of Richard Crossman,* London, Hamish Hamilton and Jonathan Cape, 1981.

Morgan, Kenneth, *Labour People: Leader and Lieutenants, Hardie to Kinnock,* Oxford and New York, Oxford University Press, 1987.

Morgan, Kenneth, *Steady as She Goes: Writing the Biography of Lord Callaghan,* Swansea, University of Wales, 1996.

Morrison, Herbert, *Government and Parliament; A Survey from the Inside*, 2nd Edition, London, Oxford University Press, 1959.

Morrison, Herbert, *Socialism and Transport*, London, Constable, 1933.

Muir, Ramsay, *How Britain is Governed*, London, R.R. Smith, 1930.

Nadal, Ira Bruce, *Biography: Fiction, Fact and Form*, London, Macmillan, 1984.

Navias, Martin, *Nuclear Weapons and British Strategic Planning 1955-1958*, Oxford, Clarendon Press, 1991.

Newman, Michael, *Harold Laski: A Political Biography*, Basingstoke, Macmillan, 1993.

Nicholson, Harold, *The Development of English Biography*, London, The Hogarth Press, 1927.

Origo, Iris, *A Need to Testify*, London, Murray, 1984.

Orwell, George, *The Lion and the Unicorn: Socialism and the English Genius*, London, Secker and Warberg, 1941.

Ovendale, Ritchie (ed.), *The Foreign Policy of the British Labour Governments 1945-51*, Leicester, Leicester University Press, 1984.

Ovendale, Richie, *The Origins of the Arab-Israeli Wars*, London, Longman, 1984.

Paige, Glenn (ed.), *Political Leadership: Readings for an Emerging Field*, New York, Free Press, 1972.

Parke, Catherine, *Samuel Johnson and Biographical Thinking*, Columbia and London, University of Missouri Press, 1991.

Pearce, Robert (ed.), *Patrick Gordon-Walker Political Diaries 1932-71*, London, Historians' Press, 1991.

Pelling, Henry, *America and the British Left*, London, A and C Black, 1956.

Pelling, Henry, *A Short History of the Labour Party*, London, Macmillan, 1961.

Pelling, Henry and Reid, Alastair J., *A Short History of the Labour Party*, Basingstoke, Palgrave Macmillan, 2005.

Pels, Dick, *Intellectual as Stranger: Studies in Spokesmanship*, London, Routledge, 2000.

Pimlott, Ben, *The Political Diary of Hugh Dalton 1918-40, 1945-60*, London, Cape in association with the LSE, 1986.

Pimlott, Ben, *The Second World War Diary of Hugh Dalton 1940-45*, London, Cape in association with the LSE, 1986.

Pimlott, Ben, *Harold Wilson*, London, HarperCollins, 1992.

Pimlott, Ben, *The Queen: A Biography of Elizabeth II*, London, HarperCollins, 1996.

Plant, Raymond, Beech, Matt and Hickson, Kevin (eds.), *The Struggle for Labour's Soul: Understanding Labour's political thought since 1945*, London, Routledge, 2004.

Ponting, Clive, *Breach of Promise: Labour in Power 1964-70*, London, Hamish Hamilton, 1989.

Pugh, Patricia, *Educate, Agitate, Organize: 100 Years of Fabian Socialism*, London, Methuen, 1984.

Pyper, Robert and Robins, Lynton (eds.), *United Kingdom Governance*, Basingstoke, Macmillan, 2000.

Radice, Giles, *Friends and Rivals*, London, Abacus, 2002.

Reed, Bruce and Williams, Geoffrey, *Denis Healey and the Politics of Power*, London, Sidgwick and Jackson, 1971.

Rush, Michael, *The Role of the Member of Parliament since 1868: From Gentleman to Players*, Oxford, Oxford University Press, 2001.

Ruston, Roger, *A Say in the End of the World: Morals and British Nuclear Weapons Policy 1941-1987*, Oxford, Clarendon Press, 1989.

Sanders, David, *Losing an Empire, Finding a Role: British Foreign Policy since 1945*, Basingstoke, Macmillan Education, 1990.

Schiff, Hilda (ed.), *Contemporary Approaches to English Studies*, London, Heinemann Educational for the English Association, 1977.

Schneer, Jonathan, *Labour's Conscience: The Labour Left 1945-51,* London and Boston, Unwin Hyman, 1988.

Seldon, Anthony (ed.), *Contemporary History: Practice and Method,* Oxford, Basil Blackwell, 1988.

Seldon, Anthony and Hickson, Kevin (eds.), *New Labour, Old Labour: The Wilson and Callaghan Government 1974-79,* London, Routledge, 2004.

Shaw, George Bernard (ed.), *Fabian Essays in Socialism,* London, The Fabian Society, 1889.

Shelston, Alan, *Biography,* London, Methuen, 1977.

Shepherd, Robert, *Iain MacLeod: A Biography,* London, Pimlico, 1994.

Shepherd, Robert, *Enoch Powell,* London, Pimlico, 1996.

Shrapnel, Norman, *The Performers,* London, Constable, 1978.

Smith, Martin, Smith, Steve and White, Brian (eds.), *British Foreign Policy: Tradition, Change and Transformation,* London, Unwin Hyman, 1988.

Stewart, Graham, *Burying Caesar,* London, Weidenfeld and Nicolson, 1999.

Strachey, John, *The Theory and Practice of Socialism,* London, Gollancz, 1936.

Tanner, Duncan, Thane, Pat and Tiratsoo, Nick, *Labour's First Century,* Cambridge, Cambridge University Press, 2000.

Tawney, R.H., *The Sickness of an Acquisitive Society,* London, The Fabian Society and George Allen and Unwin, 1920.

Tawney, R.H., *The Acquisitive Society,* London, Bell, 1921.

Tawney, R.H., *Equality,* 4th Edition, London, George Allen and Unwin, 1952.

Theakston, Kevin, *The Labour Party and Whitehall,* London, Routledge, 1992.

Theakston, Kevin, *The Civil Service since 1945,* Oxford, Blackwell Publishers, 1995.

Theakston, Kevin (ed.), *Bureaucrats and Leadership,* Basingstoke, Macmillan, 1999.

Thomas, Hugh (ed.), *Crisis in the Civil Service,* London, Blond, 1968.

Thompson, Noel, *John Strachey: An Intellectual Biography,* Basingstoke, Macmillan, 1993.

Thorpe, Andrew, *A History of the British Labour Party,* 2nd Edition, Basingstoke, Palgrave, 2001.

Tosh, John, *The Pursuit of History,* 2nd Edition, London, Longman, 1991.

Vibert, Frank (ed.), *Britain's Constitutional Future,* London, Institute of Economic Affairs, 1991.

Vickers, Rhiannon, *The Labour Party and the World: Volume 1: The Evolution of Labour's Foreign Policy 1900-51,* Manchester, Manchester University Press, 2003.

Vickers, Rhiannon, *Manipulating Hegemony: State Power, Labour and the Marshall Plan in Britain,* Basingstoke, Macmillan, 2000.

Watkins, Alan, *Brief Lives,* London, Hamilton, 1982.

Webb, Beatrice and Sidney, *A Constitution for the Socialist Commonwealth of Great Britain,* London, Longman, Green and Co, 1920.

Weber, Max, *From Max Weber: Essays in Sociology,* London, Routledge and Kegan Paul, 1948.

Wickham-Jones, Mark, *Economic Strategy and the Labour Party: Politics and Policy Making 1970-83,* Basingstoke, Macmillan, 1996.

Williams, Marcia, *Inside Number 10,* London, Weidenfeld and Nicolson, 1972.

Williams, Philip (ed.), *Diary of Hugh Gaitskell 1945-1956,* London, Cape, 1983.

Williams, Philip (ed.), *Hugh Gaitskell: A Political Biography,* London, Cape, 1979.

Wilson, Harold, *Memoirs: The Making of a Prime Minister 1916-64,* London, Weidenfeld and Nicolson and Joseph, 1986.

Woolf, Virginia, *The Death of the Moth and Other Essays,* London, The Hogarth Press, 1942.

Wright, Anthony, *British Socialism: Socialist Thought form the 1880's to 1960's,* London and New York, Longman, 1983.

Wright, Anthony, *Socialisms: Old and New,* 2nd Edition, London, Routledge, 1996.

Young, Hugo, *The Crossman Affair,* London, Hamilton and Cape for the Sunday Times, 1976.

Young, Hugo, *One of Us: A Biography of Mrs Thatcher*, London, Macmillan, 1989.
Young, John, *The Labour Governments 1964-70, Volume II: International Policy*, Manchester, Manchester University Press, 2003.
Ziegler, Philip, *Wilson*, London, Weidenfeld and Nicolson, 1993.

Articles

Attlee, Clement, "Civil Servants, Ministers, Parliament and the Public", *Political Quarterly*, 25/4, 1954.
Barnes, Susan, "The Man Who Thinks Out Loud", *Sunday Times Magazine*, 29th November 1970.
Balogh, Thomas, "The Departmental Grind", *Times Literary Supplement*, 2nd December 1977.
Beattie, Alan, "Biographies of 1992 and the limits of Biography", *Parliamentary Affairs*, 46, 1993.
Bonham-Carter, Mark, "Governing Principles", *Times Literary Supplement*, 30th January 1976.
Bonsanquet, Nick, "Sir Keith's Reading List", *Political Quarterly*, 52, 1981.
Bridges, Edward, "Haldane and the Machinery of Government", *Public Administration*, 35, 1957.
Burgess, Simon and Alderman, Geoffrey, "Centre for Policy Studies: The Influence of Sir Alfred Sherman", *Contemporary Record*, 4/1, September 1990.
Callaghan, John, "The Left and the "Unfinished Revolution': Bevanites and Soviet Russia in the 1950's", *Contemporary British History*, 15/3, Autumn 2001.
Callaghan, John, "The Fabian Society since 1945", *Contemporary British History*, 10/2, Summer 1996.
Callaghan, John, "The Cold War and the March of Capitalism, Socialism and Democracy", *Contemporary British History*, 15/3, Autumn 2001.
Campbell, John, "Crossman's Sancho Panza", *New Statesman and Nation*, 2/69, 29th September 2001.
Castle, Barbara, "Mandarin Power", *The Sunday Telegraph*, 10th June 1973.
Catterall, Peter, "Anatomising Wilson: Ben Pimlott", *Contemporary Record*, 7/2, Autumn 1993.
Clift, Ben and Tomlinson, Jim, "Tawney and the Third Way", *Journal of Political Ideologies*, 7/3, October 2002.
Crick, Bernard, "Commentary: Opening the Crossman Diaries", *Political Quarterly*, 46/1, 1975.
Croft, Pauline, "Political Biography: A Defence", *Contemporary British History*, 10/4, Winter 1996.
Crosland, Anthony, "The Future of the Left", *Encounter*, XIV/3, March 1960.
Crosland, Anthony, "On the Left Again", *Encounter*, XV/4, October 1960.
Denham, Andrew and Garnett, Mark, "The Nature and Impact of Think Tanks in Contemporary Britain", *Contemporary British History*, 10/1, Spring 1996.
Derry, John, "Political Biography: A Defence (2)", *Contemporary British History*, 10/4, Winter 1996.
Desai, Radhika, "Second-Hand Dealers in Ideas: Think Tanks and Thatcherite Hegemony", *New Left Review*, 203, Jan/Feb 1994.
Edmunds, June, "The British Labour Party in the 1980's: The Battle over the Palestinian/Israeli Conflict", *Politics*, 18/2, 1998.
Edinger, Lewis, "Political Science and Political Biography (II)", *Journal of Politics*, 26/3, August 1964, Florida.
English, Richard and Kenny, Michael, "Public Intellectuals and the Question of British Decline", *British Journal of Politics and International Relations*, 3/3, October 2001.
Gamble, Andrew, "Political Memoirs", *Politics*, 14/1, 1994.

Goodman, Geoffrey, "Harold Wilson: Leading Labour before Pipe Dreams", *The Guardian*, 24th May 1995.

Gwyn, William, "The Labour Party and the Threat of Bureaucracy", *Political Studies*, 19/4, 1971.

Hamilton, Nigel, "Wanted: Cult of Personality", *The Times Higher Education Supplement*, 10th March 2000.

Hamilton, Nigel "In Defence of the Practice of Biography", *Contemporary British History*, 10, Winter 1996.

Harris Michael, "The Centre for Policy Studies: The Paradoxes of Power", *Contemporary British History*, 10/2, Summer 1996.

Jackson, Ben, "Equality of nothing? Social justice on the British Left, c.1911-31", *Journal of Political Ideologies*, 8/1, February 2003.

James, Simon, "The Cabinet System since 1945: Fragmentation and Integration", *Parliamentary Affairs*, 47/4, October 1994.

Jenkins, Simon, "Dame Evelyn Hits Back", *The Sunday Times*, 5th October 1975.

Jones, George W., "The Value of Recent Biography, Autobiography and Diaries", *Parliamentary Affairs Journal*, 34/2, Spring 1981.

Jordan, Grant, "Central Co-ordination, Crossman and the Inner Cabinet", *Political Quarterly*, 49, 1978.

Lamb, Peter, "Harold Laski (1893-1950): Political Theorist of a World in Crisis", *Review of International Studies*, 25/2, August 1999.

Lamb, Peter, "Laski on Rights and the Problem of Liberal Democratic Theory", *Politics*, 19/1, February 1999.

Lucas, W. Scott, "Biography as History: Eden, Macmillan and Suez", *Contemporary Record*, 2/5, Spring 1989.

Lycett, Andrew, "Something Sensational", *New Statesman*, 11th December 2000.

Madgwick. P., "Leaders and Readers", *Parliamentary Affairs Journal*, 48, 1995.

McKie, David, "The Not Quite New Statesman", *The Guardian*, 18th October 1990, p.23.

Middlemas, R.K, "Cabinet Secrecy and the Crossman Diaries", *Political Quarterly*, 47/1, Jan-Mar 1976.

Miliband, Ralph, "Harold Laski: An Exemplary Public Intellectual", *New Left Review*, 200, July/Aug 1993.

Moon, Jeremy, "Post War British Political Memoir", *Parliamentary Affairs Journal*, 35, Winter 1982.

Morgan, Janet, "Book Review of Crossman: The Pursuit of Power", *Contemporary Record*, 5/1, Summer 1991.

Naftali, Timothy, "George Orwell's List", *The New York Times*, 29th July 1998.

O'Brien, Patrick, "Is Political Biography a Good Thing?" *Contemporary British History*, 10/4, Winter 1996.

Oakeshott, Michael, "Political Realities", *Times Literary Supplement*, 28th September 1962.

Oliver, Michael, "A Response to Denham and Garnett's 'The Nature and Impact of Think Tanks in Contemporary Britain'", *Contemporary British History*, 10/2, Summer 1996.

Pimlott, Ben, "The Future of Political Biography", *Political Quarterly*, 61, 1990.

Pimlott, Ben, "A Don Spills the Beans", *The Times*, Thursday 5th October 1989.

Pimlott, Ben, "Is Contemporary Biography History?" *Political Quarterly*, 70, 1999.

Pugh, Martin, "Exaggerated Reports", *Times Literary Supplement*, 3rd-9th November 1989.

Robson, William, "What the Crossman Diaries Actually Contain", *Political Quarterly*, 47/3, July-Sept 1976.

Rosen, Greg, "John P. Mackintosh: His Achievements and Legacy", *Political Quarterly*, 70/2, April 1999.

Sassoon, Donald, "Socialism in the twentieth century: an historical reflection", *Journal of Political Ideologies,* 5/1, 2000.

Schneer, Jonathan, "Hopes Deferred or Shattered: The British Labour Left and the Third Force Movement 1945-49", *The Journal of Modern History,* 56/2, June 1984.

Seldon, Anthony, "Anatomising Wilson: Philip Ziegler", *Contemporary Record,* 7/2, Autumn 1993.

Sharp, Evelyn, "Politicians", *The Listener,* 88/28, 28th September 1972.

Shell, Donald, "Labour and the House of Lords: A Case Study in Constitutional Reform", *Parliamentary Affairs,* 53/2, April 2000.

Shepherd, Robert, "The Challenge of Political Biography", *British Journalism Review,* 8/1, 1997.

Sisson, C.H., "Straight from the Trojan Horse's Mouth", *Times Literary Supplement,* 5th November 1976.

Smith, Trevor, "'Something Old, Something New, Something Borrowed, Something Blue': Themes of Tony Blair and his Government", *Parliamentary Affairs,* 56/4, October 2003.

Theakston, Kevin, "Evelyn Sharp (1903-85)", *Contemporary Record,* 7/1, Summer 1993.

Theakston, Kevin, "Richard Crossman: The Diaries of a Cabinet Minister", *Public Administration and Policy,* 18/4, Winter 2003.

Theakston, Kevin, "Prime Ministers and the Constitution: Attlee to Blair", *Parliamentary Affairs,* 58/1, 2005.

Tomlinson, Jill, "The Limits of Tawney's Ethical Socialism: A Historical Perspective on the Labour Party and the Market", *Contemporary British History,* 16/4, Winter 2002.

Turner, John, "From Left to Right and Back Again", *Times Literary Supplement,* 2nd-8th November 1990.

Various Authors, "Symposium: The Crossman Diaries Reconsidered", *Contemporary Record,* 1/2, Summer 1987.

Wilson, Harold, "A Desire to Educate", *The Listener,* 5th January 1978.

Wright, Anthony, "British Socialists and the British Constitution", *Parliamentary Affairs,* 43/3, July 1990.

Wright, Anthony, "Double Crossman", *New Statesman and Nation,* 3/124, 26th October 1990.

Unknown Author, "A Maverick in Harness", *The Observer,* 28th March 1965.

Unknown Author, "Mr Heath says Crossman diaries are malicious", *The Times,* 8th December 1975.

Pamphlets

Bevan, Aneurin, Castle, Barbara, Crossman, Richard, Driberg, Tom, Mikardo, Ian and Wilson, Harold, *It Need Not Happen: The Alternative to German Rearmament,* London, Tribune Publications, 1954.

Crick, Bernard, *Reform of the Commons,* Fabian Tract 319, London, The Fabian Society, 1959.

Fielding, Rodney, *A Socialist Foreign Policy?* Fabian Tract 401, London, The Fabian Society, July 1970.

Healey, Denis, *A Neutral Belt in Europe?* Fabian Tract 311, London, The Fabian Society, February 1958.

Mikardo, Ian, *The Second Five Years: A Labour Programme for 1950,* London, The Fabian Society, April 1948.

Labour Party Documents

Labour Party, *Cards on the Table: An Interpretation of Labour's Foreign Policy,* 1947.

Labour Party, *Your Personal Guide to the Future Labour Offers You,* 1958.

1964 Labour Party Election Manifesto, *The New Britain.*

1966 Labour Party Election Manifesto, *Time for Decision.*
Labour Party Conference Reports from 1945 to 1974.

Newspapers

Banbury Guardian
Birmingham Herald
Birmingham Post
Bristol Post
Cambridge Daily News
Cambridge Evening News
Chronicle and Echo
Coventry Express
Daily Express
Daily Herald
Daily Mail
Daily Mirror
Daily Telegraph
Daily Record
Daily Sketch
Daily Worker
Derby Evening Telegraph
Doncaster Gazette
Eastern Daily Press
Erith Observer
Evening Advertiser
Evening Chronical
Evening News
Evening Standard
Express and Echo
Financial Times
Forward
Glasgow Herald
The Gloucestershire Echo
The Guardian
Hitchin and Letchworth Pictorial
Harrow Observer
The Irish Times
The Journal
Labour Weekly
Leicester Mercury
Lincolnshire Echo
The Listener
Liverpool Daily Post
Midland Daily Telegraph
Morning Star
Morning Telegraph
New Daily
News Chronical

News of the World
New York Times
The New Statesman
Northern Echo
The Observer
Oxford Mail
Palmers Green Gazette
Policy Holder
The People
Reynolds
The Scotsman
Stafford Advertiser
Stroud News
The Sun
The Sunday Express
The Sunday Mirror
The Sunday Pictorial
The Sunday Telegraph
The Sunday Times
The Times
Tottenham and Edmond Herald
Welwyn Times
Wembley Times
Western Daily Press
Western Mail
Western Mercury
Yorkshire Evening Post

Unpublished Work

Shaw, Eric, British Socialist Approaches to International Affairs 1945-1951, May 1974, unpublished MPhil from University of Leeds.

Tanner, Duncan, Richard Crossman, the Labour Party and the Constitution. Paper given at Manchester Metropolitan University, 5th November 2004.

Theakston, Kevin, The 1964-70 Labour Governments and Whitehall Reform, University of Leeds, POLIS Working Paper No. 2, February 2004.

Other Sources

Churchill's speech including his views on a future Labour Government during the 1945 election campaign.
http://www.news.bbc.co.uk/hi/english/static/vote2001/In_depth/election_battles/19 45_camp.stm

Dalyell, Tam and Howard, A, Transcript of Great Lives Programme 9 on Dick Crossman, Series 2. http://www.bbc.co.uk/radio4/history/greatlives/dalyell_crossman.shtml

Jenkins, Roy, The Writing of Political Biography [Convocation] Lecture, given at University of Leeds Saturday 6th July 1974.

Glossary

CPS	Centre for Policy Studies
DEA	Department of Economic Affairs
EDC	European Defence Council
EEC	European Economic Community
ECSC	European Coal and Steel Community
EU	European Union
FDR	Federal Deutschland Republic
GDR	German Democratic Republic
IEA	Institute of Economic Affairs
JPC	Joint Policy Committee
NATO	North Atlantic Treaty Organisation
NEC	National Executive Committee
OPD	Defence and Overseas Policy Committee
PPS	Parliamentary Private Secretary
SEP	Steering group on Economic Planning
UN(O)	United Nations (Organisation)
WEA	Workers Educational Association

Index